Exploring the Divide:
Illness and Disability

Edited by

**Colin Barnes
and Geof Mercer**

The Disability Press

Leeds

First published 1996
by The Disability Press
School of Sociology and Social Policy
University of Leeds, Leeds LS2 9JT

Output from disk supplied and printed by University Print
Services, a division of Media Services at Leeds.

British Library Cataloguing in Publication Data
A catalogue record for this book is available from the British
Library.

Library of Congress Cataloguing in Publication Data
A catalogue record of this book has been requested.

ISBN 0-9528450-0-8 (pbk)

Contents

Preface

The majority of the chapters in this volume are revised versions of papers that were presented at a conference – *Accounting for Illness and Disability* – which was organised by the editors with the financial support of the Disability Research Unit, School of Sociology and Social Policy, University of Leeds, at Weetwood Hall in Leeds on 19-21 April 1995. The intention was to bring together some of the key contributors to debates between disability activists and theorists and medical sociologists. The central focus was on identifying issues of central concern to what had increasingly become two competing 'camps', while also exploring areas of common interest. For the purposes of this volume, additional contributions have been provided by conference participants.

Special thanks go to everyone who participated in the conference for making it such a memorable and stimulating event.

The Disability Press

The Disability Press seeks to provide an alternative outlet for work in the field of disability studies. The Disability Press acknowledges and draws inspiration from the work of all those countless disabled individuals and their allies who have, over the years, struggled to put this particular issue on to the political agenda. Its establishment is a testament to the growing recognition of 'disability' as an equal opportunities and human rights issue within the social sciences.

Funding for this first volume from the Disability Press has been provided by the Disability Research Unit. The editors also wish to record their thanks for the support and encouragement of the School of Sociology and Social Policy at the University of Leeds.

Contributors

David Ackroyd was, until recently, an Assistant Director in Stockport Social Services. For four years he was seconded to the North West Regional Health Authority with responsibility for Community Care Development. He is now working as a freelance consultant.

Colin Barnes is a member of several organisations controlled and run by disabled people and Research Director for the British Council of Disabled People (BCODP). He teaches disability studies in the School of Sociology and Social Policy at the University of Leeds, and is founder and Director of the School's Disability Research Unit.

Marian Barnes has worked in both social services and university research posts. She has researched and written for many years on aspects of user self-organisation, mental health and community care.

Nasa Begum is a research fellow at the Policy Studies Institute, London. Before joining PSI, she worked as a Project Co-Director at the King's Fund. Nasa has a background in community care, policy development and working with disabled people.

Mike Bury is Professor of Sociology and Head of Department at Royal Holloway, University of London. He teaches on the M.Sc. in Medical Sociology at Royal Holloway and has published widely on sociological aspects of chronic illness, disability, ageing and cultural dimensions of health and medicine.

Liz Crow is a disabled feminist who has been active in the disabled people's movement for the past decade. Since 1987 she has worked as a consultant on disabled people's rights, particularly in the education, arts and media, and health sectors.

Judith Emanuel is a health promotion specialist with a particular interest in community and organisational development. She is currently working on a freelance basis. Her recent work has involved training, teaching and research.

Michael P. Kelly is Head of the School of Social Sciences and Professor of Social Sciences at the University of Greenwich. He is a medical sociologist whose main interests are chronic illness, the sociology of health promotion and post-modern social theory.

Geof Mercer is a Senior Lecturer in the School of Sociology and Social Policy and a member of the Disability Research Unit, at the University of Leeds. He teaches and researches in the sociology of health and illness, and disability studies.

Mike Oliver is Professor of Disability Studies at the University of Greenwich, and an active member of the disability movement. He has published numerous books and articles, and has also made many appearances on television and radio, on disability over the last 15 years.

Ruth Pinder is Associate Research Fellow at the Centre for the Study of Health, Brunel University, and Associate GP Tutor, Northwick Park Hospital, Harrow.

Tom Shakespeare is a University Research Fellow in the School of Sociology and Social Policy, whose interests include disability studies, gender studies, cultural and identity politics, genetics and HIV/AIDS, and film production.

Polly Shardlow was a social worker for many years before she became a researcher. For the past two years, she has been working at the University of Sheffield on an ESRC-funded research project looking at the self-organisation of disabled people and people with mental health problems.

Gareth Williams is Reader in Sociology and Deputy Director of the Public Health Research and Resource Centre at the University of Salford. He has written extensively about chronic illness and disability, and lay knowledge.

CHAPTER 1

Introduction: exploring the divide

Colin Barnes and Geof Mercer

BACKGROUND

The notion that disablement is a medical problem which affects only a small proportion of the population can no longer be sustained. In the 1980s, Government social survey figures suggested that 6.5 million people had at least one 'disability' (Martin, Meltzer and Elliot, 1988). A more recent study concludes that four out of every ten adult women and men have a 'long standing illness or disability' (CSO, 1996). Internationally, there are around 50 million disabled people in Europe (Daunt, 1991) and approximately 500 million world-wide (DPI, 1992). Although there are significantly more disabled people in the under-resourced, 'developing' nations of the world, the prevalence of disablement is greatest in wealthier, developed societies (Helander, 1993). Moreover, the combination of an ageing population and new medical interventions which prolong life will ensure that the number of people with an 'impairment' or 'chronic illness' will increase substantially over the next few years. The economic, political, and social implications will be far-ranging (Hills, 1993).

The impact of disablement has stimulated a growing literature, both personal and academic, on 'chronic illness' and disability. Since the 1960s, there has been an extraordinary expansion of self-help groups and organisations controlled and run by disabled people, on a world-wide basis (Driedger, 1989). In the UK, this mobilisation of disabled people led to the emergence in 1981 of the British Council of Disabled People (BCODP), which now represents 113 national and local organisations and has a membership of over 400,000 disabled individuals (BCODP, 1996). There has been a parallel emphasis on political campaigns and demonstrations. At the same time disabled people have developed alternative perspectives to the traditional individualistic approaches to 'disability' which highlight the ways in which the medical condition constrains their daily lives. Through their actions, disabled people have sought to re-direct attention to the means by which individuals are 'disabled' by society. The focus is shifted to the level and character of social and economic disadvantage and discrimination experienced by disabled people.

Yet while there has been this politicisation of disabled people, an increasing division has emerged between 'disability theorists' and social scientists studying chronic illness, such as medical sociologists. The tendency has been to provide separate and competing, rather than joint, accounts of illness and disability. The tensions were amply illustrated in a panel discussion on chronic illness arranged during the British Sociological Association's Medical Sociology Annual Conference in 1992 (Bury, 1992). Considerable unease was expressed at the activities of disability theorists and their organisational allies, and the threat posed to the 'independence' of sociological researchers. Medical sociologists also voiced concern that disability theorists ignored complex issues in the interpretation and explanation of chronic illness and impairment in favour of political correctness and political campaigning. The trend was towards competing and more entrenched positions, whether in respect of language, theoretical approach, methods of inquiry or empirical conclusions.

It was against this background that the editors organised a conference in Leeds in April 1995 on the subject of *Accounting for Illness and Disability*. It is the participants in that event who provide the backbone to this volume. In order to contextualise these discussions, a brief review of the approaches to chronic illness and disability taken by medical sociology and disability theory will be provided together with an overview of the individual chapters.

MEDICAL SOCIOLOGY AND CHRONIC ILLNESS

The sociological analysis of health and illness typically takes as its starting point a distinction between the medical concern with disease as an abnormal bio-physical condition and its own focus on sickness as a social state. In sociological accounts, people's experience of ill-health encompasses much more than specific physiological symptoms. It extends to different levels of experience and the social meanings of illness. Two theoretical perspectives have dominated these studies: one functionalist, the other interpretative. In addition, a wide range of empirical investigations have been conducted, some influenced by a largely medical agenda, including work on the prevalence and character of chronic illness, and on patient compliance, and others interested in its associated social problems.

Talcott Parsons provided the primary stimulus to sociological theorising with his application of a functionalist analysis to a study of health and sickness (Parsons, 1951). He treated individual 'health' as central to effective task performance and the overall well-being of contemporary American society. In general terms, it was necessary for society to control those who deviated markedly from its central values and social structure. Hence, the functional significance of dealing with sickness in such a way as to eliminate any 'unconscious motivation' by individuals to avoid recovery and a resumption of their regular social obligations (Gerhardt, 1987). To obviate this particular possibility for social deviance, a special and conditionally legitimate status or 'sick role' is established, where individuals are temporarily located. As formulated by Parsons, the sick role includes both responsibilities and privileges. Thus, the sick person is not held responsible for their condition, and is granted exemption from fulfilling their 'normal' social obligations. In return, the sick person is required to take all appropriate steps to ensure their recovery, including consulting a medical practitioner.

The Parsonian approach has attracted considerable criticism within sociology (Freidson, 1970; Gerhardt, 1989). The notion of a universal role available to all sick people has been widely disputed. It has been demonstrated that access to, and granting of, the rights and privileges of the sick role are mediated by the social status and structural location of the sick person, including their gender, 'race'-ethnicity and social class. Moreover, exemption from normal social obligations is sometimes partial rather than general. A considerable literature has also developed from suggestions that some illnesses are stigmatised – perhaps the individual is 'blamed' for their condition, or the disease instils a generalised fear and dread (Goffman, 1968). Whatever the reason, the rights and privileges of the sick role are not, or only partially, granted (Freidson, 1970). A further criticism has been that Parsons wrongly narrowed the application of the sick role to 'patient' behaviour rather than the overall illness experience. Following the latter route, particular significance is accorded to studies of lay beliefs and networks (Zola, 1973). And, not least, the very notion of chronic illness runs counter to the temporary status of the sick role.

While attempts have been made to refurbish role theory, most recent studies of chronic illness have drawn inspiration instead from other sociological frameworks. The attack has been led by those located in an interpretative tradition, in particular phenomenology, which highlights the experiential aspects of illness and its underlying assumptions (Strauss and Glaser 1975; Bury, 1982). Research has documented the ways in which chronic illness influences daily living, social relationships, and people's sense of self and identity. Analysis has centred on how individuals balance the demands and uncertainties of chronic illness and its associated treatment regimes with the attempt to maintain everyday social routines. The focus has been on the meaning and experiences of chronic illness, and how far, and in what ways, people adapt to, and cope with, these constraints. In contrast to the socio-medical model, which concentrated on formal definitions and the assessment of needs, interpretative accounts have highlighted the emergent and contextual dimensions of chronic illness. The research interest has been on the ways in which the individual makes sense of their illness, and how their understandings influence social action (Anderson & Bury, 1988; Bury, 1991).

In order to understand the meanings people attribute to chronic illness, its trajectory and consequences, interpretative studies have sought to examine how these experiences are woven into individual biographies. From this standpoint, chronic illness is represented as not simply a physical challenge, but as having a more far-reaching potential for 'biographical disruption':

> 'First, there is the disruption of taken-for-granted assumptions and behaviours....Second, there are more profound disruptions in explanatory systems normally used by people such that a fundamental re-thinking of a person's biography and self-concept is involved. Third, there is the response to disruption involving the mobilisation of resources in facing an altered situation' (Bury, 1982, pp. 169-70).

The reference to individual biography implies a close link between meaning and context. Following this line of analysis, Bury (1988) distinguishes between meaning as 'consequence' and as 'significance'. The former is concerned with the 'problems which chronic illness and disability create for the individual' (p.91), such as difficulties in employment, with money, and in self-care. In an early illustration of this approach, Mildred Blaxter (1976) explored the meaning of 'disability' and its impact on social life, as well as the ways in which health and welfare systems constrain individuals. In contrast, 'meaning as significance' refers to the cultural representation of different conditions, and how the imputed stigma or other perceptions impact on individuals. Nevertheless, these meanings are not fixed or guaranteed, but are periodically 'put at risk' and perhaps revised as they are 'tested' in everyday interaction.

There is a direct link here with the work of medical sociologists in facilitating and applying the World Health Organisation's *International Classification of Impairments, Disabilities and Handicaps* (ICIDH) (WHO, 1980). This scheme provides a framework for exploring how the effects of impairment or chronic illness 'create both activity restriction (disability) and social disadvantage (handicap)' (Bury, 1988, p. 91). The intention was to conceptualise the consequences of chronic illness in such a way that practical and policy issues would be more easily identified. In practice, the widespread adoption of the WHO classification by medical sociologists stands in sharp contrast with its rejection by disability theorists. While sociologists believed that the ICIDH gave a clearer conceptual focus to the social disadvantages experienced by those with chronic illness, their disabled critics dismissed it as exhibiting little significant difference from the medical model. At the centre of the dispute was the question of how far sociological accounts elevated impairment to the determining 'cause' of disablement.

The portrayal of chronic illness by medical sociologists has also been criticised by disabled people as all too often a one-dimensional catalogue of negative consequences and meanings – the stigma, 'loss of self' and dependence – and the generally defensive coping strategies and manoeuvring. Studies which suggest a more diverse experience, or which report a positive sense of self and creative involvement in the lives of disabled people are far less in evidence. At the same time, medical sociology has tended to investigate all impairments, including stable visual or hearing impairments, from an illness perspective.

The impact and dominance of the interpretative approach in studies of chronic illness is a further source of disagreement. It is a matter of debate within medical sociology whether such research gives undue weight to subjective meanings and too little attention to wider structural forces. But it is noteworthy that non-interpretative theoretical perspectives have not made anything like the same significant or enduring contribution to the study of chronic illness. This particularly applies to studies of chronic illness and impairment in a broader political and economic context. For example, the analysis of medicine as an institution of social control, and the medicalisation of social problems, has obvious application to the study of disability and disabled people. Similar comments apply to the power and authority exercised by professionals. The Parsonian notion of a benign medical authority has been widely challenged in respect of doctor-patient relations, but sociologists have been slow to explore the potentially conflictual relations between disabled people and the professionals and other 'helpers' attached to them. This has led to a perceived disinterest in, and denial of, disability by medical sociology which has provided a powerful spur to the development of disability theory.

DISABILITY THEORY AND PRACTICE

In recent years the sociological approach to chronic illness and disability has been seriously challenged by a radical socio-political perspective that has advanced the 'social model of disability'. This was initially developed by a small but influential group of disabled activists during the late 1960s and early 70s (UPIAS, 1975, 1976). An early illustration of this socio-political approach to disability is contained in Paul Hunt's book, 'Stigma: The Experience of Disability'; which appeared in 1966. This collection of essays by six disabled men and six disabled women was one of the first to call for a focus on social rather than biological factors in understanding disability.

It was through such interventions by disabled people, that the grounds for rejecting the dominant 'medical' approach to disability were formulated. Their contention was that disablement should not be attributed to biomedical causes, and that medical or other health professional action was not the appropriate 'treatment' for a social problem. Initially, the social model focused on those with physical impairments, but it has subsequently been extended to include intellectual and sensory impairments. The main thrust of disability theory has been its analysis of the ways in which material and cultural forces have effectively 'disabled' people. Where disability had been treated as if an individual problem that stemmed inevitably from a person's impairment, this is reinterpreted as a socio-political issue. The central concern is the impact of disabling barriers and hostile social environments. The way forward has been to reconceptualise disability as a complex system of social oppression (Abberley, 1987) or institutional discrimination (Barnes, 1991):

> 'In our view, it is society which disables physically impaired people. Disability is something imposed on top of our impairments, by the way we are unnecessarily isolated and excluded from full participation in society. Disabled people are therefore an oppressed group in society. It follows from this analysis that having low incomes, for example, is only one aspect of our oppression. It is a consequence of our isolation and segregation, in every area of life, such as education, work, mobility, housing, etc.' (UPIAS, 1976, pp 3-4).

Disablism enters the political vocabulary on a par with racism and sexism. The further effect of re-defining disability as a social problem is to highlight the significance of developing organisational forms, tactics and strategies in order to advance the interests of disabled people through political struggles. The early inspiration was derived from the civil rights struggles of other oppressed groups, while the mobilisation of disabled people into more overt campaigning activity took off in the 1970s. This pressure from disabled people and their organisations has continued through the 1980s and 1990s, with the recent passing of the 1995 Disability Discrimination Act a sign of the disabled people's movement's continuing vitality (Barnes and Oliver, 1995).

The generation of the social model of disability and the politicisation of disabled people has been achieved despite what many in the disabled people's movement regard as little support, and often opposition and obstruction, from social scientists and other 'experts'. For example, in Britain, the relationship between poverty and disability was first placed on the political agenda by two disabled women, Megan du Bosson and Berit Moore, when they formed the Disablement Incomes Group (DIG) in 1965. The DIG campaign for a disability income was later joined by a host of other organisations – both 'of' and 'for' disabled people. These came together in 1972 under the umbrella of the Disability Alliance. However, the mobilisation of disabled people exacerbated tensions between disabled activists and non-disabled social scientists. These conflicts surfaced in UPIAS' critique of the Disability Alliance and its dominance by non-disabled academics (UPIAS, 1976). The Alliance was regarded as a forum where others speak on behalf of disabled people, whereas UPIAS aimed for mass participation of the disabled community:

> 'We reject also the whole idea of "experts" and professionals holding forth on how we should accept our disabilities, or giving learned lectures about the "psychology" of disablement. We already know what it feels like to be poor, isolated, segregated, done good to, stared at, and talked down to – far better than any able-bodied expert. We as a Union are not interested in descriptions of how awful it is to be disabled. What we are interested in, are ways of changing our conditions of life, and thus overcoming the disabilities which are imposed on top of our physical impairments by the way this society is organised to exclude us. In our view, it is only the actual impairment which we must accept; the additional and totally unnecessary problems caused by the way we are treated are essentially to be overcome and not accepted. We look forward to the day when the army of "experts" on our social and psychological problems can find more productive work' (UPIAS, 1976, pp. 4-5).

Other signs of the perceived paternalism, if not suspect 'support', were evident in the 1960s. Paul Hunt was again involved: on this occasion in a dispute with the staff of a Cheshire Home over the residents' demands for greater control of their lives (Miller & Gwynne, 1972). Researchers from the Tavistock Institute were called in to investigate conditions in the home. Their proposals for an 'enlightened guardian' approach to disability management provoked considerable opposition among the disabled residents:

> 'The half concealed assumption that our severe impairments actually cause our social problems is essential for Miller and Gwynne's attempt to justify their concentrating on the task of reconciling us to the inevitability of our social death, and for legitimising their research into how that sentence may most humanely be carried out' (Hunt, 1981, p. 42).

In like fashion, medical sociologists, who had long represented their starting point as a critique of the medical model of health and disease, found that their contribution was downgraded. There was a growing polarisation between social researchers and disabled activists and theorists who identified academic social science as part of the problem rather than part of the solution. The emphasis given to subjectivity and the presumed disregard for structural factors were raised as primary weaknesses in the medical sociology approach. There was little sympathy with the phenomenological interest in the complex contextual negotiation of everyday life, of identity and interaction, and the importance of treating the relationship between impairment and 'disability' as problematic and variable. It was argued that such studies deflected attention away from disablement and made no impression on removing 'disabling barriers'. This left little common ground with disability theorists and their concentration on the social exclusion and oppression of disabled people. The expanding division between disability theorists and medical sociologists included: the role of language, the causal link between impairment and disability, and the relevance of experience (Abberley, 1987; Finkelstein, 1993; Oliver, 1990; Davis, 1993).

Nevertheless, the formulation of the social model of disability has been challenged recently from within the ranks of the disabled people's movement. Two issues predominate. Firstly, there are those who wish to include 'impairment' in the account of disability. Whereas the 'orthodox' position has been that this will undermine the political force of the social model, there have been increasingly vocal claims that the individual experience of disabled people runs counter to the exclusion of the pain, fatigue and depression that often goes with impairment and chronic illness (Crow, 1992; French, 1993). A second criticism of the social model has been that it has been exclusionary to the extent that it has ignored or downplayed the significance of other structural divisions and disadvantages that affect disabled, as well as non-disabled, people. Attention is particularly drawn to the impact of sexism and racism and how these produce contrasting experiences within the disabled population (Begum, Hill and Stevens, 1994; Killin, 1993; Morris, 1991; Stuart, 1992). These debates assume considerable significance for attempts to build a positive disabled identity which incorporates and celebrates social and cultural differences.

ORGANISATION OF THE BOOK

The papers delivered at the Leeds conference on illness and disability were organised around three broad inter-related themes: definitions, identity, and environment. In practice, issues raised under one heading tended to spill-over into other areas. Therefore, it was thought inappropriate to divide the book into separate sections. Moreover, additional contributions were sought from other participants at the conference which explore key themes in detailed case studies. Just as those attending came from a wide range of backgrounds, so too the contributors to this volume include disabled activists and academics, medical sociologists, policy researchers, and people working in social services.

In chapter 2, Mike Bury surveys changes and challenges to sociological approaches to chronic illness. He traces the move from a socio-medical approach to a more explicitly sociological focus which takes an interpretative view of the individual's experience of chronic illness. Bury promotes a 'relational' approach to 'disability' which focuses on the interactions between the individual and their social location, while also noting that sociological studies have influenced policy makers away from a narrowly medical viewpoint. His review includes a robust critique of the 'social oppression' theory of disability, and maintains that disability theory is following a path which leads to an 'over-socialised' view of disability. He also takes issue with disability theorists' characterisation of the 'politics' of disability research and he concludes with a defence of the independent social researcher.

Mike Oliver provides a disability theorist's perspective on the significance of definitions in chapter 3. He identifies six main areas of contention: causality; conceptual consistency; the role of language; the normalising tendencies in both approaches; the issue of experience; and the politicisation of the definition process itself. The World Health Organisation's *International Classification of Impairments, Disabilities and Handicaps* (WHO, 1980) is criticised because it elevates impairment as a determining force in the lives of disabled people and acts as a spur to the medicalisation of disability. He contrasts it with definitions advanced by disabled people. Oliver also addresses challenges to the social model of disability from within the disabled people's movement. He argues for a concentration on the 'social barriers of disability' and those aspects of a disabled person's life which can be resolved by collective political intervention.

An alternative formulation of the relationship of impairment to the social model of disability is provided by Liz Crow in chapter 4. She emphasises the merits of the social model of disability while also arguing for its refurbishment. She contends that it runs counter to the personal experience of so many disabled people because it excludes the negative experiences associated with impairment. Her concern is that such an important part of disabled people's experience must be fully integrated into the account of disability and she calls for proper recognition of this subjective interpretation of impairment. For Crow, this does not go against the interests of disabled people in confronting disabling barriers, nor does it drive disability theory into accepting the position that all of the disadvantages experienced by disabled people are determined by their impairments.

In chapter 5, Mike Kelly draws on phenomenological perspectives to elaborate a theory of social identity which takes issue with early sociological role theory. He uses data from a study of people who have undergone total colectomy and ileostomy surgery to explore concerns about identity change and 'maintenance of self'. Kelly illustrates ways in which this illness and associated surgery are a source of potentially profound effects on the individual's self-identity and social interaction, although their salience varies across different contexts. His account highlights the significance of cultural stereotypes and self imposed negative attributions associated with this form of radical abdominal surgery, and the tensions and difficulties in confronting and overcoming these perceived threats to self-presentation and identity construction in social relationships, most particularly in intimate, and potentially sexual, encounters.

A contrasting journey through disability, identity and difference is provided by Tom Shakespeare in chapter 6. He argues that disability theorists' critique of the medical model has not gone far enough in creating space for a positive disabled identity to take root and flourish. He explores disability identity options at the personal, cultural and political levels, and draws parallels with struggles by feminists, black people, gays and lesbians. [Disabled people need to break out of the psychological prison of 'personal woes' and engage with the liberating feminist maxim that the personal is political.] Shakespeare also draws on post-structuralist writings to explore how disabled people can actively engage in constructing their own narratives and 'stories'. It is by these means that disabled people have a chance of constructing a new persona for themselves.

In chapter 7, Marian Barnes and Polly Shardlow explore the rarely documented attempts by 'users' or 'survivors' of mental health systems to achieve a positive identity. They explore one of the most fundamental objectives of such groups which is the right of 'survivors' to define their own needs, problems and solutions – rather than have this done by others. For the authors, their study of mental health user groups provides evidence of the formation of a 'new social movement'. They examine how far, and in what ways, the presumed 'passive and dependent recipients of welfare' are regaining some control over their own lives, for example, by contributing to the organisation and delivery of services. By the same token, such actions help them achieve a more positive sense of identity.

The emphasis given by medical sociologists to understanding the experience of chronic illness is illustrated in chapter 8 by Ruth Pinder. She uses two detailed case studies to point to the dilemmas and difficulties for people with arthritis in differentiating sickness and health in the labour market. She takes issue with the proponents of the social model of disability, and also rejects most attempts to 'bring impairment back in' because they do not go far enough. What is particularly lacking, she argues, is attention to the relational aspects of disability and impairment within their wider economic and socio-cultural contexts. Pinder's account examines the interplay between the body in its individual, social and political forms, and how body symbolism works at different levels, in shaping peoples' working lives.

In chapter 9, Nasa Begum, taking her lead from the social model of disability, explores the social control exercised by General Practitioners (GPs) over disabled women. Using survey data, she illustrates the ways in which doctors so often relied on stereotypes in their interactions with disabled women. Those interviewed resented the ways in which medical control operated. They felt that GPs could not see past their impairment. The disabled womens' relationship with their GPs was further complicated because the latter acted as gatekeepers to a range of non-medical resources and activities. In addition, the experiences of respondents were compounded by structural divisions located in class, and 'race'. Begum concludes by re-iterating her support for the social model of disability, while also arguing that disability theory considers further the relationship between illness, impairment and disability.

The new climate created by a reformed NHS and an internal market with purchasers and providers raises important questions about the extent to which disabled people have been meaningfully involved in decisions about their service needs and priorities. In chapter 10, Judith Emanuel and David Ackroyd report on one such initiative: the North West Regional Health Authority's development of guidelines on services for disabled people for purchasers, Health Authorities and GP Fundholders. The authors focus on a number of key questions, such as: What are the needs of disabled people? What influences the decisions taken by purchasers? How were providers to be made responsive to purchasers? The chapter elaborates how the guidelines were developed and the associated actions identified, as well as the difficulties encountered.

An exploration of the main issues in exploring the experience of impairment, disability and the environment is undertaken in chapter 11 by Gareth Williams. He identifies contrasting characterisations in rehabilitation, medical sociology and disability theory. The medical model's basic project is to deal with impairment, to which the environment is uneasily 'added on'. In medical sociology, the typical focus is on the interaction between symptoms and situation or external environment. Such accounts have been concerned primarily with subjective experience and the negotiation and re-negotiation of identity through talk. He acknowledges criticism that such studies can lose sight of the structures which shape experience. In contrast, disability theory's pre-occupation with 'social oppression' has excluded the variable social experience of chronic illness. Williams concludes by arguing for an approach which draws from both disability theory and medical sociology.

REVIEW

The impetus behind the Leeds conference, and of this volume, has been a desire to bring disability activists and theorists together with medical sociologists in order to explore areas of common concern. Over recent years there has been a widening gap, although the suggestion of protagonists lining up on opposing sides ignores the different emphases and approaches among medical sociologists and disability theorists and activists. The aim was to re-build a more positive dialogue on the key issues and concerns articulated by disability theorists and medical sociologists – and it is in this spirit that we decided to keep the editorial function to a minimum and, not least, leave the choice of terminology to participants.

We feel that the contributors in their different ways make the case for sustaining and developing such contact between the two 'disciplines' in order to generate a better understanding of the issues at stake or in dispute. Certainly, there is ample evidence that contributors remain suspicious and critical of each other's accounts of chronic illness and disability, but it is also important to highlight the common interests of disability theory and medical sociology in making the connections between the world of policy and politics and the realm of personal experiences. We hope that this volume will encourage theorists and activists to maintain the momentum towards constructive debate.

REFERENCES

ABBERLEY, P. (1987) 'The Concept of Oppression and the Development of a Social Theory of Disability', *Disability, Handicap and Society*, 2, 1, pp 5-19.

ALBRECHT, G. (1992) *The Disability Business*, London: Sage.

ANDERSON, R. & BURY, M. (eds.) (1988) *Living with Chronic Illness: the Experience of Patients and their Families*, London: Unwin Hyman.

BARNES. C. (1991) *Disabled People in Britain and Discrimination*, London: Hurst & Co.

BARNES, C. and OLIVER, M. (1995) 'Disability Rights: Rhetoric and Reality in the UK', *Disability and Society*, Vol. 10, No. 1, pp. 111-116.

BCODP (1996) *Directory of Organisations*, Derby: British Council of Disabled People.

BEGUM, N., HILL, M. STEVENS, A. (1994) *Reflections: Views of Black Disabled People on Their Lives and Community Care*, London: Central Council for Education and Training in Social Work.

BLAXTER, M. (1976) *The Meaning of Disability*, London: Heinemann.

BURY, M. (1982) 'Chronic Illness as Biographical Disruption', *Sociology of Health and Illness*, 4, pp 167-82.

BURY, M. (1988) 'Meanings at Risk: The Experience of Arthritis', in R. Anderson & M. Bury (eds.) (1988) *Living with Chronic Illness: the Experience of Patients and their Families*, London: Unwin Hyman.

BURY, M. (1991) 'The sociology of chronic illness: a review of research and prospects', *Sociology of Health and Illness*, 13, 4, pp 451-68.

BURY, M. (1992) 'Medical Sociology and chronic illness: A Comment On The Panel Discussion', *Medical Sociology News*, 18, 1, pp 29-33.

COLERIDGE, P. (1993) *Disability, Liberation and Development*, Oxford: Oxfam Publications.

CROW, L. (1992) 'Renewing the Social Model of Disability', in *Coalition*, July, pp. 5-9.

CSO (1996) *Social Trends*, London: Central Statistical Office.

DAUNT, P. (1991) *Meeting Disability: A European Response*, London: Cassell.

DAVIS, K. (1993) 'On the Movement', in Swain, J., Finkelstein, V., French, S. & Oliver, M. (eds.) *Disabling Barriers – Enabling Environments*, London: Sage, pp. 285-293.

DPI (1992) *Disabled Peoples' International: Proceedings of the Third World Congress of the Disabled Peoples' International*, Winnipeg: Disabled Peoples' International.

DRIEDGER, D. (1989) *The Last Civil Rights Movement*, London: Hurst and Co.

FINKELSTEIN, V. (1993) 'Disability: a social challenge or an administrative responsibility', in Swain, J., Finkelstein, V., French, S. & Oliver, M. (eds.) *Disabling Barriers – Enabling Environments*, London: Sage, pp. 34-44..

FREIDSON, E. (1970) *Profession of Medicine: A Study of the Sociology of Applied Knowledge*, New York: Harper Row

FRENCH, S. (1993) Disability Impairment or Something in Between, 'Disability: a social challenge or an administrative responsibility', in Swain, J., Finkelstein, V., French, S. & Oliver, M. (eds.) *Disabling Barriers – Enabling Environments*, London: Sage, pp. 17-25..

GERHARDT, E. (1987) *Ideas about Illness: An Intellectual and Political History of Medical Sociology*, Basingstoke: Macmillan.

GOFFMAN, E. (1968) *Stigma: Notes on the measurement of spoiled identity*, Harmondsworth: Penguin.

HELANDER, E. (1993) *Prejudice and Dignity: An Introduction to Community Based Rehabilitation*, Geneva: World Health Organisation.

HILLS, J. (1993) *The Future of Welfare: A guide to the debate*, York: Joseph Rowntree Foundation.

HUNT, P. (1966) *Stigma: The Experience of Disability*, Geoffrey Chapman, London.

HUNT, P. (1981) 'Settling Accounts With The Parasite People: A Critique of "A Life Apart" by E. J. Miller and G. V. Gwynne', *Disability Challenge*, 1, pp. 38-50.

KILLIN, D. (1993) 'Independent Living, Personal Assistance, Disabled Lesbians and Disabled Gay Men', in C. Barnes, (ed.) *Making our Own Choices*, Derby: The British Council of Disabled People, pp. 55-58.

KLEINMAN, A. (1988) *The Illness Narratives: Suffering, Healing and the Human Condition*, New York: Basic Books.

MARTIN, J., MELTZER, H., & ELLIOT, D. (1988) *OPCS Surveys of Disability in Great Britain: Report 1 – The prevalence of disability among adults*, London: HMSO.

MILLER, E. J. & GWYNNE, G. V. (1972) *A Life Apart*, London: Tavistock.

MORRIS, J. (1991) *Pride Against Prejudice*, London: Women's Press.

OLIVER, M. (1990) *The Politics of Disablement*, Basingstoke: Macmillan and St.Martin's Press.

OLIVER, M. (1992) 'Changing the Social Relations of Research Production', *Disability, Handicap and Society*, 7, 2, 101-114.

OLIVER, M. (1993) 'Re-defining disability: a challenge to research', in Swain, J., Finkelstein, V., French, S. & Oliver, M. (eds.) *Disabling Barriers – Enabling Environments*, London: Sage.

OLIVER, M. (1996) *Understanding Disability: From Theory to Practice*, Basingstoke: Macmillan and St.Martin's Press.

PARSONS, T. (1951) *The Social System*, New York: Free Press.

RADLEY, A. (1994) *Making Sense of Illness*, London: Sage.

SHAKESPEARE, T. (1993) 'Disabled People's Self Organisation, A New Social Movement?', *Disability and Society*, 8, 3, pp. 249- 264.

STONE, D. (1985) *The Disabled State*, London: Macmillan.

STRAUSS, A. L. and GLASER, B. (1975) *Chronic Illness and the Quality of Life*, St. Louis: C.V. Mosby and Co.

STUART, O. (1992) 'Race and Disability: What Type of Double Disadvantage', *Disability, Handicap and Society*, 7, 2, pp

SWAIN, J., FINKELSTEIN, V., FRENCH, S. & OLIVER, M. (eds.) *Disabling Barriers – Enabling Environments*, London: Sage..

TOWNSEND, P. (1979) *Poverty in the UK*, Harmondsworth: Penguin.

UPIAS (1975) *Policy Statement*, London: Union of the Physically Impaired Against Segregation.

UPIAS (1976) *Fundamental Principles of Disability*, London: Union of the Physically Impaired Against Segregation.

WHO (1980) *International Classification of Impairments, Disabilities and Handicaps*, Geneva: World Health Organisation.

ZOLA, I. K. (1973) 'Pathways to the Doctor: From Person to Patient', *Social Science and Medicine*, 7, pp. 677-89.

CHAPTER 2

Defining and Researching Disability: challenges and responses

Mike Bury

INTRODUCTION

It is something of a cliché to say that we are living in a period of rapid social change. Yet it seems clear that a fundamental process of cultural as well as economic and social transformation is underway, and on a global scale. Arguments have proliferated as to the directions of such change. For some, the changes represent little more than cultural fragmentation, perhaps even degeneration, for others they represent renewal (Featherstone, 1992). What is less in doubt is that assumptions underpinning a range of social and intellectual activities are under strain. Nowhere is this more in evidence than in the health field. Not only is modern medicine being challenged on all sides, from managerialism to alternative medicine, but the very categories that have underpinned modern health and welfare systems are being severely scrutinised.

In this chapter, a preliminary sketch of change in one area of health and welfare is presented, namely that of disability. The chapter first examines the recent history of defining and researching disability, and identifies the emergence of a 'socio-medical' model, particularly in the British context. It then notes the development of a more explicit sociological view, which has emerged from these concerns and from more theoretical considerations. Second, the chapter examines recent arguments put forward by a number of 'disability theorists', that disability should be defined and researched primarily as a form of 'social oppression'. Critiques of the socio-medical model and sociological work which have been informed by these arguments will be examined. Finally, the chapter considers the impact this controversy is having on the field of disability studies, and on the relationship between researchers and researched.

THE EMERGENCE OF DISABILITY

In the immediate post-war world, at least in Britain, health care and social welfare in the disability area were characterised, in Topliss' terms, by a mixture of neglect and humanitarian concern (Topliss, 1979). The effects of war and industrial injury slowly gave way to the impact of chronic disease and disability in an ageing population. Though, of course, not all disability at this time was associated with chronic illness, and not all such illness involved disability, the relationship between the two was becoming increasingly evident (Taylor, 1976). In addition, disability in earlier stages of the life course, from the effects of congenital abnormalities, and from injuries caused by high risk sports and leisure activities was also becoming significant. The relationship between age, life course, disability and such factors as gender and ethnicity has subsequently received more attention, especially in social research (Arber and Evandrou, 1993).

During the same period medical specialties grew, and this has sometimes led to accusations, mentioned in more detail below, of the medicalisation of disability. Since then, areas such as rheumatology, stroke and rehabilitation services have grown rapidly, alongside the massive expansion of services for patients with a wide variety of other chronic disabling conditions. Specialist facilities for treating the effects of trauma, whether on the sports field or the roads have also grown. Medical research on these conditions and on the general profile of disability has also expanded at a rapid rate.

In Britain, research on the social dimensions of chronic illness and disability began in earnest in the 1960s, though it has to be said, within a less theoretical framework than in the U.S. (Bury, 1991). Collaboration between public health oriented rehabilitation specialists such as Michael Warren, and sociologists such as Margot Jefferys, focused on the definition and assessment of motor impairment in prevalence studies (Jefferys et al., 1969). As Donald Patrick has pointed out, such work was linked to the task of estimating medical need and the possibility of developing preventive strategies (Patrick and Peach, 1989, p. 21).

This and other work culminated in the first OPCS national study of 'impairment and handicap' carried out by Amelia Harris and her colleagues, and published in 1971. This showed, for the first time, the extent of impairment in Britain, and suggested that just under 4% of the population aged 16-64 and just under 28% population over the age of 65 suffered from some form of impairment (Harris et al., 1971). Importantly, gender differences were noted, with twice the level of impairment in women compared with men (Patrick and Peach, 1989, p. 22). Comparable studies were carried out in the U.S. at this time (ibid.).

Subsequently, in Britain, Wood and his colleagues sought to clarify the terminology that was being used in this research, especially in the light of confusion, present even in the Harris survey, where different definitions (e.g. of impairment and handicap) were evident, with the terms sometimes being used synonymously. In 1980 the World Health Organisation published the results of this work in the form of the International Classification of Impairments, Disabilities and Handicaps (ICIDH) which provided a more consistent definition of the terms involved (WHO, 1980). In this classification, *impairment* referred to abnormality in the structure of the functioning of the body, whether through disease or trauma; *disability* referred to the restriction in ability to perform tasks, especially those associated with everyday life and self care activities; and *handicap* referred to the social disadvantage that could be associated with either impairment and/or disability. The latter term was particularly emphasised as a means of revealing needs created as a consequence of chronic illness interacting with a sometimes hostile social environment.

The widespread use of this schema helped focus the socio-medical model that earlier work had been building, and provided the basis for both developments and debate in the years that followed. Community based studies, such as that in Lambeth, South London, provided the framework for the exploration of prevalence of impairment, health care and rehabilitation needs in disability and social aspects of handicap, such as material hardship and the role of social support. This kind of research helped to explore the mediating relationship between the various planes of experience that the WHO schema described (Patrick and Peach, 1989).

National and local studies underlined, in particular, the economic dimensions of disability, and the hardship experienced by many, particularly in a period of growing recession. Though the Harris survey had been associated with the 1970 Chronically Sick and Disabled Persons Act, which for the first time obliged local authorities in Britain to estimate and meet the needs of the disabled, various research findings reinforced the view held by Mechanic and others in earlier U.S. work, that the consequences of disability were most obviously seen in financial hardship. In fact, a less well publicised volume of the Harris study revealed the extent of financial hardship among the disabled (Harris et al., 1971b). Townsend's compendious work on *Poverty in the United Kingdom* gave additional weight to the link between disability and inequality (Townsend, 1979).

Though the socio-medical model provided the grounds for identifying and drawing attention to the various needs of disabled people, many problems remained. At the research level, it had long been recognised that the definition of disability, unlike disease was less categorical and more 'relational' in character. It was pointed out that the term disability was conceptually 'slippery' and difficult to pin down (Topliss, 1979), and involved complex interactions between the individual and the social environment. Moreover, the boundaries between impairment, disability and handicap were recognised as less than clear cut in everyday settings, and difficult to operationalise in research, even though the distinctions remained important in directing attention to different planes of experience (Bury, 1987).

At the policy level, though the consequences of disability were being identified, financial compensation and greater emphasis on disabled people's own views was not much in evidence. In part this arose from the continuing part that medicine played, within administrative circles, in adjudicating access to benefits. In order to tackle this problem, and provide new estimates of disability based on a broader definition, a new national study was commissioned by the OPCS in 1984, and several surveys, including one on children, were carried out between 1985 and 1988. The main purpose of this new initiative was to inform a review of social security in the disability field, and pave the way for such benefits to be based on a more systematic appreciation of the relational character of disability.

As a result of this orientation, the OPCS developed an approach to measuring disability which would be more sensitive to the difficulties encountered in earlier work. By combining judgements of professionals, researchers and disabled people themselves, and by using the basic definition of disability as laid down in the WHO classification, the OPCS was able to operationalise a new approach that gave a wider picture. Scales were developed on key areas of disability ranging from problems with locomotion, through seeing, hearing and personal care, to difficulties with communication (Martin et al., 1988, p. 10).

The development of these scales, at the pilot stage, was conducted in close co-operation with groups involved in disability at the time. A large number of people and organisations was invited to comment on the pilot interview-based questionnaires. A somewhat smaller number was involved in consultations in actually developing the scales, including, for example MIND, MENCAP, Royal National Institute for the Deaf (RNID), the Disablement Income Group (DIG) the Disability Alliance and the Royal National Institute for the Blind (RNIB) (Martin, 1995). By focusing directly on the nature and impact of disability on everyday life (but not on impairment) this approach shifted the centre of gravity of the socio-medical model towards defining the severity of disability in terms of its effects, including, again, employment and financial difficulties.

For present purposes, two main findings are of note. First, the association of disability with age was once more confirmed. This is of particular importance in the OPCS survey, which was innovatory in assessing the level of disability without, at the point of interview, an age reference; in other words, if a person could not perform a particular activity they were counted as disabled irrespective of age. However, when the data from the survey were analysed, they showed that of six million people living in Great Britain with at least one form of disability (based on the relatively low threshold used in the survey) almost 70% of disabled adults were aged 60 and over, and nearly half were aged 70 and over (Martin et al., 1988, p. 27). The very old emerged as those most likely to be affected, with 63% of women and 53% of men over the age of 75 being disabled. When severity is taken into account, the very old again predominate, with 64% of adults in the two highest categories aged 70 or over, and 41% aged 80 or over (Martin et al., 1988). I will return to the significance of some of these findings later in the chapter.

For the moment however, it is the predominance of chronic disease as the cause of disability, which is of particular note in the OPCS study. Many of the disorders associated with later life, especially arthritis, and hearing loss (the former helping to explain much of the gender difference in disability rates) were most frequently associated with disability, underlining the long term trend away from disabilities caused by trauma and medical conditions in early life, to disorders in later life.

Important though this study was in developing and improving the picture available from the Harris study, the role of chronic illness in the findings did expose one of the tensions to be found in work of this kind. For, no matter how justifiable the attempt is to influence the direction of the operation of welfare, and notably social security, away from medical adjudication, a full picture of disablement in contemporary populations inevitably exposes its health and illness dimensions. From the viewpoint of everyday experience, therefore, different aspects of health and welfare needs may be relevant. Moreover, these dimensions have implications for different forms of intervention on the impairment, disability, and handicap continuum. The presence of chronic illness as a causal factor in disability may highlight the need for greater attention to preventive measures, better delivery of health care and medical treatment, the provision of home adaptations, or the need for financial or social support.

Some needs may, therefore, be condition specific, depending upon the particular illness or impairment concerned. A follow up study by the RNIB, for example, involving further interviews with a sample of visually impaired people from the OPCS survey, and a more detailed analysis of the relevant OPCS material, was able to provide a more in depth picture of the special needs of people with visual impairments, including their health needs (Bruce et al., 1991). The relationship between the general profile of disability and the specific needs of groups within the population clearly needs to be appreciated.

This issue, for sociologists, at least, has underpinned their growing concern with the meaning of disability, and not simply its definition or prevalence. Alongside work on the socio-medical model, therefore, a more independent sociological voice began to emerge. This set out a more distinctive research approach, in comparison with the medical and policy agendas, which had dominated the field until then. This approach began to apply more explicitly sociological concepts to the area.

In Britain, Mildred Blaxter's book *The Meaning of Disability* (Blaxter, 1976), and in the U.S., Strauss and Glaser's book, *Chronic Illness and the Quality of Life* (Strauss and Glaser, 1975) captured the spirit of these concerns. Using different methods, both books explored the range of problems encountered by people with disabilities. In the case of Blaxter's book, she showed that over time the impact of disability on social life was particularly marked, even when other more practical problems had been resolved. She also showed how the complicated relationship between health and welfare systems hampered individuals and their families in adapting to disability. Strauss and his colleagues looked particularly at the balance people sought to strike between the demands of illness and treatment regimens and the need to maintain a normal everyday life.

Since these pioneering studies, more sociological work on specific disabling illnesses have now been undertaken, documenting both the problems people face and the active steps they take to overcome them. The emphasis on meaning in this work has revealed, in more depth, the issues that people find most difficult in adapting to in disabling illness. Such studies have also highlighted the constraints of societal responses and the availability or the lack of resources needed to tackle them (Bury, 1991). The exploration of the contextual and emergent nature of disability in sociological work of this kind has acted as a counter point to the more formal definitions and assessments in the socio-medical model, as described above.

However, despite, or perhaps because of this wider body of work, in both the U.S. and U.K., new challenges have developed, not least from among people with chronic disorders and disabilities themselves. As services and research have expanded so the boundaries that have separated fields of activities, notably those between professionals and patients/clients have shifted. And as numerous sources of information have emerged these have inevitably provided grounds for more critical perspectives to develop. Indeed, under conditions of information explosion and media interest, as Anthony Giddens has pointed out in a more general cultural context, experts and expert knowledge become 'chronically contestable' (Giddens, 1991).

Though the field of chronic illness and disability has long contained a large number of lay charitable and self help groups, whose interests and views have often departed from those in the medical and academic establishments, new forms of organisation and outlook have recently emerged. While some groups, especially those linked to specific chronic diseases, continue to concentrate on supporting medical and, to a lesser extent, social research, others have begun to adopt and develop a more critical position with respect to both the definition and study of disability.

The emergence of the 'disability movement', characterised by an increasingly challenging attitude to the discrimination and 'exclusionary practices' which have historically affected the disabled in modern society, has gained considerable momentum. New forms of political, educational and professional activities have proliferated as expressions of these developments. In addition, help lines, lobbyists, and rights activists, have provided numerous opportunities for challenges to existing policies and practices to gain ground. Many of these activities have drawn on a range of writings that seek to confront current research. For example, a special issue of *Disability, Handicap and Society* was given over to the topic in 1992, following a conference supported by the Rowntree Foundation. It is to the main lines of the criticisms found here and elsewhere that the chapter now, therefore, turn. Following a brief outline of the definitional and theoretical issues addressed in these recent arguments, the implications for social research are then addressed.

DISABILITY AS A FORM OF SOCIAL OPPRESSION

Perhaps the sharpest challenge to existing ideas about disability is the argument that disability should be seen as a form of 'social oppression' (Oliver, 1990; 1992). Although this term is not clearly defined, the basic position is clear. In contrast to existing notions of disability, which, it is argued, portray it as a characteristic of individuals, 'disability' is seen, instead, as a wholly social phenomenon. Mike Oliver, whose writing may act as an exemplar in this context, states, for example, that 'disability as a category can only be understood within a framework, which suggests that it is culturally produced and socially constructed' (Oliver, 1990, p. 22). 'Disability' is seen to be a function of those practices and perceptions linked to certain bodily mental or behavioural states which are so designated. Here the ICIDH definition of 'disability' is rejected, in favour of an approach which at times is similar to that of the ICIDH definition of 'handicap', that is, the social disadvantage experienced by disabled people.

From the 'social oppression' viewpoint, disability is not the resulting limitations caused by chronic illness, impairment or trauma, but the way such matters are responded to and categorised by the wider society. Disability is the product of definitions and practices that seek to exclude individuals who might be seen to deviate from the socially constructed norms of the 'able bodied'. In short, 'disability' is what a 'disablist' society decides so to call. The links with labelling theory developed by sociologists in the 1960s are immediately apparent in such an argument. It is not the 'inherent' nature of disability that matters, but the labelling process, which categorises people by virtue of their position in relation to the dominant structures and values of the society.

The important starting point for 'oppression theory', is that 'disability' should not be conceptualised as an individual attribute, but as the result of 'exclusionary practices'. In a capitalistic society, these designate which attributes are seen as productive and acceptable and which are abnormal or deviant. Definitional questions, according to this argument, therefore flow not from the 'personal tragedy' of disability, but from the needs of the social system to distinguish between people in industrial and educational environments, and the need to decide who is to be excluded or segregated (Oliver, 1990, p.28).

State involvement in people's lives, throughout the modern period, is seen to be preoccupied with the sorting and segregating of individuals, especially in terms of their abilities to meet the dictates of the work place, and, in general, to ensure that social order is maintained by regulating exclusions in matters such as eligibility for state benefits. Thus disability turns out to be a central rather than peripheral matter to the development and maintenance of modern welfare states (Stone, 1984; Albrecht, 1992).

In addition to the 'exclusionary practices' that result from this process, the tendency to portray disability as a feature of the individual, it is held, reinforces an 'ideology of individualism'. This, to stay with Oliver's argument, is held to be at the heart of our current concepts. In extending his 'political economy' view of disability, to cover this point, Oliver argues:

> 'It is not the ideological construction of property owning, self interested or rational individuals that is important (in discussing disability). Rather it is the construction of "able bodied" and "able minded" individuals which is significant' (Oliver, 1990, pp.45-46).

The 'theory of medicalisation' is then added to this approach in order to explain the role of medicine in regulating and managing disability. Rather than accepting medicine as a means of meeting the needs of individuals, Oliver, again, casts medicine's role as essentially the handmaiden to the capitalist order. Referring to Zola's (1972) theory of medicalisation and social control, Oliver argues that medical labels 'stick to some groups and not others'. This process is held to be a function of the ideological and material needs of the system, rather than the health and welfare needs of individuals. Indeed the latter act as a screen behind which discriminatory practices take place. In this sense, the argument that medical knowledge is 'socially constructed' (Bury, 1986) is also invoked.

Given the apparent lack of effective treatment for many chronic disorders, the only explanation Oliver can find for medicine's involvement in disability is a regulatory and 'imperialistic' one. Though the expanding role of medicine, including surgery, in treating a variety of different 'impairments' is left unclear, Oliver echoes Finkelstein's employment of the idea of 'medical dominance' of disability to account for the development of specialisms such as rehabilitation medicine (Finkelstein, 1980). In so doing such writers draw on a range of medical sociology writings from the nineteen seventies which, as Gerhardt (1989) has noted, portrayed medicine as the result of the (largely arbitrary) artful practices of the medical profession, rather than as the application of objective knowledge to the patient's condition. In an attempt to turn the tables on this process Oliver asks, 'who should be in charge of the rehabilitation process, disabled people or the professionals?' (Oliver, 1993, p. 61).

RESEARCHING DISABILITY

As has been stated, one of the purposes of this chapter is to trace how these critical ideas about disability are being applied to the area of research. Perhaps one of the first questions that arises, in this connection, is why 'disability theorists' should be particularly concerned with research in the first place. If disability, from a 'social oppression' viewpoint, is self evidently entirely 'social' and therefore 'political' in character (Oliver, 1992) a social movement espousing such a position might well be expected to concern itself primarily with political action against a 'disablist society' and use social research findings, wherever possible, for these purposes, rather than focus on the activities of research and researchers as such. Indeed, Oliver has done precisely that, using the OPCS study and its estimates (which, as I will show, has been severely criticised elsewhere by 'disability theorists') in support of disability rights (Barnes and Oliver, 1995).

In fact, disability groups have long adopted this approach, in their campaigning as the reference to the RNIB earlier in this chapter indicates. Others, such as the Disability Alliance, have long used the research findings of Townsend and others in pamphleteering, campaigning and advancing their case. Recent campaigns for 'disability rights' legislation in the British parliament have employed similar tactics. It could be argued that in such activity, challenging definitions and research approaches has not been a high priority. The majority of those arguing for disability rights seem more concerned with other, more substantive issues. The position of 'disabled people' has been advanced without the need for a radical 'deconstruction' of the term, as defined, for example, by WHO/ OPCS. These 'second order' constructs have not been the focus of concern. It seems that appeals to generally accepted definitions of disability, rather than 'social oppression' theory, have been more than adequate for the political tasks in hand.

However, the role that medical and social research has played in the recent history of disability is often held by others, especially the 'disability theorists', to be negative and part of the problem to be addressed, rather than a potential (if limited) part of its solution.

As a result, 'disability theorists' have developed critiques both of the putative effects of recent research, and the research process itself. In so doing they have drawn links between their general critiques of the variety of professional discourses on disability, and recent research activities. Here, both medical and social research have become the focus of 'struggle', because they have been seen, like other professional activities, as largely self serving. As Oliver has stated:

> 'The idea that small groups of "experts" can get together and set a research agenda for disability, is again, fundamentally flawed' (Oliver, 1992, p. 102).

This suggests that 'disability theorists' should extend their arguments to fashion a different research agenda and possibly a new methodology. Whilst this immediately opens up the possible counter charge that 'disability theorists' may be making a similar play to establish themselves as a groups of 'experts' – especially as many now hold university posts, and run research projects and units – the main thrust is to argue a strong case against the activities of the present research community.

Current research on disability, it is held, is grossly unsatisfactory for two main reasons. First, it is alleged that most, if not all, research in the area is an alienating experience for disabled people. Though, as far as I can see, this charge is not supported by any systematic empirical evidence, it is forcibly argued from first principles that, as the disabled are the object of research rather than its authors, 'almost all social research has been alienating' (Oliver, 1992, p. 103, quoting Rowan, 1981). Because, it is held, the disabled themselves have not carried out the research, this is taken to mean that its execution is wholly negative. Though it would be difficult to know, in most cases, of course, whether individual researchers were or were not impaired or disabled (Oliver and others write as if they know that all previous research was carried out by the 'able bodied') this is held, importantly, by 'disability theorists' to add to the sense of exclusion and oppression, identified in the general critique of disability as it is currently defined. Although it is not at all clear what this might mean, from here it is a short step to argue that research on disability should only be carried out or controlled by disabled people themselves (Zarb, 1992).

Second, the effects of research in terms of its impact on policy is also seen as largely or wholly negative. The WHO and OPCS approaches have attracted particular opprobrium, from broadsides by Finkelstein (1980) onwards. According, to Oliver, for example, in discussing the OPCS study:

> 'despite promises to the contrary, the Government has failed to take any coherent policy initiatives based upon it (i.e. the OPCS survey)' (Oliver, 1992, p. 103).

One reading of this comment could be that it suggests that the government could have taken policy initiatives, and that it is the politicians who are at fault. It appears that broken promises rather than poor research are the problem here. Moreover, it would also seem to follow from this, that in such a political climate, a more 'radical' style of research might run into even more difficulties at the political level. In either case, criticism of the research and of the researchers would not seem to be, in principle, the key issue, but the lack of action by governments, on the evidence they have paid to be collected. In fact, the OPCS survey *did* have an impact on policy in the U.K., especially in the formulation and implementation of the Disability Living Allowance (DLA) and the Disability Working Allowance (DWA). The DLA has increased the number eligible for benefit on the lower threshold set by the survey, and medical tests for the DWA now use functional scales and everyday language; only in extreme cases is reference made to medical conditions.

However, the OPCS survey, in particular, has continued to come in for intense criticism from 'disability theorists', and, it should be noted, other lobbying groups in the field, including some of those who were not just 'the object' of enquiry, but participated in it. Even though, as argued earlier, the survey was based on a more detailed appreciation of the perceptions of disabled people themselves, in comparison with any previous equivalent study, this has not been accepted by the critics as a sign of progress. Thus, research of this kind has been held to be at best useless and at worst a further source of 'oppression'.

The background to this takes us back to the underlying conception of disability discussed earlier. While critics such as Finkelstein and Oliver recognise that research endeavours such as Harris's 1971 survey, Wood's WHO classification and the OPCS survey contain a social component, they remain dismissive of them because, they argue, such 'research is based on the idea that disability and handicap arise as a direct consequence of individual impairments' (Oliver, 1990, p.7). This argument is advanced despite the fact that the WHO approach expressly underlined the complexities of the relationships between the different dimensions, and that the disability movement's own conception of disability also begins with some form of underlying impairment, whether through disease or trauma. French (1993), for example, has made the point that though she agrees with:

'the basic tenets of the ('disability theorists') model', she believes, 'that some of the most profound problems experienced by people with certain impairments are difficult, if not impossible, to solve by social manipulation' (French, 1993, p.17).

Here, French seems to recognise the dangers of an 'oversocialised' view of disability, creating a reductionist perspective in its zeal to exclude the role that different factors plays.

In fact, the idea that impairment and disability are closely related, but distinct proves difficult to reject. Without some underlying initial problem, social responses would, so to speak, have nothing to respond to. If labelling theory is invoked, some form of 'primary deviation' is necessary, if societal reactions are to have any meaning. Labels have to be attached to a restricted range of phenomena if they are to be effective (positively or negatively) as labels at all. Moreover, while the role of impairment (especially as the result of chronic illness) was clearly conceptualised in the WHO approach, this was not the most important aspect of the schema. It was the emphasis on handicap which mattered most, in its attempt to point to the social disadvantage which may result from the social reactions and conditions within which disability is experienced.

As mentioned earlier, as a result of the 'relational' character of the processes at work, the distinctions between disability and handicap are inevitably problematic (Bury, 1987). Both disability and handicap can be seen as a product, from this viewpoint, *of the interaction of the individual and the social environment*. The distinction between them is simply designed to direct attention to the different dimensions of experience, that is, the difference between restricted activity (which, following French's comment, may be more or less 'social produced' in character) and related social disadvantage. Without such a distinction, the ability to know that disadvantage has increased or reduced would be difficult indeed to establish. The 'disability theorists' critique, however, rejects this distinction and asserts that disability is wholly a product of social circumstances.

Once this uni-dimensional view of disability is adopted, the next step in their critique of research is fairly easily taken. If research is based on an unacceptable definition of disability, all research which fails to adopt the 'disability theorists' conception becomes a target as part of the 'oppression' of disabled people. This reinforces the argument that research should be a field of struggle in which 'disability as oppression' can be produced or resisted.

Oliver states:

> 'This view (the WHO approach to research) can and does have oppressive
> consequences for disabled people and can be quite clearly in the methodology
> adopted by the recent OPCS survey in Britain' (Oliver, 1990, p.7).

In order to develop this argument, Oliver then goes on to examine in some
detail the questionnaire items from the OPCS survey. It may be helpful at
this point to follow his line of attack. The questionnaire, he contends,
contains items such as:

- Can you tell me what is wrong with you?
- How difficult is it for you to get about your immediate neighbourhood on
  your own?
- Does your health problem/disability make it difficult for you to travel by
  bus?

Oliver comments:

> 'These questions clearly ultimately reduce the problems that disabled people face
> to their own personal inadequacies or functional limitations' (Oliver, 1990, p. 7;
> see, also Abberley, 1992, p. 140).

In fact, the first of the above 'questions' was not actually part of the survey
proper, and was not coded, being used only to establish the terms in which
individual respondents normally talked about their disability. However,
though it is hard to see how the construction of 'personal inadequacy' can
simply be read off from the other questions about transport and work
difficulties, specifically designed to elicit people's problems in working and
moving around, a critical view of the precise nature of the questions and the
assumptions on which they are based is, of course, a justifiable exercise.
However, instead of analysing these questions in any detail, especially in
relation to the aims of the survey, Oliver goes on to put forward an
alternative set of questions, based on the 'social oppression' approach. These,
Oliver argues, would include such questions as the following:

- Can you tell me what is wrong with society?
- Are there any transport or financial problems which prevent you from
  going out as often or as far as you would like?
- Do poorly designed buses make it difficult for someone with your health
  problem/disability to use them? (Oliver, 1990, p. 8).

While we might wonder just what sort of answer a researcher might expect to the first (presumably ironic) question; 'What is wrong with society?', and how this might help in a study of disability, the other examples do offer a more persuasive alternative to the OPCS approach. But these questions, in turn, raise similar difficulties to those they replace. The second alternative question about transport, for example, could be asked of anyone and therefore loses its value as a question about disability. In order for the question to work, the respondent would need to have a prior and identified 'health problem/disability' in order to be the focus of research in the first place. If this is not accepted, then the idea that 'the disabled' should have control over the research process evaporates. If it is, then some prior question about what is 'wrong' with the person seems inescapable. In both contexts 'disability' must have some degree of independence from the social consequences associated with it.

The recognition of the role of impairment, alone, does not circumvent these dilemmas. Without a working and restricted definition of disability involving activity restriction, the strong form of relativism in the 'social oppression' approach threatens to negate any meaningful form of enquiry, as it seems to refer to any form of difficulty that the 'disability theorists' wish to include. Asking people in the general population about transport problems, for example, is hardly likely to form the basis of effective, let alone radical action to reduce 'disabling barriers'.

Moreover, there is not much point asking such people about specific issues, such as the design of buses, or other environmental barriers if they present no problem. Indeed the third example alternative question on bus design, given above, has to mention, if it is to make sense at all, the person's 'health problem or disability'. The inadequacy of buses can only be judged (and, indeed campaigned against) if there is good evidence of what they are inadequate for, and this inevitably takes us back to disability among people in specific contexts. Poorly designed buses do not in this sense *create or construct* disability. If a person has difficulty climbing steps as a result of paraplegia or arthritis, for example, the presence of steps on buses has not created the person's disability, in the sense of reduced mobility. What it means is that these technologies have not been designed to help the disabled person have access and overcome mobility restriction.

I think it also has to be recognised that while 'struggles' over which barriers need to be tackled and to what extent they can be overcome or removed is the understandable focus of political arguments and action, they raise all manner of problems about the different needs, interests and values in different social groups, including those among the disabled. The removal of some barriers might be at the expense of tackling others, as one group may articulate their needs more effectively. For example, the elderly chronically sick and disabled have traditionally had less of a voice than younger people. For older people, resources spent on removing some barriers may be of less importance than resources for care in the home. Rolling up the different aspects of disability into the one dimension of 'oppression' fails to recognise these potential differences, which carefully conducted research is likely to reveal

This also suggests that the alternative form of questioning in survey research, advocated by Oliver, may make sense to some disabled people but not to others. Diversity in experience arguably cuts across an approach to research methodology directed by an ideological argument about 'oppression'. From this viewpoint the alternative approach advocated by Oliver and others, in opposition to survey work such as that of the OPCS, all too often reads like a list of somewhat confused 'politically correct' statements about the position of disabled people. Challenging though these may at first sight seem, the present discussion suggests that they do not provide a thought through alternative research strategy, or an adequate approach to the diverse views and experiences of disabled people in different contexts.

The idea of research as a field of 'struggle' becomes even more complicated as attacks on qualitative social research are added to the campaign of 'disability theorists'. Survey work, such as the OPCS study, carried out by epidemiologists and government departments is in one sense a readily identifiable target, partly because it exemplifies a 'positivist' approach, and can be seen as part of official medical and state responses to disability (Abberley, 1992). Qualitative research however, carried out largely by sociologists, presents a slightly different challenge to 'disability theorists', and has received separate attention because of the difficulty identifying, 'which side is it on?' (Becker, 1963; Oliver, 1992).

Though sociologists may have thought that they were dealing with chronic illness and disability from the patient or person viewpoint, and especially, as argued earlier, addressed its meaning in a social context, these assumptions are also now being challenged by the 'theorists'. Far from bringing new perspectives to bear, it is argued, qualitative research has not addressed which side it is on; the world of the disabled or the world of the expert. Although interpretive or qualitative research in this area is recognised as a possible improvement on the 'dominant' positivistic paradigm, all is, unfortunately, not well here either. According, again, to Oliver:

> 'Interpretive research has still a relatively small group of powerful experts doing work on a larger number of relatively powerless research subjects. To put the matter succinctly, interpretative research is just as alienating as positivistic research because what might be called the "social relations of production" have not changed one iota' (Oliver, 1992, p. 106).

While many sociologists may be surprised to see themselves regarded as 'powerful experts' the intention is clear. In order to bring about a change in research activity and method, a new kind of research is called for; 'what has variously been called critical enquiry, praxis or emancipatory research' (Oliver, 1992, p.107). Because, it is held, previous research has made no difference to the position of disabled people, and brought about no beneficial results, a new 'emancipatory' approach is called for which:

> 'is about the facilitating of the politics of the possible by confronting social oppression wherever it occurs. Central to the project is a recognition of and confrontation with power which structures the social relations of research' (Oliver, 1992, p. 110).

Qualitative social research as much as survey work is now being exhorted, therefore, to abandon its existing orientation and join the struggle against 'social oppression'. Definitional and research issues are now being linked together in a common endeavour, in which researchers of any hue are being asked to put themselves and their skills at the disposal of the 'theorists' and their particular approach to disability politics.

THE FUTURE OF RESEARCHING DISABILITY

The scene is set, therefore, for a lively period in both 'official' research and sociological work. It appears that this may involve a struggle for influence, and possibly control over the direction and funding of research in disability. Quoting Gollop (cited in Oliver, 1992), Oliver has argued that the new emancipatory paradigm should be based on 'reciprocity, gain and empowerment'. In effect this means that, 'researchers have to learn how to put their knowledge and skills at the disposal of their research subjects' (Oliver, 1992, p.111). In this way a new research agenda will, apparently be fashioned. Moreover, research relationships, as expressed in traditional social research methods, are likely to be the focus of considerable critical debate.

Partly as a result of these developing arguments and criticisms (though also for other reasons) researchers are already coming under greater pressure to examine their assumptions and methods. In many respects this is to be welcomed, and is already having the effects of bringing 'client' and patient groups into the research process. However, this chapter has said enough to suggest that there are also grounds for concern with the alternatives being argued. Two main reservations about their implications for research relationships may act as an appropriate conclusion to the present discussion.

First, this chapter has tried to show that the 'social oppression' approach to disability is open to the criticism of reductionism, especially as an 'over socialised' conceptualisation of the processes at work. If this is accepted, the models it seeks to replace may be of continuing use, both in research, and in the policy process. There is a danger, in adopting the 'social oppression' approach of caricaturing alternatives, and generating hostility where collaboration and rational debate would be of greater value. While the relationship between researchers and the researched is always a sensitive issue, and needs to be approached with care, it is difficult to sustain the argument, that either survey methods or qualitative research in themselves are inherently 'alienating'.

Second, the idea that research should become a site for 'struggle' suggests a politicisation of research that may have a number of unintended consequences. While it may be taken as axiomatic that individuals have a unique insight into their own experiences, it does not logically follow that they are qualified or able to undertake research. Moreover, such a view also runs the risk that the status of being disabled should be the main criteria for carrying out research on the subject. This sits uneasily in an argument in which the very idea of 'disability', as a defining characteristic of individuals, is being challenged.

Taken to its logical conclusion this could also mean a direct threat to the independence of research. Given the political climate in which we now live, this argument needs to be approached with caution. The independence of research has long been guarded by researchers, and others, including the disabled. Independence in this context does not mean a lack of engagement with social issues, or a naive view of 'value free' research, or most importantly an unwillingness to work closely with those being researched (Bury, 1996). What it does mean, though, is that research findings need to be based on the use of 'publicly available methods' (Hammersley, 1992) if they are to withstand hostile scrutiny, especially by governments. Threats from neo-conservative sources to social research have seriously reduced this independence throughout the 1980s and 90s. Margaret Thatcher, in particular, was associated with a view that research should serve political interests. It would be an irony indeed if 'disability theorists' in emphasising empowerment and autonomy of people with disabilities were to add to this trend. Instead, a process of open debate and mutual tolerance would seem to offer a more productive way forward.

REFERENCES

ABBERLEY. P. (1992) 'Counting Us Out: a discussion of the OPCS disability surveys', *Disability, Handicap and Society*, 7, 2, pp. 139-155.

ALBRECHT, G. (1992) *The Disability Business*, London: Sage.

ARBER, S. & EVANDROU, M. (eds.) (1993) *Ageing, Independence and the Life Course*, London: Jessica Kingsley Publishers.

BARNES, C. & OLIVER, M. (1995) 'Disability Rights: rhetoric and reality in the UK', *Disability and Society*, 10, 1, pp. 111-116.

BECKER, H. (1963) *Outsiders: Studies in the Sociology of Deviance*, New York: Free Press.

BLAXTER, M. (1976) *The Meaning of Disability*, London: Heinemann.

BRUCE, I., McKENNEL, A. & WALKER, E. (1991) *Blind and Partially Sighted People in Great Britain*, London: HMSO.

BURY, M. (1986) 'Social Constructionism and the Development of Medical Sociology', *Sociology of Health and Illness*, 8, 2, pp. 137-169.

BURY, M. (1987) 'The International Classification of Impairments, Disabilities and Handicaps: A Review of Research and Prospects', *International Disability Studies*, 9, 3, pp. 118-122.

BURY, M. (1991) 'The Sociology of Chronic Illness: a review of research and prospects', *Sociology of Health and Illness*, 13, 4, pp. 451-468.

BURY, M. (1996) 'Disability and the Myth of the Independent Researcher: A Reply', *Disability and Society*, 11, 1, pp. 111-114.

FEATHERSTONE, M. (1992) 'The Heroic Life and Everyday Life', *Theory, Culture and Society*, 9, 159-182.

FINKELSTEIN, V. (1980) *Attitudes and Disabled People: Issues for Discussion*, New York: World Rehabilitation Fund.

FRENCH, S. (1993) 'Disability, impairment or something in between?', in Swain, J., Finkelstein, V., French, S. & Oliver, M. (eds.) *Disabling Barriers – Enabling Environments*, London: Sage.

GERHARDT, U (1989) *Ideas About Illness: an intellectual and political history of medical sociology*, London: Macmillan.

GIDDENS, A. (1991) *Modernity and Self Identity*, Cambridge: Polity Press.

HAMMERSLEY, M. (1992) 'On Feminist Methodology', *Sociology*, 26, 2, 187-206.

HARRIS, A., COX, E. & SMITH, C. (1971) *Handicapped and Impaired in Great Britain*, Vol. 1, London: HMSO.

HARRIS, A., COX, E. & SMITH, C. (1971b) *Handicapped and Impaired in Great Britain, Economic Dimensions*, London: HMSO.

JEFFERYS, M., NULLARD, J. B., HYMAN, M. & WARREN, M. D. (1969) 'A set of tests for measuring motor impairment in prevalence studies', *Journal of Chronic Diseases*, 28, 303-309.

MARTIN, J., MELTZER, H. and ELLIOT, D. (1988) *The Prevalence of Disability Among Adults*, London: HMSO.

MARTIN, J. (1995) personal communication

OLIVER, M. (1990) *The Politics of Disablement*, London: Macmillan.

OLIVER, M. (1992) 'Changing the Social Relations of Research Production', *Disability, Handicap and Society*, 7, 2, 101-114.

OLIVER, M. (1993) 'Re-defining disability: a challenge to research', in Swain, J., Finkelstein, V., French, S. & Oliver, M. (eds.) *Disabling Barriers – Enabling Environments*, London: Sage.

PATRICK, D. & PEACH, H. (eds.) (1989) *Disablement in the Community*, Oxford: Oxford Medical Publications.

ROWAN, J. (1981) 'A dialectical paradigm for research', in Reason, P. and Rowan, J. (eds.) *Human Inquiry: a sourcebook of new paradigm research*, Chichester: John Wiley.

STONE, D.A. (1984) *The Disabled State*, London: Macmillan.

STRAUSS, A. L. and GLASER, B. (1975) *Chronic Illness and the Quality of Life*, St. Louis: C.V. Mosby and Co.

TAYLOR, D. (1976) *Physical Impairment: Social Handicap*, London: Office of Health Economics.

TOPLISS, E. (1979) *Provision for the Disabled (2nd ed.)*, Oxford: Blackwell with Martin Robertson.

TOWNSEND, P. (1979) *Poverty in the United Kingdom*, Harmondsworth: Penguin Books.

WORLD HEALTH ORGANISATION (1980) *International Classification of Impairments, Disabilities and Handicaps*, Geneva: WHO.

ZARB, G. (1992) 'On the Road to Damascus: first steps to changing the relations of disability research production', *Disability, Handicap & Society*, 7, 2, 125-138.

ZOLA, I. (1972) 'Medicine as and Institution of Social Control', *Sociological Review*, 20, 487-504.

CHAPTER 3

Defining Impairment and Disability: issues at stake

Mike Oliver

INTRODUCTION

For the past fifteen years the social model of disability has been the foundation upon which disabled people have chosen to organise themselves collectively. This has resulted in unparalleled success in changing the discourses around disability, in promoting disability as a civil rights issue and in developing schemes to give disabled people autonomy and control in their own lives. Despite these successes, in recent years the social model has come under increasing scrutiny both from disabled people and from others working in the field of chronic illness.

What I want to explore in this chapter are some of the issues that are at stake in these emerging criticisms and suggest that there is still a great deal of mileage to be gained from the social model and that we weaken it at our peril. I will do this by briefly outlining the two alternative schemas which have emerged in the articulation of conflicting definitions of chronic illness, impairment and disability. I will then discuss six issues that, I suggest, go to the heart of the debate as far as external criticisms from medical sociologists are concerned. These are: the issue of causality; the question of conceptual consistency; the role of language; the normalising tendencies contained in both schemas; the problem of experience; and finally, the politicisation of the definitional process.

Having identified the issues at stake externally, I will discuss a number of internal criticisms that have emerged from disabled people themselves around the place of impairment, the incorporation of other oppressions and the use and explanatory power of the social model of disability. While remaining sceptical about these criticisms, I will finally suggest that a start can be made towards resolving some of them by focusing on what disabled people would call impairment and medical sociologists would call chronic illness.

THE PROBLEM OF DEFINITIONS

Since the 1960s there have been various attempts to provide and develop a conceptual schema to describe and explain the complex relationships between illness, impairment, disability and handicap. This has led to the adoption of the International Classification of Impairments, Disabilities and Handicaps (ICIDH) by the World Health Organisation (WHO) (Wood, 1980) which has been used as the basis for two national studies of disability in Britain (Harris, 1971; Martin, Meltzer and Elliot, 1988).

Not everyone has accepted the validity of this schema nor the assumptions underpinning it. Disabled people's organisations themselves have been in the forefront of the rejection of the schema itself (Driedger, 1988), others have rejected the assumptions which underpin it (Oliver, 1990) and the adequacy of it as a basis for empirical work has also been questioned (Abberley, 1993). This is not the place to discuss these issues in detail; rather I intend to look at some of the dimensions of the debate that is currently taking place. In order to facilitate this, I reproduce the two alternative schemas below for those who are not familiar with either or both:

The WHO International Classification of Impairments, Disabilities and Handicaps:

> 'IMPAIRMENT: In the context of health experience, an impairment is any loss or abnormality of psychological, physiological, or anatomical structure or function ...

DISABILITY: In the context of health experience, a disability is any restriction or lack (resulting from an impairment) of ability to perform an activity in the manner or within the range considered normal for a human being ...

HANDICAP: In the context of health experience, a handicap is a disadvantage for a given individual, resulting from an impairment or a disability, that limits or prevents the fulfilment of a role that is normal (depending on age, sex, social and cultural factors) for that individual' (Wood, 1980, pp 27-29).

The Disabled People's International (DPI) definition:

'IMPAIRMENT: is the functional limitation within the individual caused by physical, mental or sensory impairment.

DISABILITY: is the loss or limitation of opportunities to take part in the normal life of the community on an equal level with others due to physical and social barriers' (DPI, 1982).

THE ISSUE OF CAUSALITY

The search for causality has been a major feature of both the scientific and the social scientific enterprise. What is at stake for the disability schemas described above is how to explain negative social experiences and the inferior conditions under which disabled people live out their lives. For those committed to the WHO schema, what they call chronic illness is causally related to the disadvantages disabled people experience. For those committed to the DPI schema however, there is no such causal link; for them disability is wholly and exclusively social. Hence each side accuses the other of being incorrect in causal terms.

Causality in the two schemas

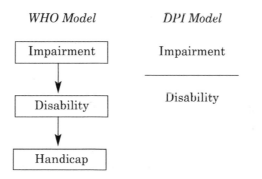

WHO Model   *DPI Model*

Impairment   Impairment

Disability   Disability

Handicap

These schemas appear to be incompatible and have led one medical sociologist critically to suggest:

> 'Sometimes, in seeking to reject the reductionism of the medical model and its institutional contexts, proponents of independent living have tended to discuss disablement as if it had nothing to do with the physical body' (Williams, 1991, p. 521).

Ironically that is precisely what the DPI definition insists, disablement is nothing to do with the body. It is a consequence of the failure of social organisation to take account of the differing needs of disabled people and remove the barriers they encounter. The schema does not, however, deny the reality of impairment nor that it is closely related to the physical body. Under this schema impairment is, in fact, nothing less than a description of the physical body.

The appearance of incompatibility however, may be precisely that: appearance. It may well be that this debate is in reality, the result of terminological confusion; that real similarities exist between chronic illness and impairment and that there is much scope for collaboration between supporters of both schemas if this confusion can be sorted out.

THE QUESTION OF CONCEPTUAL CONSISTENCY

This terminological confusion is not just a matter of agreeing to use the same words in the same way. It is also about understanding and appeared when a policy analyst attempted to relate her own experience to policy issues in the area of disability.

> 'I found myself puzzled by arguments that held that disability had nothing to do with illness or that belief in a need for some form of personal adaptation to impairment was essentially a form of false consciousness. I knew that disabled people argue that they should not be treated as if they were ill, but could see that many people who had impairments as a result of ongoing illness were also disabled. My unease increased as I watched my parents coming to terms with my mother's increasing impairments (and disability) related to arterial disease which left her tired and in almost continual pain. I could see that people can be disabled by their physical, economic and social environment but I could also see that people who became disabled (rather than being born with impairments) might have to renegotiate their sense of themselves both with themselves and with those closest to them' (Parker, 1993, p.2).

The DPI schema does not deny that some illnesses may have disabling consequences and many disabled people have illnesses at various points in their lives. Further, it may be entirely appropriate for doctors to treat illnesses of all kinds, though even here, the record of the medical profession is increasingly coming under critical scrutiny. Leaving this aside, however, doctors can have a role to play in the lives of disabled people: stabilising their initial condition, treating any illnesses which may arise and which may or may not be disability related.

The conceptual issue underpinning this dimension of the debate, therefore, is about determining which aspects of disabled people's lives need medical or therapeutic interventions, which aspects require policy developments and which require political action. Failure to distinguish between these up to now has resulted in the medicalisation of disability and the colonisation of disabled peoples lives by a vast army of professionals whon perhaps, political action (i.e. civil rights legislation) would be a more appropriate response.

THE ROLE OF LANGUAGE

Despite recent attempts to denigrate those who believe in the importance of language in shaping reality, largely through criticisms of what has come to be called 'political correctness', few would argue that language is unimportant or disagree that attempts to eradicate terminology such as cripple, spastic, wobbler and mongol are anything other than a good thing.

This role of language, however, is more complex than simply the removal of offensive words. There is greater concern over the way language is used to shape meanings and even create realities. For example, the language used in much medical discourse including medical sociology is replete with words and meanings which many disabled people find offensive or feel that it distorts their experiences. In particular the term chronic illness is for many people an unnecessarily negative term, and discussions of suffering in many studies have the effect of casting disabled people in the role of victim.

The disabling effects of language is not something that is unique to disabled people. Other groups have faced similar struggles around language. Altman in his study of collective responses to AIDS points out:

> '... in particular the Denver Principles stressed the use of the term "PWA" as distinct from "victims" or "patients", and the need for representation at all levels of AIDS policy-making "to share their own experiences and knowledge" ' (Altman, 1994, p.59).

The struggles around language are not merely semantic. A major bone of contention is the continued use of the term 'handicap' by the WHO schema. This is an anathema to many disabled people because of its connections to 'cap in hand' and the degrading role that charity and charitable institutions play in our lives.

THE NORMALISING TENDENCIES OF BOTH SCHEMAS

Underpinning both schemas is the concept of normality and the assumption that disabled people want to achieve this normality. In the WHO schema it is normal social roles and in the DPI schema it is the normal life of the community. The problem with both of these is that increasingly the disability movement throughout the world is rejecting approaches based upon the restoration of normality and insisting on approaches based upon the celebration of difference.

From rejections of the 'cure', through critiques of supposedly therapeutic interventions such as conductive education, cochlea implants and the like, and onto attempts to build a culture of disability based upon pride, the idea of normality is increasingly coming under attack. Ironically it is only the definition advanced by the Union of the Physically Impaired Against Segregation (UPIAS) that can accommodate the development of a politics of difference. While its definition of impairment is similar to that of DPI, its definition of disability is radically different:

> 'DISABILITY: the disadvantage or restriction of activity caused by a contemporary social organisation which takes no or little account of people who have physical impairments and thus excludes them from the mainstream of social activities' (UPIAS, 1976).

Again, this is not just a matter of semantics but a concerted attempt to reject the normalising society. That some organisations of disabled people have not fully succeeded cannot be explained only as a matter of dispute between different political positions within the disability movement but also as evidence of just how ingrained and deep-rooted the ideology of normality is within social consciousness more generally.

THE PROBLEM OF EXPERIENCE

Recently, a number of sociologists working in the general area of medical sociology and chronic illness have expressed concern over the growing importance of the 'social oppression theory' of disability, associated research methodologies, and their implications for doing research in the 'chronic illness and disability fields' (Bury, 1992).

Whilst these writers feel the need to 'positively debate' these developments, the basis of their concern is similar to that expressed by Hammersley with respect to some aspects of feminist research, i.e. the tendency to 'privilege experience over sociological research methodology' (Hammersley, 1992). In short, this privileging of experience is perceived as a threat; firstly, to 'non disabled' researchers doing disability research; secondly, to the traditional role of the sociologist giving voice to the voiceless' – in this case 'older' disabled people whose interests are said to be poorly served by 'social oppression theory'; and, thirdly, to the 'independence' of sociological activities within the 'medical sociology world'.

As a social researcher, I have some sympathy for these concerns but the problem is that most social research has tended to privilege methodology above experience and, as a consequence, does not have a very good track record in faithfully documenting that experience; whether it be the black experience, the experience of women, the experience of disability and so on. Additionally, scientific social research has done little to improve the quality of life of disabled people. Finally, it is difficult to demonstrate that so called 'independent research' has had much effect on policy, legislation or social change (Oliver 1992).

THE POLITICISATION OF THE DEFINITIONAL PROCESS

By now it should be clear that defining impairment or disability or illness or anything else for that matter is not simply a matter of language or science; it is also a matter of politics. Altman captures this in respect of the definitional battles surrounding AIDS:

> 'How AIDS was conceptualised was an essential tool in a sometimes very bitter struggle; was it to be understood as a primarily bio-medical problem, in which case its control should be under that of the medical establishment, or was it rather, as

most community-based groups argued, a social and political issue, which required a much greater variety of expertise?' (Altman, 1994, p.26).

This battle is related to two political processes; exclusion and inclusion as far as disabled people and disability definitions are concerned. The ways in which disabled people have been systematically excluded from the definitional process has recently been described in one incident which captures the nature of this exclusion more generally.

> 'It is a hot summer day in London in the late 1980's. Gathered together in one of the capital's most venerable colleges is a large number of academics, researchers and representatives of research funding bodies. Their purpose? A symposium on researching disability comprising presentations on a variety of different methodological and other themes, given and chaired by a panel of experienced disability researchers.

> Those convening the seminar are proud that it will shine a spotlight on a usually neglected area of social science research. But some in the audience (and one or two others who have chosen not to attend) hold a different view. What credibility can such a seminar muster, they ask, when none of those chairing or presenting papers are themselves disabled? What does it say about current understanding of disability research issues that such an event has been allowed to go ahead in this form, when a symposium on researching gender issues given entirely by men, or race relations research given entirely by white people, would have been laughed out of court?' (Ward and Flynn, 1994, p.29).

It should be pointed out that this exclusion has been systematic and disabled people have not been properly consulted by organisations such as WHO and the Office of Population Censuses and Surveys who have been most heavily funded in Britain to undertake such work. Where claims that this is not the case have been made, the reality is that research organisations have demonstrated that they don't even understand the difference between organisations *for* and organisations *of* disabled people and while they may have consulted the former, they have not consulted the latter.

However, disabled people have begun to resist this situation by producing their own research based upon their own definitions (Barnes, 1991; 1992), the British Council of Disabled People (BCODP) has established its own research sub-committee and in Canada disabled people have produced their own guidelines on what is acceptable and not acceptable research for disability organisations to be involved in (Woodhill, 1993).

These initiatives have begun to have some impact on not only the research community but on Government as well. Altman discusses the role of people with AIDS (PWAs) in AIDS research and argues that it is in everyone's interest to encourage such developments:

> '.. CRI (Community Research Initiative) has proved that a community model of research, involving PWAs themselves in decision making, could run effective trials – partly because it was able to successfully access suitable patients and encourage them to participate – and could resolve the complex ethical questions of such research successfully' (Altman, 1994, p.70).

At a recent meeting of disabled people from all over Europe, the group decided to reaffirm their own definition of disability and to spell out the implications of this for the WHO schema.

> 'A Disabled Person is an individual in their own right, placed in a disabling situation, brought about by environmental, economic and social barriers that the person, because of their impairment(s), cannot overcome in the same way as other citizens. These barriers are all too often reinforced by the marginalising attitudes of society. It is up to society to eliminate, reduce or compensate for these barriers in order to enable each individual to enjoy full citizenship, respecting the rights and duties of each individual'.

> 'By supporting this resolution this meeting on human rights expresses its non-support for the current classification of impairment, disability and handicap operated by the World Health Organisation. We call upon the WHO to enter into a dialogue with disabled people's organisations to adopt a new definition in line with the above resolution' (DPI, 1994).

DEVELOPING A SOCIAL MODEL OF IMPAIRMENT?

Whatever happens to this call for a dialogue between organisations of disabled people and the World Health Organisation, disabled people have begun their own internal dialogue around the social model of disability. It is to some of the dimensions of this dialogue that I now turn before considering some of the implications.

A major criticism that some disabled people have made of the social model concerns the way it connects, or rather doesn't connect with the experience of impairment. French (1993), for example, argues that her visual impairment imposes some social restrictions which cannot be resolved by the application of the principles of social model. She cites as examples her inability to recognise people and read or emit non-verbal cues in social interactions.

Clearly, most disabled people can come up with similar examples. As a wheelchair user when I go to parties I am more restricted than some other people from interacting with everyone else and what's more, it is difficult to see a solution – houses are usually crowded with people during parties and that makes circulation difficult for a wheelchair user. But other people may find circulation difficult as well but for other reasons; they may simply be shy. The point that I am making is that the social model is not an attempt to deal with the personal restrictions of impairment but the social barriers of disability as defined earlier by DPI and UPIAS.

Other disabled people have criticised the social model for its assumed denial of 'the pain of impairment', both physical and psychological. In many ways some of these criticisms mirror those made from without although they are not beset by the same terminological confusion between illness and impairment.

> '... there is a tendency within the social model of disability to deny the experience of our own bodies, insisting that our physical differences and restrictions are entirely socially created. While environmental barriers and social attitudes are a crucial part of our experience of disability – and do indeed disable us – to suggest that this is all there is to it is to deny the personal experience of physical or intellectual restrictions, of illness, of the fear of dying' (Morris, 1991, p.10)

This denial of the pain of impairment has not, in reality been a denial at all. Rather it has been a pragmatic attempt to identify and address issues that can be changed through collective action rather than medical or other professional treatment.

> 'If a person's physical pain is the reason they are unhappy then there is nothing the disability movement can do about it. All that BCODP can do is facilitate the politicisation of people around these issues. Of course this politicisation is fairly difficult to make practical progress with – much easier to achieve anti-discrimination legislation than a total review of how society regards death and dying, I imagine. This might explain why these subjects haven't been made a priority, but their day will come' (Vasey, 1992, p.43).

These criticisms are taken further by Crow (1992) who argues that the way forward for the social model of disability is to fully integrate the experience of impairment with the experience of disability. However, up to now and for very important reasons, the social model has insisted that there is no causal relationship between impairment and disability.

> 'The achievement of the disability movement has been to break the link between our bodies and our social situation, and to focus on the real cause of disability, i.e. discrimination and prejudice. To mention biology, to admit pain, to confront our

impairments, has been to risk the oppressors seizing on evidence that disability is "really" about physical limitation after all' (Shakespeare, 1992, p.40).

Finally the social model of disability is criticised because it was written (if it ever was?) by healthy wheelchair users. According to one recent commentator:

'The social model of disability appears to have been constructed for healthy quadriplegics. The social model avoids mention of pain, medication or ill-health' (Humphrey, 1994, p.66).

The social model of disability does indeed avoid mention of such things, not because it was written by healthy quadriplegics, but because pain, medication and ill-health properly belong within either the individual model of disability or the social model of impairment.

OTHER INTERNAL CRITICISMS OF THE SOCIAL MODEL OF DISABILITY

A further internal criticism comes from other oppressed groups who feel that these other oppressions such as racism (Hill, 1994), sexism (Morris, 1991) and homophobia (Hearn, 1991) have not been incorporated into the social model. Again, it is certainly true that the social model of disability has not explicitly addressed the issue of multiple or simultaneous oppression but then such issues are only just beginning to be explored in respect of both impairment and disability (Begum, Hill and Stevens, 1994; Zarb and Oliver, 1993; Priestley, 1995).

This dissatisfaction has been expressed not simply because the social model does not adequately reflect experience of oppression of all disabled people but also because it may 'oversimplify' some of the issues raised in Disability Equality Training (DET).

'For some time I have been dissatisfied with the oversimplified "social model" of disability we are obliged to use in Disability Equality Training and have read with interest the recent arguments re-introducing "impairment" into that model.

'Although the "social model" has for some time served us well as a way of directing attention away from the personal to the political, I feel now that the debate has been hampered by the rather rigid genealogy of disability thinking. My own literary, linguistic and therapeutic background led me to post-modernist thinkers such as Foucault, Derrida, Barthes and Lacan in an attempt to make sense of the personal and political aspects of the disability debate' (Cashling, 1993, pp.199-200).

While it is undeniably true that some DET trainers may have used the social model in an over rigid way, those like myself who draw on Marxist rather than post-modernist thinking call this reification; that is, the elevation of a concept into a thing, a social construction into reality. And it remains to be seen whether post-modernist explanations of the oppression of disabled people as simply a manifestation of society's hatred of us, will take us as far as the social model of disability in challenging that oppression. Cashling suggests they might but I have my doubts. For me our oppression is ultimately due to our continued exclusion from the processes of production, and not because of society's hatred (real or imagined) of us.

Such criticism, however, raises questions about the way the model is used, rather than the model itself. If we expect models to explain, rather than aid understanding, then they are bound to be found wanting. Many of those arguing for the incorporation of impairment have confused models and theories. I suggest that the continuing use and refinement of the social model of disability can contribute to rather than be a substitute for the development of an adequate social theory of disability. As both Abberley (1987) and myself (Oliver 1990) have argued, an adequate social theory of disability must contain a theory of impairment.

A final criticism comes from one of the founding fathers of the social model, Vic Finkelstein, who is also critical of the adequacy of the social model's explanatory power. Recently he has questioned the ability of the social model to explain fully the social position of disabled people in modern society, and suggests that there are at least two variants: the social death model and the social barriers model (Finkelstein, 1993). He then goes on to suggest that the administrative model is the only one which has sufficient scope to fully explain societal responses to disabled people.

> 'In my view administrative approaches dominate all forms of helping services for disabled people in the UK, whether these are provided by statutory agencies or voluntary bodies, or demanded by pressure group organisations. The cure or care forms of intervention are administered within the rehabilitation and personal-care services respectively' (Finkelstein, 1993, p.37).

For me, the administrative model is similar to the position I took in trying to locate disability historically within the rise of capitalist society.

> 'As the conditions of capitalist production changed in the twentieth century, so the labour needs of capital shifted from a mass of unskilled workers to a more limited need of skilled ones. As a result of this, the Welfare State arose as a means of ensuring the supply of skill, and in order to "pacify" the ever increasing army of the

unemployed, the under-employed and the unemployable' (Manning and Oliver, 1985, p.102).

While I think Finkelstein and I are basically saying the same thing, for me it is important not to stretch the explanatory power of models further than they are able to go. For me the social model of disability is concerned with the personal and collective experiences of disabling social barriers and how its application might influence professional practice and shape political action. It is not a substitute for social theory, it is not an attempt to provide a materialist history of disability and it is not an explanation of the failure of welfare state in respect of services to disabled people.

THE SOCIAL MODEL OF DISABILITY IS ALIVE AND WELL

These are some of the major internal debates going on around the social model. One of the things they have in common is their concern to somehow integrate impairment into the social model of disability. Personally I have no interest in such attempts because, as Vasey (1992) has already pointed out, the collectivising of experiences of impairment is a much more difficult task than collectivising the experience of disability. Our own history has taught us this in the way in which we have been classified and segregated by our impairments and the way in which single impairment organisations have failed to provide an adequate basis for collective self-organisation amongst disabled people in the past (Campbell and Oliver, 1996).

Additionally there is still much mileage in the social model of disability. It has the power to transform consciousness in a way that a social model of impairment never will. David Hevey describes his own transformation:

'The second flash on this road to Damascus as a disabled person came when I encountered the disability movement. I had learnt to live with my private fear and to feel that I was the only one involved in this fight. I had internalised my oppression. As a working class son of Irish immigrants, I had experienced other struggles but, in retrospect, I evidently saw epilepsy as my hidden cross. I cannot explain how significantly all this was turned around when I came into contact with the notion of the social model of disability, rather than the medical model which I had hitherto lived with. Over a matter of months, my discomfort with this secret beast of burden called epilepsy, and my festering hatred at the silencing of myself as a disabled person, "because I didn't look it", completely changed. I think I went through an almost evangelical conversion as I realised that my disability was not, in fact, the epilepsy, but the toxic drugs with their denied side-effects; the medical regime with its blaming of the victim; the judgement through distance and silence of bus-stop crowds, bar-room crowds and dinner-table friends; the fear; and, not least, the employment problems. All this was the oppression, not the epileptic seizure at which I was hardly (consciously) present' (Hevey, 1992, pp.1-2).

While it has the power to transform consciousness in the way described above, its demise is surely premature.

Finally, the hegemony of the individual model of disability may have begun to be challenged by the social model, but it has not yet replaced it. Hence, engaging in public criticism may not broaden and refine the social model; it may instead breathe new life in the individual model with all that means in terms of increasing medical and therapeutic interventions into areas of our lives where they do not belong.

Despite my reservations about the project, the development of a social model of impairment to stand alongside a social model of disability appears inevitable. This being the case, those disabled people concerned may wish to develop a dialogue with medical sociologists working on the experience of chronic illness. In so doing, the issues identified earlier in this chapter may well help the dialogue to develop. In any case, our understandings of the experience of impairment may well be enhanced and the enterprise of medical sociology enriched.

CONCLUSIONS

In this chapter I have looked at some of the definitional issues involved in impairment and disability. Subsequently, my argument has centred on three key points. Firstly, we must not assume that models in general and the social model of disability in particular can do everything; that it can explain disability in totality. It is not a social theory of disability and it cannot do the work of social theory. Secondly, because it cannot explain everything, we should neither seek to expose inadequacies, which are more a product of the way we use it, nor abandon it before its usefulness has been fully exploited. Finally, if a social model of impairment is to be developed, a dialogue between disabled people and medical sociologists may enrich the process.

REFERENCES

ABBERLEY, P. (1993) 'The Significance of the OPCS Disability Surveys', in Oliver, M. (ed.) *Social Work: Disabled People and Disabling Environments*, London: Jessica Kingsley Publishers.

ALTMAN, D. (1994) *Power and Community: Organisational and Community Responses to AIDS*, London: Taylor and Francis.

BARNES, C. (1991) *Disabled People in Britain and Discrimination*, London: Hurst & Co.

BARNES, C. (1992) *Disabling Imagery and the Media: An Exploration of the Principles for Media Representation of Disabled People*, Derby: Ryburn Publishing and BCODP.

BEGUM, N., HILL, M. and STEVENS, A. (eds.) (1994) *Reflections: Views of black disabled people on their lives and community care*, London: Central Council for Education and Training in Social Work.

BURY, M. (1992) 'Medical Sociology and chronic illness: A Comment On The Panel Discussion', *Medical Sociology News*, 18, 1, pp 29-33.

CAMPBELL, J. and OLIVER, M. (1996) *Disability Politics in Britain: Understanding Our Past, Changing Our Future*, London: Routledge.

CASHLING, D. (1993) 'Cobblers and Song-birds: the language and imagery of disability', *Disability, Handicap and Society*, 8, 2, 199-206.

DPI (1982) *Proceedings of the First World Congress*, Singapore: Disabled People's International.

DPI (1994) 'Agreed Statement', at Human Rights Plenary Meeting in Support of European Day of Disabled Persons, London: Disabled People's International.

DRIEDGER, D. (1989) *The Last Civil Rights Movement*, London: Hurst and Co.

FINKELSTEIN, V. (1993) 'Disability: a social challenge or an administrative responsibility', in Swain, J. et al., (eds.) *Disabling Barriers – Enabling Environments*, London: Sage.

FRENCH, S. (1993) 'Can you see the rainbow?', in Swain, J. et al., (eds.) *Disabling Barriers – Enabling Environments*, London: Sage.

HAMMERSLEY, M. (1992) 'On Feminist Methodology', *Sociology*, 26, 2, 187-206.

HARRIS, A. (1971) *Handicapped and Impaired in Britain*, London: HMSO.

HEARN, K. (1991) 'Disabled Lesbians and Gays Are Here to Stay', in Kaufman, T. and Lincoln, P. (eds.) *High Risk Lives: Lesbian and Gay Politics After the Clause*, Bridport: Prism Press.

HEVEY, D. (1992) *The Creatures Time Forgot: Photography and Disability Imagery*, London: Routledge.

HILL, M. (1994) 'Getting things right', *Community Care 'Inside'*, 31 March, p 7.

HUMPHREY, R. (1994) 'Thoughts on Disability Arts', *Disability Arts Magazine*, 4, 1, pp 66-67.

MANNING, N. and OLIVER, M. (1985) 'Madness, Epilepsy and Medicine', in Manning, N. (ed.) *Social Problems and Welfare Ideology*, Aldershot: Gower.

MARTIN, J., MELTZER, H. and ELLIOT, D. (1988) *OPCS Surveys of Disability in Great Britain: Report 1 – The prevalence of disability among adults*, London: HMSO.

MORRIS, J. (1991) *Pride against Prejudice*, London: Women's Press.

OLIVER, M. (1990) *The Politics of Disablement*, Basingstoke: Macmillan and St Martins Press.

OLIVER, M. (1992) 'Changing the social relations of research production', *Disability, Handicap and Society*, 7, 2, pp 101-114.

PARKER, G. (1993) *With This Body: Caring and Disability in Marriage*, Milton Keynes: Open University Press.

PRIESTLEY, M. (1995) 'Commonality and Difference in the Movement: an association of Blind Asians in Leeds', *Disability and Society*, 10, 2, pp 157-70.

RIOUX, M. and BACH, M. (eds.) (1994) *Disability Is Not Measles: New Research Paradigms in Disability*, Ontario: Roeher Institute.

SHAKESPEARE, T. (1992) 'A Response to Liz Crow', *Coalition*, September 1992, pp 40-42.

SWAIN, J., FINKELSTEIN, V., FRENCH, S. and OLIVER, M. (eds.) (1993) *Disabling Barriers – Enabling Environments*, London: Sage.

VASEY, S. (1992) 'A Response to Liz Crow', *Coalition*, September 1992, pp 42-44.

WARD, L. and FLYNN, M. (1994) 'What Matters Most: Disability, Research and Empowerment', in Rioux, M. C. and Bach, M. (eds.) *Disability Is Not Measles: New Research Paradigms in Disability*, Ontario: Roeher Institute.

WILLIAMS, G. (1991) 'Disablement and the Ideological Crisis in Health Care', *Social Science and Medicine*, 33, 4, pp. 517-524.

WOOD, P. (1980) *International Classification of Impairments, Disabilities and Handicaps*, Geneva: World Health Organisation.

WOODHILL, G. (1993) *Independent Living and Participation in Research*, Toronto: Centre for Independent Living in Toronto (CILT).

ZARB, G. and OLIVER, M. (1993) *Ageing with a Disability: What do they expect after all these years?*, London: University of Greenwich.

CHAPTER 4

Including All of Our Lives: renewing the social model of disability

Liz Crow

INTRODUCTION

This chapter has its origins in an article written for Coalition – one of the journals of the British disabled people's movement. In the four years since it appeared in that initial form, both discussions with other disabled people and my own circumstances have influenced my thinking. During that time, we have started to talk more freely about our experiences of impairment and the more fully developed form of the social model of disability that is advocated here is already beginning to be applied informally within the disabled people's movement.

My life has two phases: before the social model of disability, and after it. Discovering this way of thinking about my experiences was the proverbial raft in stormy seas. It gave me an understanding of my life, shared with thousands, even millions, of other people around the world, and I clung to it.

This was the explanation I had sought for years. Suddenly what I had always known, deep down, was confirmed. It wasn't my body that was responsible for all my difficulties, it was external factors, the barriers constructed by the society in which I live. I was being dis-abled – my capabilities and opportunities were being restricted – by prejudice, discrimination, inaccessible environments and inadequate support. Even more important, if all the problems had been created by society, then surely society could un-create them. Revolutionary!

For years now this social model of disability has enabled me to confront, survive and even surmount countless situations of exclusion and discrimination. It has been my mainstay, as it has been for the wider disabled people's movement. It has enabled a vision of ourselves free from the constraints of disability (oppression) and provided a direction for our commitment to social change. It has played a central role in promoting disabled people's individual self-worth, collective identity and political organisation. I don't think it is an exaggeration to say that the social model has saved lives. Gradually, very gradually, its sphere is extending beyond our movement to influence policy and practice in the mainstream. The contribution of the social model of disability, now and in the future, to achieving equal rights for disabled people is incalculable.

So how is it that, suddenly, to me, for all its strengths and relevance, the social model doesn't seem so water-tight anymore? It is with trepidation that I criticise it. However, when personal experience no longer matches current explanations, then it is time to question afresh.

In contrast to many critics, I come to this discussion as a proponent of the social model of disability, as someone who lives it daily. My concern is less to develop a theoretical construct as to reach an understanding of disabled people's experiences which we can then apply through our civil rights movement. The social model works well on a large scale – it is succeeding in tackling discriminatory social structures and demonstrating our need for civil rights legislation. Where it currently lets us down is at the personal level – its capacity to include and represent fully the range of disabled individuals.

This debate has no need to denigrate the social model: at a fundamental level it already works; now is our chance to make it work better.

DISABILITY IS 'ALL'?

The social model of disability has been our key to dismantling the traditional conception of impairment[1] as 'personal tragedy' and the oppression that this creates. Mainstream explanations have centred on impairment as 'all' – impairment as the cause of our experiences and disadvantage, and impairment as the focus of intervention. The World Health Organisation's International Classification of Impairments, Disabilities and Handicaps (ICIDH), provides the following definitions:

> *Impairment:* Any loss or abnormality of psychological, physiological, or anatomical structure or function *Disability:* Any restriction or lack (resulting from impairment) of ability to perform an activity in the manner or within the range considered normal for a human being. *Handicap:* A disadvantage for a given individual, resulting from an impairment or disability, that limits or prevents fulfilment of a role that is normal, depending on age, sex, social or cultural factors' (WHO, 1980).

Within this framework, which is often called the medical model of disability, a person's functional limitations (impairments) are the root cause of any disadvantages experienced and these disadvantages can therefore only be rectified by treatment or cure.

The social model, in contrast, shifts the focus from impairment onto disability, using this term to refer to disabling social, environmental and attitudinal barriers rather than lack of ability. Thus, while impairment is the functional limitation(s) which affects a person's body, disability is the loss or limitation of opportunities resulting from direct and indirect discrimination. Social change – the removal of disabling barriers – is the solution to the disadvantages we experience. This way of seeing things opens up opportunities for the eradication of prejudice and discrimination.

In contrast, the medical model makes the removal of disadvantage contingent upon the removal or 'overcoming' of impairment – full participation in society is only to be found through cure or fortitude. Small

---

[1] Along with many Disabled people, I feel some discomfort at the word 'impairment' because it has become so imbued with offensive interpretation. Perhaps we need to replace impairment with an alternative term.

wonder, therefore, that we have focused so strongly on the importance of disabling barriers and struggled to dismantle them.

In doing so, however, we have tended to centre on disability as 'all'. Sometimes it feels as if this focus is so absolute that we are in danger of assuming that impairment has no part at all in determining our experiences. Instead of tackling the contradictions and complexities of our experiences head on, we have chosen in our campaigns to present impairment as irrelevant, neutral and, sometimes, positive, but never, ever as the quandary it really is.

Why has impairment been so excluded from our analysis? Do we believe that admitting there could be a difficult side to impairment will undermine the strong, positive (SuperCrip?) images of our campaigns? Or that showing every single problem cannot be solved by social change will inhibit or excuse non-disabled people from tackling anything at all? Or that we may make the issues so complex that people feel constructive change is outside their grasp? Or even that admitting it can sometimes be awful to have impairments may fuel the belief that our lives are not worth living?

BRING BACK IMPAIRMENT!

The experience of impairment is not always irrelevant, neutral or positive. How can it be when it is the very reason used to justify the oppression we are battling against? How can it be when pain, fatigue, depression and chronic illness are constant facts of life for many of us?

We align ourselves with other civil rights movements and we have learnt much from those campaigns. But, we have one fundamental difference from other movements, which we cannot afford to ignore. There is nothing inherently unpleasant or difficult about other groups' embodiment: sexuality, sex and skin colour are neutral facts. In contrast, impairment means our experiences of our bodies *can* be unpleasant or difficult. This does not mean our campaigns against disability are any less vital than those against heterosexism, sexism or racism; it does mean that for many disabled people personal struggle related to impairment will remain even when disabling barriers no longer exist.

Yet our insistence that disadvantage and exclusion are the result of discrimination and prejudice, and our criticisms of the medical model of disability, have made us wary of acknowledging our experiences of impairment. Impairment is safer not mentioned at all.

This silence prevents us from dealing effectively with the difficult aspects of impairment. Many of us remain frustrated and disheartened by pain, fatigue, depression and chronic illness, including the way they prevent us from realising our potential or railing fully against disability (our experience of exclusion and discrimination); many of us fear for our futures with progressive or additional impairments; we mourn past activities that are no longer possible for us; we are afraid we may die early or that suicide may seem our only option; we desperately seek some effective medical intervention; we feel ambivalent about the possibilities of our children having impairments; and we are motivated to work for the prevention of impairments. Yet our silence about impairment has made many of these things taboo and created a whole new series of constraints on our self-expression.

Of course, the suppression of concerns related to impairment does not mean they cease to exist or suddenly become more bearable. Instead this silencing undermines individuals' power to 'cope' and, ultimately, the whole disabled people's movement. As individuals, most of us simply cannot pretend with any conviction that our impairments are irrelevant because they influence so much of our lives. External disabling barriers may create social and economic disadvantage but our subjective experience of our bodies is also an integral part of our everyday reality. What we need is to find a way to integrate impairment into our whole experience and sense of our selves for the sake of our own physical and emotional well-being, and, subsequently, for our individual and collective capacity to work against disability.

As a movement, we need to be informed about disability *and* impairment in all their diversity if our campaigns are to be open to all disabled people. Many people find that it is their experience of their bodies – and not only disabling barriers such as inaccessible public transport – which make political involvement difficult. For example, an individual's capacity to attend meetings and events might be restricted because of limited energy. If these circumstances remain unacknowledged, then alternative ways of contributing are unlikely to be sought. If our structures and strategies – *how* we organise and offer support in our debates, consultation and demonstrations – cannot involve all disabled people, then our campaigns lose the contributions of many people. If our movement excludes many disabled people or refuses to discuss certain issues then our understanding is partial: our collective ability to conceive of, and achieve, a world which does not disable is diminished. What we risk is a world which includes an 'elite' of people with impairments, but which for many more of us contains no real promise of civil rights, equality or belonging. How can we expect anyone to take seriously a 'radical' movement which replicates some of the worst exclusionary aspects of the society it purports to challenge?

Our current approach to the social model is the ultimate irony: in tackling only one side of our situation we disable ourselves.

REDEFINING IMPAIRMENT

Our fears about acknowledging the implications of impairment are quite justified. Dominant perceptions of impairment as personal tragedy are regularly used to undermine the work of the disabled people's movement and they rarely coincide with disabled people's understandings of their circumstances. They are individualistic interpretations: our experiences are entirely explained by each individual's psychological or biological characteristics. Any problems we encounter are explained by personal inadequacy or functional limitation, to the exclusion of social influences.

These interpretations impose narrow assumptions about the varying experiences of impairment and isolate experience from its disabling context. They also segregate us from each other and from people without impairments. Interpreting impairment as personal tragedy creates fear of impairment and an emphasis on medical intervention. Such an interpretation is a key part of the attitudes and actions that disable us.

However, the perception of impairment as personal tragedy is merely a social construction; it is not an inevitable way of thinking about impairment. Recognising the importance of impairment for us does not mean that we have to take on the non-disabled world's ways of interpreting our experience of our bodies.

In fact, impairment, at its most basic level, is a purely objective concept which carries no intrinsic meaning. Impairment simply means that aspects of a person's body do not function or they function with difficulty. Frequently this is taken a stage further to imply that the person's body, and ultimately the person, is inferior. However, the first is fact; the second is interpretation. If these interpretations are socially created then they are not fixed or inevitable and it is possible to replace them with alternative interpretations based on our own experience of impairment.

We need a new approach which acknowledges that people apply their own meanings to their own experiences of impairment. This self-interpretation adds a whole new layer of personal, subjective interpretations to the objective concept of impairment. The personal interpretation incorporates any meaning that impairment holds for an individual (i.e. any effects it has on their activities), the feelings it produces (e.g. pain) and any concerns the individual might have (e.g. how their impairment might progress). Individuals might regard their impairment as positive, neutral or negative, and this might differ according to time and changing circumstances. With this approach, the experiences and history of our impairments become a part of our autobiography. They join our experience of disability and other aspects of our lives to form a complete sense of ourselves.

Acknowledging the relevance of impairment is essential to ensuring that people are knowledgeable about their own circumstances. An individual's familiarity with how their body works allows them to identify their specific needs. This is a precursor to meeting those needs by accessing existing information and resources. Self-knowledge is the first stage of empowerment and gives a strong base for individuals to work collectively to confront disability and its impact upon people with impairments.

We need to think about impairment in three, related, ways:

- First, there is the objective concept of *impairment*. This was agreed in 1976 by the Union of Physically Impaired Against Segregation (UPIAS, 1976) and has since been developed by Disabled People's International (DPI) to include people with a range of non-physical impairments:

    'Impairment: lacking all or part of a limb, or having a defective limb, organism or mechanism of the body' (UPIAS, 1976).

- Second, there is the individual interpretation of the *subjective experience of impairment* in which an individual binds their own meanings to the definition of impairment to convey their personal circumstances.

- Finally, there is the impact of the wider *social context* upon impairment, in which misrepresentation, social exclusion and discrimination combine to disable people with impairments.

It is this third aspect to impairment which is not inevitable and its removal is the primary focus of the disabled people's movement. However, all three layers are currently essential to an understanding of our personal and social experiences.

RESPONSES TO IMPAIRMENT

We need to reclaim and acknowledge our personal experiences of impairment in order to develop our key debates, to incorporate this experience into the wider social context and target any action more precisely. One critical area of concern is the different responses to impairment, for ultimately these determine our exclusion or inclusion.

Currently, the main responses to impairment divide into four broad categories:

- *avoidance/'escape'*: through abortion, sterilisation, withholding treatment from Disabled babies, infanticide and euthanasia (medically assisted suicide) or suicide;
- *management*: in which any difficult effects of impairment are minimised and incorporated into our individual lives, without any significant change in the impairment;
- *cure*: through medical intervention;
- *prevention*: including vaccination, health education and improved social conditions

The specific treatments that emerge from these responses differ markedly according to whether they are based on the medical or social model. Currently, the treatment available is dominated by the medical model's individualistic interpretation of impairment as tragic and problematic and the sole cause of disadvantage and difficulty. This leads policy-makers and professionals to seek a 'solution' through the removal of impairment. Each of these responses is considered, at different times and in different contexts, to be valuable in bringing about the perceived desired outcome of reducing the number of people with impairments. The result is often a fundamental undermining of our civil and human rights.

For example, although not currently legal in Britain, euthanasia and infanticide are widely advocated where the 'quality of life' of someone with an impairment is deemed unacceptably low. An increasing number of infanticide and euthanasia cases have reached the courts in recent years, with judgements and public responses implying increasing approval. Infanticide is justified on grounds that 'killing a defective infant is not morally equivalent to killing a person. Very often it is not wrong at all' (Singer, 1979). Suicide amongst people with impairments is frequently considered far more rational than in people without, as though impairment renders it the obvious, even the only, route to take.

Assumptions of the inevitable poor quality of life of people with an impairment dominate the development of pre-natal screening and abortion. The express aim of screening is to offer abortion where impairment is indicated[2]. Where foetal screening indicates impairment, 86% of the general public in Britain 'approve' of abortion (de Crespigny with Dredge, 1991). Screening is rarely offered so that parents can plan for their child. These approaches have created a huge research industry and foetal screening and abortion are now major users of impairment-related resources.

Prevention of impairment through public health measures receives only minimal consideration and resourcing. The isolation of impairment from its social context means that the social and economic causes of impairment often go unrecognised. The definitions of prevention are also questionable, in that foetal screening and subsequent abortion are categorised by mainstream approaches as preventative, whereas in reality such action is about elimination of impairment.

Where removal of impairment is not possible, mainstream approaches extend to the management of impairment, although this remains one of the most under-resourced areas of the health service. However, much of the work in this area, rather than increasing an individual's access to and control over the help that they might need, is more about disguising or concealing impairment. Huge amounts of energy and resources are spent by medical and rehabilitation services to achieve this. For example, many individuals are prescribed cosmetic surgery and prostheses which have no practical function and may actually inhibit an individual's use of their body. Others are taught

[2] Section 1, (i) (b) of the 1967 Abortion Act permits abortion if 'there is substantial risk' of the child being born with a severe handicap.

to struggle for hours to dress themselves when the provision of personal assistance would be more effective.

There are a number of critical flaws in mainstream interpretations of impairment and associated responses. First, little distinction is made between different people's experience of impairment or different aspects of a single impairment – or indeed, whether there may be positive aspects to some impairments. Instead, resources are applied in a generalised way to end impairment, regardless of the actual experience and interpretations of the people concerned. With the development of genetic screening, intervention aims to eliminate people with specific types of impairment altogether. Rarely is consideration given to the positive attributes of impairment. For example, the cystic fibrosis gene confers resistance to cholera which is an important benefit in some parts of the world. Associations are being identified between some impairments and creative or intellectual talent, while impairment in itself requires the development of more co-operative and communitarian ways of working and living – an advantage in a society with so much conflict to resolve.

Second, impairment is presented as the full explanation, with no recognition of disability. Massive resources are directed into impairment-related research and interventions. In contrast, scant resources are channelled into social change for the inclusion of people with impairments. For example, research will strive to 'cure' an individual of their walking difficulty, whilst ignoring the social factors which make not walking into a problem. There is little public questioning of the distribution of funds between these two approaches. Additionally, such assumptions inhibit many disabled people from recognising the true causes of their circumstances and initiating appropriate responses.

A third criticism is that, while these responses to impairment are seen as representing the interests of disabled people, they are made largely by people with no direct experience of impairment, yet are presented as authoritative. Disabled people's knowledge, in contrast, is frequently derided as emotional and therefore lacking validity. Although mainstream interventions are presented as being for the benefit of disabled people, in fact they are made for a non-disabled society. Ingrained assumptions and official directives make it clear that there is an implicit, and sometimes explicit, intention of population control. Abortion, euthanasia and cure are presented as 'quality of life' issues, but are also justified in terms of economic savings or 'improvement' to populations [3].

It is counteracting these and related concerns which motivates the disabled people's movement. The social model of disability rejects the notion of impairment as problematic, focusing instead on discrimination as the key obstacle to a disabled person's quality of living. The logical extension of this approach is to seek a solution through the removal of disability and this is what the disabled people's movement works towards.

As a result, the overriding emphasis of the disabled people's movement is on social change to end discrimination against people with impairments. There is a strong resistance to considering impairment as relevant to our political analysis. When impairment is discussed at all within the disabled people's movement it tends to be in the context of criticising mainstream responses. We have, for example, clearly stated that foetal screening for abortion and the implicit acceptance of infanticide for babies with significant impairments are based on assumptions that our lives are not worth living. Our intervention in public debates in recent years about medically assisted suicide (euthanasia) has exposed the same assumption. In contrast, we have asserted the value of our lives and the importance of external disabling barriers, rather than impairment in itself, in determining quality of life. The same perspective informs our criticisms of the resources spent on attempting to cure people of their impairments.

It is this rejection of impairment as problematic, however, that is the social model's flaw. Although social factors *do* generally dominate in determining experience and quality of life – for example requests for euthanasia are more likely to be motivated by lack of appropriate assistance than pain (Seale and Addington Hall, 1994) – impairment *is* relevant. For fear of appearing to endorse mainstream interpretation, we are in danger of failing to acknowledge that for some individuals impairment – as well as disability – causes disadvantage.

Not acknowledging impairment also lays the disabled people's movement open to misappropriation and misinterpretation. For example, disabled people's concerns about genetic screening and euthanasia have been used by pro-life groups to strengthen their arguments. Equally, the movement's

[3] In 1991 a new screening test for Down's Syndrome was recommended for all pregnant women on the grounds that the £88 test would reduce the cost per 'case' discovered (and presumably, aborted) from the current £43,000 to £29,500 (Pulse, 25 May, 1991).

rejection of medical and rehabilitation professionals approaches to treatment and cure has not been accompanied by an exploration of what forms of intervention *would* be useful. Our message tends to come across as rejecting all forms of intervention when it is clear that some interventions, such as the alleviation of pain, in fact require more attention and resources. In both cases, the reluctance of the disabled people's movement to address the full implications of impairment leaves its stance ambiguous and open to misuse.

It is also clear that, by refusing to discuss impairment, we are failing to acknowledge the subjective reality of many disabled people's daily lives. Impairment *is* problematic for many people who experience pain, illness, shortened lifespan or other factors. As a result, they may seek treatment to minimise these consequences and, in extreme circumstances, may no longer wish to live. It is vital not to assume that they are experiencing a kind of false consciousness – that if all the external disabling barriers were removed they would no longer feel like this. We need to ensure the availability of all the support and resources that an individual might need, whilst acknowledging that impairment *can* still be intolerable.

This does not imply that *all* impairment is intolerable, or that impairment causes *all* related disadvantage; nor does it negate the urgency with which disability must be confronted and removed. It simply allows us, alongside wider social and political change, to recognise people's experiences of their bodies. Without incorporating a renewed approach to impairment we cannot achieve this.

A RENEWED SOCIAL MODEL OF DISABILITY

We need to take a fresh look at the social model of disability and learn to integrate all its complexities. It is critical that we recognise the ways in which disability and impairment work together. The social model has never suggested that disability represents the total explanation or that impairment doesn't count – that has simply been the impression we have given by keeping our experiences of impairment private and failing to incorporate them into our public political analysis.

We need to focus on disability *and* impairment: on the external and internal constituents they bring to our experiences. Impairment is about our bodies' ways of working and any implications that holds for our lives.

Disability is about the reaction and impact of the outside world on our particular bodies. One cannot be fully understood without attention to the other, because whilst they can exist independently of each other, there are also circumstances where they interact. And whilst there are common strands to the way they operate, the balance between disability and impairment, their impact and the explanations of their cause and effect will vary according to each individual's situation and from time to time.

We need a renewed social model of disability. This model would operate on two levels: a more complete understanding of disability and impairment as social concepts; and a recognition of an individual's experiences of their body over time and in variable circumstances. This social model of disability is thus a means to encapsulating the total experience of both disability and impairment.

Our current approach is based primarily on the idea that once the struggle against disability is complete, only the impairment will remain for the individual and there will be no disadvantage associated with this. In other words, when disability comes to an end there will be no socially-created barriers to transport, housing, education and so on for people with impairments. Impairment will not then be used as a pretext for excluding people from society. People with impairments will be able to participate in and contribute to society on a par with people who do not have impairments.

In this non-disabling society, however, impairment may well be unaltered and some individuals will find that disadvantages remain. Removal of disability does not necessarily mean the removal of restricted opportunities. For example, limitations to an individual's health and energy levels or their experience of pain may constrain their participation in activities. Impairment *in itself* can be a negative, painful experience.

Moreover, whilst an end to disability means people with impairments will no longer be discriminated against on those grounds, they may remain disadvantaged in their social and economic opportunities by the long-term effects of earlier discrimination. Although affirmative action is an important factor in alleviating this, it is unlikely to be able to undo the full scale of discrimination for everyone.

Our current interpretation of the social model also tends to assume that if impairment ceases, then the individual will no longer experience disability. In practice, however, they may continue to be disabled, albeit to a lesser degree than previously. Future employment opportunities, for example, are likely to be affected by past discrimination in education even when impairment no longer exists.

In addition, an end to impairment may also trigger a massive upheaval to those aspects of an individual's self-identity and image formed in response to disability and impairment. It can also signal the loss of what may be an individual's primary community. These personal and collective identities are formed in response to disability. That further changes may be required in changing circumstances is a sign of the continuing legacy of disability.

Our current approach also misses the fact that people can be disabled even when they have no impairment. Genetic and viral testing is now widely used to predict the probability of an individual subsequently acquiring a particular impairment. Fear has been expressed that predisposition to impairment will be used as a basis for discrimination, particularly in financial and medical services (Disability Awareness in Action, 1994).

There are also circumstances in which disability and impairment exist independently, and change in one is not necessarily linked to change in the other. For example, disability can dramatically ease or worsen with changes to an individual's environment or activities even when their particular impairment is static. Leaving a purpose-built home to go on holiday, for example, may give rise to a range of access restrictions not usually encountered, even though an individual's impairment remains the same. Equally, an employee with an impairment may find their capacity to succeed at work is confounded within one organisation but fully possible in another simply because of differences in the organisations' equality practices.

Where impairment increases, disability does not necessarily follow suit if adequate and appropriate resources are readily available to meet changes in need. A new impairment, a condition which fluctuates or a progressive impairment may mean that an individual needs additional or changing levels of personal assistance, but disability will remain constant if that resource is easily accessed, appropriate and flexible.

Perhaps most importantly, however, disability and impairment interact. Impairment must be present in the first instance for disability to be triggered: disability is the form of discrimination that acts specifically against people with (or who have had) impairments. This does not mean that impairment causes disability, but that it is a precondition for that particular oppression.

However, the difficulties associated with a particular impairment can influence the degree to which disability causes disadvantage. For example, an individual with a chronic illness may have periods in which their contact with the social world is curtailed to such an extreme that external restrictions become irrelevant. At times of improved health the balance between impairment and disability may shift, with opportunities lost through discrimination being paramount.

Impairment can also be caused or compounded by disability. An excessively steep ramp, for example, might cause new impairment or exacerbate pain. An inaccessible health centre can restrict the availability of health screening that would otherwise prevent certain impairments, whilst inadequate resourcing can mean that pain reduction or management techniques are not available to many of the people who need them. Medical treatments, including those used primarily for cosmetic purposes, can cause impairment – for example, it has now emerged that a side effect of growth hormone treatment is the fatal Creutzfeldt-Jakob Disease.

Discrimination in general can also cause major emotional stress and place mental health at risk. Our reluctance to discuss impairment obscures this aspect of disability. If we present impairment as irrelevant then, even where impairment is caused by disability, it is, by implication, not a problem. This limits our ability to tackle social causes of impairment and so diminishes our campaigns.

Like disability, other inequalities can also create or increase impairment. For example, abuse associated with racism or heterosexism, sexist pressure to modify physical appearance and lack of basic provision because of poverty can all lead to impairment. A significant proportion of people become active in the disabled people's movement as a result of such experiences, or through a recognition of these (and other) links that exist between oppressions.

Different social groups can also experience diverse patterns of impairment for a variety of social and biological reasons. Impairment for women, for example, is more likely to be associated with chronic pain, illness and old age (Morris, 1994). Excluding the implications of impairment risks reducing the relevance of the social model of disability to certain social groups. For example, the most common cause of impairment amongst women is the chronic condition, arthritis, where the major manifestation of impairment is pain. Unless the social model of disability incorporates a recognition of the patterns of impairment experienced by different social groups, there will be a failure to develop appropriate services.

Impairment can also be influenced by other external factors, not necessarily discriminatory, which may be physical, psychological or behavioural. Differences in cultural and individual approaches to pain and illness, for example, can significantly affect the way a person feels, perceives and reacts to pain. The study of pain control has revealed that pain can be significantly reduced by a range of measures, including by assisting individuals to control their own treatment programmes and through altered mental states associated with meditation or concentration in activity. The limited availability of such measures to many people who could benefit extends this to the sphere of disability.

Social factors can, at the most fundamental level, define what is perceived as impairment. Perceptions of norms and differences vary culturally and historically. As mainstream perceptions change, people are defined in and out of impairment. Many people labelled 'mentally ill', for example, simply do not conform to contemporary social norms of behaviour. Other inequalities may contribute to the identification of impairment. For example, racist classifications in the school psychological service have led to a disproportionately high number of Black compared to white children in segregated units for 'the emotionally and behaviourally disturbed', whilst it is relatively recently that the sexuality of lesbians and gay men has ceased to be officially defined as 'mental illness'.

Mainstream perceptions tend to increase the boundaries of impairment. The logical outcome of a successful disabled people's movement is a reduction in who is perceived as having an impairment. An absence of disability includes the widespread acceptance of individuality, through the development of a new norm which carries an expectation that there will be a wide range of attributes within a population. With an end to disability, many people currently defined as having an impairment will be within that norm. Impairment will only need definition as such if *in itself* it results in disadvantages such as pain, illness or reduced opportunities.

CONCLUSION

I share the concerns expressed by some disabled people that some of the arguments I have put forward here might be used out of context to support the medical model of disability, to support the view that the experience of impairment is nothing but personal tragedy. However, suppression of our subjective experiences of impairment is not the answer to dealing with these risks; engaging with the debates and probing deeper for greater clarity might well be. I believe that the value of this renewed social model of disability to our campaigns and the way we live our lives means we must do this.

I am arguing for a recognition of the implications of impairment. I am not supporting traditional perspectives on disability and impairment, nor am I advocating any lessening of the energies we devote to eliminating disability. Acknowledging our personal experiences of impairment does not in any way disregard the tremendous weight of oppression, nor does it undermine our alignment with other civil rights movements. Certainly, it should not weaken our resolve for change. Disability remains our primary concern, *and* impairment exists alongside.

Integrating those key factors into our use of the social model is vital if we are to understand fully the ways that disability and impairment operate. What this renewed social model of disability does is broaden and strengthen the current social model, taking it beyond grand theory and into real life, because it allows us to incorporate a holistic understanding of our experiences and potential for change. This understanding needs to influence the structure of our movement – how we organise and campaign, how we include and support each other. A renewed approach to the social model is vital, both individually and collectively, if we are to develop truly effective strategies to manage our impairments and to confront disability. It is our learning and support within our own self-advocacy and political groups, peer counselling, training and arts that enable us to confront the difficulties we face, from both disability and impairment. It is this that allows us to continue working in the most effective way towards the basic principle of equality that underpins the disabled people's movement.

It is this confronting of disability and aspects of impairment that underpins the notion of disability pride which has become so central to our movement. Our pride comes not from 'being disabled' or 'having an impairment' but out of our response to that. We are proud of the way we have developed an understanding of the oppression we experience, of our work against discrimination and prejudice, of the way we live with our impairments.

A renewed approach to the social model is also relevant in our work with non-disabled people, particularly in disability equality training. Most of us who run such courses have avoided acknowledging impairment in our work, concerned that it confirms stereotypes of the 'tragedy' of impairment or makes the issues too complicated to convey. Denying the relevance of impairment, however, simply does not ring true to many non-disabled people: if pain, by definition, hurts then how can it be disregarded? We need to be honest about the experiences of impairment, without underplaying the overwhelming scale of disability. This does not mean portraying impairment as a total explanation, presenting participants with medical information or asking them to fantasise impairment through experiential exercises. Instead, it allows a clear distinction to be made between disability and impairment, with an emphasis on tackling disabling barriers.

The assertion of the disabled people's movement that our civil and human rights must be protected and promoted by the removal of the disabling barriers of discrimination and prejudice has gained significant public support in recent years. It is this social model of disability which underpins the civil rights legislation for which we campaign, and civil rights will remain the centre of our political attention.

At a time when so many people – disabled and non-disabled – are meeting these ideas afresh, we need to be absolutely clear about the distinction between disability and impairment. The onus will remain upon disabled people to prove discrimination and there will still be attempts to refute our claims by using traditional perceptions of impairment. To strengthen our arguments we must peel away the layers and understand the complexities of the way disability and impairment work so that our allegations of discrimination are water-tight. This is necessary now in our campaigning for full civil rights and will remain necessary when we claim justice under the legislation which will inevitably follow that campaign.

At this crossroads in disabled people's history, it is time for this renewed approach to the social model and the way we apply it. Disability is still socially created, still unacceptable, and still there to be changed; but by bringing impairment into our total understanding, by fully recognising our subjective experiences, we will achieve the best route to that change, the only route to a future which includes us all.

REFERENCES

DE CRESPIGNY, L. with DREDGE, R. (1991) *Which Tests for My Unborn Baby?*, Australia: Oxford University Press.

DISABILITY AWARENESS IN ACTION (1994) 'Further Examples of Threats to Life', *Disability Awareness in Action Newsletter*, 13.

MORRIS, J. (1994) 'Gender and Disability' in: FRENCH, S. (ed.) *On Equal Terms: Working with disabled people*, London: Butterworth-Heinemann.

SEALE, C. and ADDINGTON-HALL, J. (1994) 'Euthanasia: Why people want to die earlier', *Social Science and Medicine*, 39, 5, pp. 647-654.

SINGER, P. (1979) *Practical Ethics* , Cambridge: Cambridge University Press,

UPIAS (1976) *Fundamental Principles of Disability*, London: Union of the Physically Impaired Against Segregation.

WORLD HEALTH ORGANISATION (1980) *International Classification of Impairments, Disabilities and Handicaps*, Geneva: WHO.

This article is a version of 'Including All of Our Lives' by Liz Crow, which is published in: Morris, J., ed. (1996) *Encounters with Strangers: Feminism and Disability,* London: The Women's Press.

CHAPTER 5

Negative Attributes of Self: radical surgery and the inner and outer lifeworld

Michael P. Kelly

INTRODUCTION

This chapter considers the impact on self and on public identity construction of radical abdominal surgery. The surgery is total colectomy and ileostomy which is performed to cure the disease ulcerative colitis. The mechanisms whereby self presentations are constrained in various ways by the after-effects of surgery, are explored. These constraints, it will be argued, are twofold. First, they derive from the immediate problems which are generated by wearing a surgical appliance and being faecally incontinent. These impact directly on the centre of the lifeworld of the person who has had the surgery (Schutz, 1964; 1967; 1970). In turn these problems may be significant in identity construction in social interaction. Second, the after-effects of surgery impact on self and identity via an inter-subjectively understood notion of the symbolic meaning of this particular procedure and its sequelae. The inter-subjectivity derives from a range of negative cultural categories which actors draw upon pre-morbidly and post-operatively. Pre-morbidly the negative categories are of marginal significance to the lifeworld of the person. Post-operatively they are central. It will be shown that those inter-subjective understandings may have profound effects on the actor, regardless of any physical constraints produced by the surgery, and to some extent independent of publicly constructed identities. In other words, the negative attributions are imposed internally rather than externally (cf. Scambler and Hopkins, 1986). It will be shown that the problems are particularly acute in intimate and potential sexual encounters.

This essay draws on earlier published material (Kelly, 1991; 1992a; 1992b; 1994a; 1994b; Kelly and Field, 1996), However, new data are presented and the theoretical arguments are developed with reference to a specific phenomenological perspective.

BACKGROUND

Ulcerative colitis is an inflammatory disease of the lining layer of the gut. The inflammation results in symptoms of chronic unpredictable diarrhoea, loss of copious blood in the stool, pain, weight and appetite loss, and raised temperature. The causes of the disease are not known at present, and there is no medical cure for the condition. It is a disease of unpredictable course, sometimes occurring in acute form where the patient's life is threatened within a matter of days or weeks. In other cases, the sufferer may have a much more low grade experience of symptoms lasting for many years with periods of exacerbation and remission. The standard medical treatments when this research was originally conducted were the administration of oral or topical steroids and the use of an anti-inflammatory agent called Sulphasalazine (Salazopyrin). Steroids tend to be most effective in first onset and appear to be less efficacious thereafter. This leaves Sulphasalazine, which may itself have side effects such as nausea and male sterility, as the main palliative treatment.

When a patient is in an acute phase of the illness their life will revolve around going to the toilet. One of the great difficulties faced by a patient with colitis is the urgent need to evacuate. They not infrequently will have the sensation of requiring to open their bowels at once. In such circumstances they will have to stop what they are doing and go immediately to a toilet. As this urge is often quite uncontrollable, episodes of self-soiling are not uncommon. The sufferer may need to evacuate up to a dozen times a day and in very severe cases twenty or so or more times in 24 hours. The person with colitis therefore always has to know where the nearest toilet is, and simple tasks such as travelling, shopping, going away on holiday, going to social events become occasions fraught with danger and uncertainty. Of course, when the illness is at its most severe, the person will be too unwell to go out of the house anyway, and the sheer exhaustion which accompanies the loss of blood, the dehydration and the fever will lay them low. People whose symptoms are in remission will still have to attend to the potential unpredictability of their bowel motions. Even if they are apparently well, they may only get a few seconds warning of the start of a new attack.

There are some very serious complications of colitis. However, two are of especial note: toxic megacolon and cancer. Toxic megacolon is the disease process where the bowel literally expands until it bursts causing potential life threatening peritonitis. Colitis is a risk factor for bowel cancer. In persons who have had colitis for more than 10 years, there is a very greatly enhanced risk of the development of cancer, even where the symptoms have been low grade and apparently benign. This means that a person who is diagnosed as having colitis should be monitored regularly to ascertain whether any pre-cancerous changes are occurring in the bowel. This involves two highly invasive procedures, barium enema and colonoscopy. In barium enema the barium is drained under gravity through the back passage into the colon. X-ray photographs are then taken. A colonoscope is a fibre optical instrument allowing the physician or surgeon to visualise the colon's surface and take out microscopic samples for investigation, again entering via the back passage. Both procedures are painful and highly undignified.

If pre-cancerous changes are observed, if the patient's life is threatened by some other complication, or their health and quality of life is extremely poor, then the only treatment option is radical surgery. This may involve the complete removal of the large bowel (colectomy) and the redirection of the small bowel through the abdominal wall (ileostomy). Following surgery, an appliance – a bag – must be worn by the patient who is made permanently faecally incontinent. When the research on which this chapter is based was done, this was the standard surgical procedure in use. More recently, other techniques have been perfected in which an internal reservoir or pouch is constructed. For some, these pouches still require external drainage with a catheter. Alternatively, the pouch is linked to the anus, so something approximating to normal defecation can occur. All these procedures are major. For elective as against emergency cases however they carry very few risks, but they do carry a considerable post-operative residue with which the 'cured' patient has to live for the rest of their life.

Colitis tends to be a disease of early adulthood. So not only do sufferers have to contend with a major illness they are also often in the throws of coping with all the problems and difficulties associated with taking on adult statuses and responsibilities, jobs, relationships and children.

METHODS

The data for this paper were collected in a series of semi structured interviews with people who had colitis and were waiting for surgery, or who had had surgery after a previous period of time with the disease. These interviews initially took the form of a guided conversation about the principal features of the natural history of the disease. However, after the first couple of interviews had been completed it became clear that with one simple question i.e. 'Could you tell me when you first noticed there was something wrong?', the respondents were able to talk at considerable length with a minimum of guidance. The objective was to get the people to talk as freely and as openly as possible.

Some 50 or so interviews were originally conducted. However, only 45 were analysed in depth, because some of the subjects when interviewed turned out not to have had colitis, or to have had some other kind of surgery. In a couple of cases the tape recorder failed to record, in two further cases relatives interfered with the interview and effectively took it over. All the interviews were tape recorded and then transcribed longhand. Then a simple thematic analysis was undertaken on the basis of the main features of the disease, what the literature on chronic illness suggested should be key ideas, and themes generated *de novo* from the transcripts themselves. These were cross referenced on a manual card index and sorted for purposes of generating categories and theoretical constructs. A great variety of themes emerged in the process but one of the most significant concerned ideas of self and identity. A limited amount of data relating to those concepts are presented in this chapter.

The sample itself was generated in several ways. In the area where the research was done, the names of people who might be prepared to be interviewed were obtained from several surgeons and from nurses engaged in stoma care. Also two branches of the Ileostomy Association were visited and volunteers recruited. At the beginning of each interview the volunteers were told what the purpose of the visit was – which was to obtain information about the experience of colitis and surgery from the patient's perspective.

THEORETICAL STARTING POINTS

The conceptual structure of the chapter begins with a simple distinction (following Ball, 1972) between self and identity. In Ball's view, self is ego as known to ego i.e. that idea that each and every individual has in their mind's eye of who and what they are. Identity, in contrast, is ego as known to others, i.e. the way the individual is seen, perceived and defined by others. In this view, self is not some biologistic or psychologistic 'thing'. It is rather the way that internally the individual objectifies themself to themself. Self is both experience in the here and now, and, a remembered past and an anticipated future having apparent existential continuity. The medium which links the self of experience to the self of past and future, is language and particularly the narrative stories and accounts that the individual uses to present their self to themself, and to others. Through language self can objectify. That is it can think about itself in the same way that it can think about objects in the immediate, imagined or remembered environment. It can therefore imagine how it appears to others and can anticipate various identities that may emerge in interaction.

As interaction unfolds, self may become aware that the way it wants to be recognised and understood by others, is not happening. Everyone sometimes feels uncomfortable in the situation in which they find themselves and notices that they are misperceived by others. Some aspects of self and public identity on the other hand are rarely equivocal. Gender, approximate age, racial grouping are not generally ambiguous, although particular individuals may go to great lengths to deceive others in this regard. However, it is when the major axes of social differentiation are left behind and the focus is on social roles and behaviours which are not unambiguous, that the potential for misunderstanding arises. Guessing a stranger's correct occupation, or the type of school they went to, for example, is both a party game and the heart of a good deal of interaction between strangers. The rituals of interaction between people who do not know each other involve subtle processes of revealing identity markers, and covering up *faux pas* and misunderstandings. In certain settings key badges of office such as a doctor's white coat or stethoscope, or the fitter's tool bag help to establish relative identities. But in the absence of badges of office, interaction between strangers is about uncovering enough to establish identities and to allow interaction to proceed. Props of all kinds are routinely used in interaction, and costumes and well rehearsed starter scripts like 'Hello, how do you do?' 'Very well thank you' are all widely used to assist in these processes. Underlying obvious identity markers are a range of other facets. Selves and identities both attract and may try to attach themselves to particular moral, social and emotional characteristics. Self may lay claim to certain virtues, vices, beliefs, values, attitudes and so on, and identity may be linked to these moral characteristics too if such virtues or vices are publicly acknowledged.

So far the model presented here is based on the notion that interaction is problematic, people have to work to make interaction a success (i.e. it is a highly skilful activity) and that language and talk underlies the process. These are common enough ideas drawn as they are from observations of writers like Schutz (1964, 1967, 1970), Garfinkel (1967), Goffman (1969), Mead (1934), James (1892), Stone (1962), and Rosenberg (1981). What is of particular interest in this chapter is the impact on self and identity of illness and surgery, and the attempts to present self and the processes of legitimation which then come into play. When someone has an illness or a condition that actually or potentially cuts across interaction a new dynamic is established in that interaction. The extracts chosen to demonstrate this phenomena relate to an area of human conduct where feelings of self and socially constructed and negotiated identities are especially acute anyway. This relates to sexual or romantic encounters. Notwithstanding sex education, reams of advice and a good deal of media coverage and role modelling, arguably most potential new sexual encounters are intrinsically problematic. Most people, at least at some point in their lives, find them embarrassing, difficult and awkward. This chapter considers what happens to self and identity following major surgery, which creates faecal incontinence, and the need to wear an appliance on the abdomen. It also examines the impact on interaction and for self of cultural stereotypes in these processes.

THE DATA

Several extracts from the various interviews are now presented. The first series of extracts is from the interview with Georgina (a pseudonym). When Georgina had surgery she was 35. She had had colitis for about five years and her health had deteriorated to such a degree that an operation was recommended. She was a manual worker, unmarried and living on her own after the break-up of a long-standing relationship. Her mother and father lived nearby in the same town. Before the operation she expressed many fears about what her body would look like after surgery, and she also expressed a great deal of anxiety about the pain that would ensue after the operation. Although she was both by her own admission, and visibly, very poorly, she had been a very reluctant recruit to surgery and had had to be talked into it by the stoma nurse. Georgina discussed at length issues relating to appearance, and attractiveness. She is here describing what happened when the stoma therapist had been in to the hospital to change the appliance for her:

> 'She changed the bag for me one day. But we had an awful carry on. Cos every time she just went to put a new one, a new bag on, it just started leaking again. Cos, I wasn't, the first stages where it was solidifying or anything. I thought "Oh my God", it was horrid. I thought it was really, really horrible y'know. But, I thought, "Have I got to look at that all the time?" '

Georgina here is describing the not uncommon revulsion which many people with ileostomies feel when they first have their operation. The physical alteration to their body and the physical presence of the stoma seems to have done something profound to them in a way that is unwelcome and disagreeable. Many patients are discharged when they still have feelings of profound doubt and worry about their body, and a degree of uncertainty about their self. For many, and Georgina was a case in point, their whole sense of who and what they are has been undermined, or at least severely jolted by the experience of the surgery and the physical presence of the stoma and the appliance. What also happens is that while they are in hospital their overriding identity as far as their doctors, nurses and family and carers have been concerned, is as a patient and as someone undergoing major surgery. In that sense, the patient's anxieties are reflected back to them in the institutional structures of the hospital environment. Once they leave hospital and they resume other roles again, the incongruities between self and identify really begin to emerge. Here Georgina describes an early outing when she still felt delicate and uncertain:

> '..There was a bloke stopped me in the pub on Saturday night when I was out wi' me pals .... And he says "You're looking fine now", he says, "You're getting on". And I says, "How do you [inaudible]", and he says "You looked absolutely horrible", and I says, "Oh thanks very much, ha ha"! He says, "No, but you're looking fine now, and everybody's saying that" '.

While this little interchange could be put down to nothing more than good manners on the part of the 'bloke' it nevertheless presented a dilemma for Georgina. She was flattered, and pleased, but also her apparently normal external appearance was at odds with the way she herself felt and she knew herself to look underneath her clothes. She felt disgusted and she thought others there would be disgusted also.

Georgina had continuing doubts about how she would cope:

> 'I'm not so bad now, but I found when I just came home, I sat. Came home, I spent half my day in the toilet. Every two minutes I was away thinking, "I'd better empty this, I'd better empty this". And same as when I go to the pub. I sit and I go, "Oh God, I think this is needing [emptying]". And rather than go in a public toilet, I go home and every thing. I don't have any confidence. And my pal says "You canna carry on like that, ya have to". And I say "I can't go to these toilets and stand, in the pub, with everybody drunk and I just thought "Oh no". But I'll just have to get used to it'.

Here we have a situation where Georgina's friends and acquaintances are attempting to construct an identity for her as a well or a recovered person, while she herself does not feel that she is either of those things. Furthermore, she does not believe that others really feel like that either. It is not the fundamental effects on self of the experience which define her self concept, nor the attempts by others to try to welcome her back from the sick role which defines her identity, but rather her own concern about the way she anticipates that others will respond which dominates her thinking. Ultimately Georgina remained very worried about embracing the 'well' or 'recovered' identity which her apparent 'well' appearance demanded. She was concerned because this would ultimately test her self – and her altered self might be revealed for what it truly was:

> 'I says to my pal, how could I be going out with somebody for a couple of weeks and then say "I've got something to tell you". I have a fear of somebody turning round and saying "Oh yeah" and going out the door and never coming back. Cos I think if someone done that, it would really hurt you. You'd feel depressed about it'.

One of the important transitions that occurs for someone who leaves hospital is the change from being someone whose whole identity is defined with reference to their acquisition of an ileostomy i.e. their time in hospital, to one where while their own sense of self is still defined with reference to the stoma, their public identity is defined without any reference to the stoma at all. The latter occurs where the individual finds themselves in social situations where others with whom they are interacting are quite oblivious to the surgery. Non-disease and non-surgical cues provide the basis for identity construction. In these circumstances, in the ordinary run of things, there is no need for the person with the ileostomy to say anything about their ileostomy to others at all. Their own concerns about their stoma are, and can remain, private. However, that is not the case where potential sexual or romantic encounters are concerned. Knowing how to, and feeling confident about handling this aspect of presentation of self can be a major source of anxiety. In certain circumstances the person with the ileostomy feels uncomfortable about passing themselves off as someone without an ileostomy. At the same time they have no easy way to manage the presentation of self involved. One young respondent eloquently expressed problems generated by this tension. She is Frances (again a pseudonym). She was 21 when interviewed. She was a clerical worker who at the time of the interview had had her stoma for four months and was still feeling acutely embarrassed by the whole thing. She had had a very sudden onset of colitis and had got to surgery in less than a year from when she believed the first symptoms had appeared:

> Frances: 'I can't really face telling anyone about it. People [by whom she meant professionals involved in her care] keep saying it's nothing to be ashamed of. But I just don't feel ready to tell anyone about it. So no one actually knows apart from my family. I don't want to tell anyone just now. I think that's probably a bad thing in a way as well, cos I'm kinda keeping it all in. But I just don't want to. I think its going to be quite hard going, going back to work as well'.

> Researcher: 'Why'?

Frances: 'Just getting back and facing everyone, just getting back into a routine'.

The interview then began to explore some of those feelings, and the impact on self can be seen clearly:

Frances: 'I would get upset if I thought about it often enough'.

Researcher: 'What would upset you about it do you think'?

Frances: 'Em, I just think you feel unattractive really with it. I think it just makes you feel like that. Just, unfeminine .... I was lucky. If I had been married, if I'd got married when I was supposed to get married, I think, I don't know, I think I'm glad I didn't, looking back. I'd rather be on my own'.

Researcher: 'Really'?

Frances: 'Mmmm .

Researcher: 'Why'?

Frances: 'Not forever. I just mean just now. Just until I can come to terms with the thing myself. I think it would be hard to tell someone, I think it would take me a long time before ......'.

Researcher: 'What do you mean? A prospective partner'?

Frances: 'I'd have sort of feel. They would have to get to know me first, before I'd tell them. I wouldn't just go out with someone for a couple of dates and then tell them'.

Frances is grappling with several things. First, she has a view that her particular condition will be stigmatised by prospective partners. She does not believe this on the basis of any evidence that the ileostomy will be the defining aspect of her identity. She had no direct experience of this happening. At the time of the interview she had told no-one outside of her family circle. Her anticipation was not on the basis of bitter experience. Her anticipation was however on the basis of cultural values and norms which she was drawing upon where her own sense of recoil from the stoma was objectified onto others. In a Meadian sense she is role taking and imagining the way others might perceive her (Mead, 1934). By drawing inter-subjectively upon various cultural norms relating explicitly to femininity, and implicitly to attractiveness, she finds herself wanting and believes others will do so too. Second, she is objectifying her own self. There is the self which is impacted on by the stoma, and there is the 'true' self – the real her which is more important than the self defined with reference to the stoma. She has concluded that she must have time with a prospective partner so he can get to know her. By this she has some idea of a life in which the stoma is unimportant. Frances wants the opportunity to construct an identity which is not one based on her stoma. What she had yet to do, at the time of interview, was to find a way to deal with this herself and carry off the presentation of self in which 'I am more important than the stoma' was the dominant motif.

That Frances should feel like this is hardly surprising. Another subject offers a graphic account of why this is so. She is Lana, a nurse. She was 20 when interviewed having first been diagnosed as having colitis when she was 18. Here she is describing her experiences in hospital after she had had her operation and at the point when she was mobile enough to be taken to have a bath:

> 'I remember the first time I had a bath. And they decided they were gonna change it [the appliance], y'know. And the bags that y'get in hospital, y'know they've got the brown stuff all around, and it all sticks to you, and every thing. And it wouldn't come off. And it was all over the bathwater and oh! And I started crying in the bathroom y'know, because it was all over the place, and, I just think, I thought that when they [the nurses] looked at me, they must be disgusted. Because they see this, and it was horrible, y'know'.

What is so interesting about this quotation is that as Lana does the role taking she is not simply imagining in a vacuum what the nurses might feel. She is a nurse herself and she had nursed stoma patients. She knew how she felt about that, and therefore she thought she had a pretty shrewd idea as to how the people nursing her would feel. She had access to 'privileged' back-stage talk, which she knew was negative. The problem of access to what is otherwise privileged discourse, caused further problems for Lana. She dearly wanted to keep public knowledge of her condition to a minimum. However, she lived in a small village some 15 miles from the main town, where the hospital was where she had had her operation. She found the local gossip (which is of course a form of public identity construction) hard to cope with:

> Lana: 'I mean people have said to me, back in Budling, mm, all I say, I'm not lying, but I'm not telling the truth. I just say I had to get a bit of my bowel taken out, and they don't know ...... They don't know that it's a whole total colon, or with Crohn's disease you can get a resection, I mean they don't have a clue, so they don't know'.

Researcher: 'Is it important to you not to tell them'?

Lana: 'Just now'.

Researcher: 'Why do you think that is'?

Lana: 'Er, don't know. Budling's such a small place and they all look at you, y'know. And the girl said to my sister, well a woman actually, who'd found out. And she said to my sister "Oh God, what a shame. That's terrible, y'know, that poor girl, She's such a bonnie lassie and she's had to get that horrible operation?" And I thought, "Oh God, if this is what I've to face when I come home I'm not telling anyone". Y'know, cos my sister told me, but, I had, I've had a really bad time since I came home, because I got out on 18th February, that was Thursday night. Friday night we were having fish. So I went out to the fish shop [she met someone who asked her how she was feeling] And I say "Oh fine". Being such a small town I thought, "Oh she's heard I've been in hospital", y'know. And eh, and I thought that was as far as the conversation was going to go. And she said, er, "That was a terrible operation that y've had". Y'know she's standing looking at my tummy, y'know, she says "How do you cope with that bag thing"? y'know. I sort of looked at her because I hadn't told anybody outside my family, and I know that nobody would tell her, and I thought "How the hell do you know"? And I didn't look annoyed and I just said, "Do you mind telling me how you found out"? "Oh my sister's a staff nurse in theatre" '.

This breach of professional etiquette caused Lana enormous distress, because her inability to define not just her identity, but her own sense of self as reflected back to her was removed. Selves and identities are not static things. They are in a relationship of constant flux with each other. Self is presented, identity is negotiated and self is redefined and represented in a never ending process. What is crucial here is that as self is presented, it is not or only partially legitimated, and instead a very particular definition of identity is applied which Lana had not wanted but she was now powerless to do much about. Small wonder that later in the interview she made this comment.

Lana: 'Every night when I go to my bed, and that's where I do most of my thinking. And you lie and think about it. And it's, it's the thought "God I've got this for the rest of my life", y'know, em, people keep saying "It'll become part of your life", but I don't know yet'.

These concerns are not simply psychological worries and fears but they relate to the fact that the sense of self is tied into the technical efficiency of the appliance. This helps explain why and how the ileostomy can become such a dominant concern. In order to feel confident and to engage in presentation of self in a way that appears to be unexceptional and ordinary requires that the ileostomy be bracketed out of feelings about self and therefore bracketed out of interaction more generally. If an appliance leaks or falls off, the game is up. It will make a mess. It will smell and a replacement will have to be found. The wearer's fear is that this might happen at any moment. Steven explains:

> ' Y'see I'm a very active person, and I thought y'know "Is this gonna come apart"? No, I thought if I'm really active and hill walking and things like that, "How am I gonna hill walk for a full day"? Y'know, walk 20, 25 miles. How am I gonna be in that time? So the stoma therapist provided me with ... the belt ... so that gives you confidence, because that is what I was needing. I had confidence till I had a few failures [leaks]. I had a few failures, and the confidence soon goes. It goes very quickly'.

> Researcher: 'You had some accidents [leaks] did you'?

> Stephen: 'Well one, one came adrift and er that ..... it was in the house, but I thought if I was in the middle of a hill, or the middle of a shoot and that happened, I'm in deep trouble. So that's when I lost confidence and got very depressed about it. That's when, I say, I suddenly realised. Oh, I knew it was for life certainly but eh, but it really got home to me at that point'.

What Steven is struggling with here is that he wanted other things in his life to be more important than his stoma. The country life of walking and shooting, was an expression of the self he wanted to be. He was however concerned that the unreliability of the stoma would override his efforts. In this sense he is quite right since the presentation of self and the recognition of this by others, is for the person with an ileostomy critically dependent on the ileostomy, being under the control of the person who has it. This can never be an entirely taken-for-granted aspect of life for the person in this position. The forceful salience of the ileostomy will vary, but it can never be entirely ignored or forgotten about.

Nevertheless it does seem to be the physical scarring and the stoma itself which seem to exert the most profound influence on self, and not just in people who are anticipating relationships, but to people in long-lasting ones. Tricia, a clerical worker, for example, was 49 and had been married for more than 25 years. She was less than a year away from surgery when interviewed. She explained her anxieties:

> 'It was just that I em, when I looked at my body, and saw the big scar, and this [the appliance] at the side, I thought "Oh Heavens will Gregor [her husband] ever look at me again". Which is really ridiculous. Y'know. He is a very loving person'.

She explained how this concern had caused her to cry. Tricia was someone whose marriage was very secure, and where husband and wife had in fact been through many shared difficulties over the years. And yet she still felt that her identity as defined by her husband might be fundamentally transformed. The power of the negative feelings about self to be extended to others, is considerable. And this happened in spite of the fact that she herself felt quite positive about how she managed her stoma:

> ' I'm amazed how I've adapted to it. And er, honestly I forget that I've got it at times, and I've, and it's not until I feel the bag getting heavy or swollen, y'know, if there's any wind in it, that I realise that there's something there. It, y'know, I've been amazed at how, I have adapted to it and I've found myself in the kitchen the other day, y'know when y'r working away with both hands, you sort of shut the drawer with the hip bone and realising "oh! better not do that", y'know having completely forgotten that it was there'.

This quotation helps to illustrate another facet of self. For some people with ileostomies, as time goes by, the salience of the stoma and the appliance fade and other more mundane aspects of life and subjectivity assume importance, or reassume importance. There is a clear imperative that life goes on and the post-operative patient has in some way to integrate with or to obey the imperative. In hospital their entire sense of self and their whole public identity was rooted in the presence of the stoma and in the experience of surgery. Profound as these experiences are, there is status passage onward. However, as these extracts also suggest while self may grow more comfortable with the surgical residue, self also is acutely aware of the possibly negative aspects attaching to when the stoma is public – even with the most intimate of associates.

Barbara, a young respondent (22 when interviewed) and at that time unemployed and unmarried, shows some of the acute concern that negative identity construction will occur.

> 'One thing I can remember, eh, the day that they told me, that I was going to get out of the hospital. When they said right, you're O.K., you're gonna get out the next day, er, I didn't want to go home, because I was sorta secure in the hospital. Well I did want to go home, but I didn't at the same time, and er, the day that I got out I just felt like bursting into tears. I didn't like, I'm the kind of person that hides my emotions, but I really felt like bursting into tears because I'd left the security of the hospital, and I didn't know how other people were gonna react'.

Barbara took a very direct approach in the end and used this directness to try and influence the way identity construction occurred in relationships, with varying results. She describes two of her relationships:

'Well you don't have to tell them because, I mean, I don't know, people, I suppose I well you don't have to tell them unless you're in any situation where you feel you must, I s'pose. My last boyfriend, I told him, er. I sorta put it off because, eh, I had this boy before right, and er, I'd just been out wi' him a couple of times right, and I sorta. He sensed that there was something wrong with me. I just sorta, I don't know, I just sorta clamped up, em, and I just sorta, I thought to myself, right, I'm gonna tell him because, because, it just wasna doing any good, right. So I told him, and he says "God, what does that matter"? He says er, "I mean", he says, "To tell you the truth, my grandad's gone through the same operation". And I thought it was really genuine and everything. The next time he saw me, he never spoke to me or anything, and that sorta put me off, y'know telling anybody, cos he seemed really genuine about it. Ah, "Oh God, that's nothing, I mean my grandad's had that operation, and I mean I know what its like, and why should you bother about what people think"? And all the rest of it. And the next time he saw me he never even spoke to me. And I thought. And I thought "God", and it really knocked me back. So then, er, my last boyfriend em, I'd been going out with him a couple of months and er, I searched, I kept putting off. I wanted to tell him. But I just sorta kept putting it off. I thought, should I tell him straight away, so I will know whether it will bother him or not. So he can just sorta go away and that will be it. And if it doesn't bother him, sorta keep going out with him. So I knew straight away whether he was bothered or not, and I just sorta put it off and put it off, and then one night I just told him. And I mean, he just sorta sat back and thought, "God, what's this"? He says, "I'm really shocked"... Cos I'd been going out with him for about three months. I mean he never had any notion, never thought anything about it, never noticed or anything. And he just accepted it. He just didn't bother at all. He says, "It doesn't bother me", he says, "God, I've been going with you for three months", he says, "I really like you", he says, "You don't think something like that's gonna bother me". I'm no going out with him by the way. But that was, I mean we fell out about something else'!

This final extract demonstrates some of the ambiguities and difficulties involved. Sooner or later if the relationship is to progress, the person with the ileostomy has to present this aspect of their self to others. That aspect of self may be something they are very comfortable with, or it may be something from which they metaphorically recoil. Either way, when they reveal this aspect of their self to another, or as in the case of Tricia, they want to resume a normal life with a spouse, there is a potential danger that it will not be some of the positive facets of self which will be acknowledged and legitimated by the other person. It might be precisely that aspect of self which is so negatively evaluated by self, which could from the core of the identity imposed, negotiated or developed, by the others.

This happens in non-sexual relationships too and the issues being described here apply more broadly. A version of self is proffered in speech, deportment and dress, and a response is made in which identity is confirmed or developed. Interaction is by definition a processual thing and in that sense all interaction is potentially unstable. For the person with an ileostomy, the ileostomy itself provides for an added dimension of potential instability.

DISCUSSION

In the previous sections a model of the relationship between self and identity has been sketched out and some data have been presented to illustrate the proposed model. In schematic terms this may be restated as follows: self is a multifaceted phenomena borne on the data of internalised talk and presented to others via speech, dress and deportment. Self is not a thing, and exists only in the present here and now. However, through language it does have a sense of itself in the past and in an anticipated future. Before, during and after interaction self anticipates the response of others to its presentation and draws upon a stock of cultural knowledge, beliefs or experience to do the anticipations. During interaction, identity emerges as a consequence of the presentation of self and the responses of others (which are themselves similar processes of self-presentation). In the case of the operations described here, the surgery has a profound influence on, and is a highly salient facet of self. Although it may cease to be prominent in the internal lifeworld, it remains a significant feature of anticipated and actual interaction, especially where degrees of intimacy are involved. That significance is drawn from inter-subjectively shared understandings of the world. Self and identity are forever in a process of becoming and are not ever in any sense complete. They are constructed and reconstructed constantly in interaction, in memory and in talk. However, despite the malleability and mutability and the process of becoming, certain key markers provide points of anchor for self and identity. The obvious ones associated with age, gender and ethnicity provide aspects of self and identity which for most people carry over time and place. Social roles, occupations and statuses, while less dominant in an analytic sense, nevertheless provide for key constants in many people's lives. Chronic illness or body altering surgery are other constants, and their implications for social interaction are potentially profound. However, the term 'potentially' is used here quite deliberately to try to capture some of the tenuousness of the processes involved.

Old fashioned role theory not infrequently tended to assume a fit between people and the roles they played (Dahrendorf, 1968). Early sociological theory held that becoming a human involved learning particular social roles and playing out the appropriate performance. While it was recognised that people might interpret roles somewhat differently, the notion of a fit between person and role was assumed. There is a sense in which having a chronic illness or having particular types of surgery or for that matter other forms of impairment, could be conceptualised in this rather old fashioned sense. Sadly however this kind of thinking leads to some unhelpful stereotypical accounts of illness or 'disability'. The person is the role. In these cases the person becomes an ileostomist or an ulcerative colitic. What happens is that the person becomes the role and the role becomes a social category loaded with meaning. Sociologists and writers involved with the disability movement have rightly criticised the naivety of the original theoretical position and the ideological nature of the social categories thus generated. However, just because they are theoretically naive and politically incorrect does not render such categories unimportant.

Certain categories such as chronic sick, colitic, ileostomist and others are part of the cultural capital of society. As with all stereotypes, these categories are drawn upon by cultural actors and serve not just ideological purposes, but also act as a functional shorthand. For most social actors those categories exist in what Schutz called the outer zones of relevance of the life-world (Schutz, 1964, 1967, 1970). For persons who do not have to confront the reality of disease or surgery in the here and now, the categories function as a reference point out of their immediate range of interest. In this they co-exist with many hundreds of similar categories of more or less relevance.

Once illness and surgery enter the immediate lifeworld of the person and their family, the issue the person has to deal with is coping with the practical problems generated by the illness. Most assuredly there is not a one to one fit between the person and the illness, because as these data show the nature of the illness and the surgery has varying degrees of salience depending on place, time and context. At the level of self, the individual will not only have to confront the daily graft of managing the illness and the post-operative sequelae, but also have to manage all the other aspects of their lifeworld too.

However, and this is where the processes conjoin, the erstwhile categories from the outer zones of relevance do not vanish and are not expunged. They remain a significant resource. At the level of self, the individual will be cognisant with the fact that they are much more than their ileostomy or their colitis, and they are a 'real' person not just a stoma. However, in the anticipations that they make of other people's responses to them, they draw not only on their own experiences of illness and surgery, but also on the cultural categories derived from their understandings of those things before they were ill. They anticipate that others, who do not have their inner knowledge, will respond according to broad cultural stereotypes. In part, their task is breaking through the stereotype, of rendering it irrelevant, so that they can reveal their true self and develop a social identity in which other more important aspects of themselves are given precedence over the illness or surgery. In the case of the disease and surgery described here, that is more than possible in many interactive settings. When they are fully clothed their ileostomy is not visible, and for many people with colitis, for a good deal of the time they will not look desperately ill. The problem reaches acute dimensions in intimate or potentially intimate relationships when being undressed will render the appliance visible, or when diarrhoea might start at any moment. This is overlaid by another set of cultural categories about body shape, size and appearance which are highly loaded with meaning in the context of sexual attraction. The cultural stereotypes of sickness and stoma surgery would seem to be diametrically opposed to visions of loveliness and sexual desirability.

What this essay has tried to capture is two notions. The first is that while cultural stereotypes may be offensive, unhelpful and damaging, they are very real. They form part of a backdrop of cultural meanings which for most able bodied people are in the outer zones of relevance of the lifeworld. They are drawn upon heavily, however, by persons with the condition, not necessarily in their self concepts – although these stereotypes may form a clear part of some facets of self – but will particularly form a strong component of anticipated responses from others in the negotiation of identity in presentation of self.

REFERENCES

BALL, D. (1972) 'Self and identity in the context of deviance: the case of criminal abortion', in Scott, R. A. and Douglas, J. D. (eds.) *Theoretical Perspectives on Deviance*, New York: Basic Books.

DAHRENDORF, R. (1968) *Essays in the Theory of Society*, London: Routledge and Kegan Paul.

GARFINKEL, H. (1967) *Studies in Ethnomethodology*, New Jersey: Prentice Hall.

GOFFMAN, E. (1969) *The Presentation of Self in Everyday Life*, London: Penguin.

JAMES, W. (1892) *Psychology: The Briefer Course*, New York: Holt, Rinehart and Winston.

KELLY, M. P. (1991) 'Coping with an ileostomy', *Social Science and Medicine*, 33, 2, 115-125.

KELLY, M. P. (1992a) 'Self, identity and radical surgery', *Sociology of Health and Illness*, 14, 3, 390-415.

KELLY, M. P. (1992b) *Colitis*, London: Routledge.

KELLY, M. P. (1994a) ' Patients' decision making in major surgery: the case of total colectomy', *Journal of Advanced Nursing*, 19, 1168-1177.

KELLY, M. P. (1994b) 'Coping with Chronic Illness: A Sociological Perspective', Inaugural Professorial Lecture delivered the University of Greenwich, London: University of Greenwich Press.

KELLY, M. P. and FIELD, D. (1996) 'Medical Sociology, Chronic Illness and the Body', *Sociology of Health and Illness*, 18, 241-57.

MEAD, G. H. (1934) *Mind, Self and Society: From the Standpoint of a Social Behaviourist*, Chicago: University of Chicago Press.

ROSENBERG, M. (1981) 'The Self-Concept: Social Product and Social Force', in Rosenberg, M. and Turner, R. (eds.) *Social Psychology: Sociological Perspective* New York: Basic Books.

SCAMBLER, G. and HOPKINS, A. (1986) 'Being epileptic: Coming to terms with Stigma', *Sociology of Health and Illness*, 8, 26-43.

SCHUTZ, A. (1953) 'Common-sense and scientific interpretation of human action', *Philosophy and Phenomenological Research*, 14, 1-37.

SCHUTZ, A. (1964) *Collected Papers: II Studies in Social Theory*, (edited and with an introduction by Broderson, A.) The Hague: Martinus Nijhoff.

SCHUTZ, A. (1967) *The Phenomenology of the Social World*, trans. G. Walsh and F. Lehnert, Evanston, Illinois: North Western University Press.

SCHUTZ, A. (1970) *On Phenomenology and Social Relations: Selected Writings*, (ed.) Chicago: University of Chicago Press.

STONE, G. (1962) 'Appearance and the Self', in Rose, A. (ed.) *Human Behaviour and Social Process*, London: Routledge and Kegan Paul.

CHAPTER 6

Disability, Identity and Difference

Tom Shakespeare

INTRODUCTION

Within social theory, questions of disability identity bridge key contemporary debates, including the structure/ agency problem and the biology/ society dualism. It is my purpose to survey some of these issues and try to chart a way through these dichotomies. Identity is a complex field, and social psychologists, sociologists, political scientists, cultural critics and philosophers all use the word variously and in different contexts. Furthermore, the demands of a political movement and the development of social theory may run in contradictory directions – one pragmatic and instrumental, the other more concerned with complexity and nuance. Disability Studies prioritises faithfulness to lived experience, certainly, but also internal coherence and theoretical adequacy.

Initially, I want to foreground two specific uses of identity which illustrate a significant tension in the disability debate. First, we can talk about identifying as an active verb, as much as to say *uncovering* disabled people or *discovering* disabled people. Second, we can use identity in a reflexive sense, in terms of *identifying oneself*, which is about staking a claim to membership of a collective or a wider group. Michel Foucault talks about these differences in the concept of identity. He suggests we are made into subjects from above, through surveillance and control operating through the state, through schools and other agencies, and we make ourselves into subjects from below, where he mainly talks about the processes of confession and communication, people 'speaking the truth about themselves'. I think this distinction is also what he meant, from personal experience, when he argued 'one should not be a homosexual, but one who clings passionately to the idea of being gay' (quoted by Kritzman, 1988, xxiii).

This paper seeks to contextualise the social model within wider models of disability, and to look at the identity options for disabled people. Parallels are drawn with the experiences of women, lesbians and gays, and black people, and post-structuralist concepts are used to problematise the issue of identity. I suggest that recent political developments offer disabled people new opportunities in how they identify. A useful metaphor is that of story telling: identity is an aspect of the stories we tell to ourselves, and to others. Sociology itself could be conceived in terms of form of story-telling. For example, Ken Plummer's recent work uses the concept of story to explore the way that people understand and represent their sexual experiences – for example, as lesbians and gays 'coming out' (Plummer, 1995). I suggest that similar processes in self-understanding are going on in the field of disability identity. Previously there was a limited range of narrative devices and themes available to people with impairment: now, new stories are being told, and we are creating ourselves for ourselves, rather than relying on the traditional narratives of biomedical intervention or rehabilitation, of misery, decline and death. Doing it for ourselves, perhaps we can reconcile tensions and produce alternative, happier endings.

IDENTIFYING DISABLED PEOPLE

Let me distinguish two main approaches to identifying disabled people as a group, one based in a physical or medical understanding, the other based in a socio-cultural understanding: this may be simplistic, but I find the distinction useful for heuristic purposes. I will then go on to subdivide the social identifications further.

The first approach conceives of disability as the outcome of impairment: it is a form of biological determinism, because it focuses on physical difference. Disabled people are defined as that group of people whose bodies do not work; or look different or act differently; or who cannot do productive work. The key elements of this analysis are performing and conforming: both raise the question of normality, because this approach assumes a certain standard from which disabled people deviate.

Often, this approach does not identify 'the disabled' as such, but focuses on particular groups of people with impairment – for example 'the blind' or 'epileptics'. Here we see a denial of the common social experiences which unite disabled people, and a focus on medical dimensions of difference. It is as if we did not speak of Black British people, but instead highlighted Bangladeshi, Jamaican, Guyanese or Sri Lankan people in Britain. Obviously, there are times when ethnic origin is important, but there is a danger of overlooking the unities in the experience of Black British people, and also of essentialising difference.

A wider problem, which is revealed in the confusions of quantitative social research such as the 1988 OPCS Disability Surveys, or exhaustive categorisations such as the International Classification of Impairments, Disabilities and Handicaps, is that everyone is impaired (Sutherland, 1981). We are dealing with an aspect of the human condition, not with the attribute of a specific and identifiable minority. There are differences of degree, although it proves contentious to draw a line, but these are not qualitative differences. If everyone is impaired, we face difficulties if we seek to identify disabled people on the basis that they experience particular physical deficits not shared by the majority population. For example, recent Human Genome research has highlighted the fact that everyone carries four or five recessive genes which would cause genetic disease in an offspring, if the other parent was also a carrier.

Furthermore, I believe that a situation where disabled people are defined by their physicality can only be sustained in a situation where non-disabled people have denied their own physicality (Shakespeare, 1994). If everyone is impaired, then we should look at the ways in which a specific group in society, namely non-disabled people, ignore their experience of impairment and physical limitation. Perhaps the maintenance of a non-disabled identity in the context of physical limitation is a more useful problem with which to be concerned: rather than interrogating the other, let us rather deconstruct the normality-which-is-to-be-assumed. This way of thinking about identity has recently been usefully explored in the context of HIV/AIDS (Crawford, 1994). Moving on to the second approach, disability has been conceived as an outcome of social processes or as a constructed or created category. The social model concept, arising from the social movement of disabled people, and developed by Disability Studies sociologists is the classic example. But one of the points of the current paper is to suggest that while this materialist approach is one route to the social identification of disabled people, there are other fruitful options.

Let me highlight five options for identifying disability as a social process:

1.   *The social model*, which focuses on the disability as a relationship between people with impairment and a discriminatory society: disability is defined as the outcome of disabling barriers imposed by environmental or policy interventions. It suggests a strategy of barrier removal, or education to remove prejudice, with the goal of inclusion. Disabled people, in this approach, do not want anything extra, but wish to be treated the same as non-disabled people. In the social model, there is nothing to distinguish people with impairment who are socially disabled, from people with dependent children who are socially disabled. A whole range of people may in fact be disabled by barriers or prejudices.

2.   *The minority group approach*, in which disabled people are an oppressed group. This is a weaker claim than the social model, focusing on power politics and identity politics, while not necessarily problematising disability itself. It could be associated with North American disability movement approaches, and has a general resonance within self-organised disability politics. That is, it often co-exists with the first option, although I will argue that there are tensions between a focus on removing disabling barriers, and opposing the oppression of disabled people as a minority group. For example, a minority group approach may advocate special measures, or a comprehensive disability income, or a bigger share of social resources. In a pioneering, if ultimately unsatisfactory analysis, Helen Liggett has highlighted the dangers of a minority group approach which reinforces the constitution of disability (Liggett, 1988, p. 271).

3.   *A Weberian or Foucauldian approach* in which disability is a category of social policy. This is epitomised by the work of Deborah Stone (Stone, 1985). A parallel could be drawn with Mary McIntosh's work locating the creation of a homosexual role (McIntosh, 1968): in the same way, we could look at how the development of industrial capitalism in the nineteenth century, through the 1834 Poor Law Amendment Act, set up a distinction between the deserving and the undeserving poor which has influenced social

policy up to the present day and led to the identification of the disability category. As with other approaches, this shifts the attention from the person with impairment to the statutory or policy processes which construct him/her as officially disabled. Robert Scott's work, from a labelling perspective, could usefully be included under this heading (Scott, 1969).

4.   *Disability as the outcome of definitions inherent in social research methods*, for example in the OPCS Disability Surveys. The work of Abberley (1992) and others shows how survey instruments construct a category fairly arbitrarily, resulting in the idea that there are approximately six million disabled people in Britain. Methodological criticism of the type advanced by Kitsuse and Cicourel (1963), or by Hindess (1973), illustrates the weaknesses of such empiricism.

5.   *Disability as a cultural category.* This approach, drawing upon the notion of cultural representation, has precedents in the work of Sontag (1991), and is also related to Foucault's concept of discursive formations. Elsewhere I have looked at this in terms of prejudice, focusing on stereotypes, language and the creation of meaning. Using the notion of otherness, I suggested that the processes of denial and projection are involved in the cultural construction of disability (Shakespeare, 1994).

By offering a range of ways of understanding disability as a social construction, I do not thereby intend to abandon the social model's stress on material, environmental and policy factors. But rather than reducing the category 'disability' to a straightforward social relation, I think an analysis of discursive practices offers a richer and more complex picture of disability. It is in this sense, rather than the narrow phenomenological sense, that I would say disability is socially constructed, and would highlight the benefits of a Foucauldian analysis, regarding disability as a process of subjection.

Ian Hacking has developed an interesting account of what he calls 'making up people' which draws upon McIntosh's 'homosexual role hypothesis' and has relevance to my argument here. Thus he describes as 'dynamic nominalism' the suggestion that:

> 'numerous kinds of human beings and human acts come into being hand in hand with our invention of the categories labelling them' (Hacking, 1986, p. 236).

This casts light on the various forms of social construction of disability outlined above. To me, this also indicates that we would be right to see recent disability politics as opening up new narrative possibilities for individual identity, which may have been unavailable before. As Hacking argues:

> 'Making up people changes the space of possibilities for personhood' (Hacking, 1986, p. 229).

Below I will consider some of these developments.

DISABLED PEOPLE IDENTIFYING

Medical approaches consider negative self identity to be an outcome of physical impairment, and focus on the need for adjustment, mourning, and coming to terms with loss. Social approaches view negative self-identity as a result of the experience of oppressive social relations, and focus attention on the possibilities for changing society, empowering disabled people, and promoting a different self-understanding.

A particularly useful metaphor for understanding both approaches is provided by the concept of identity as narrative, which focuses on the stories we tell about ourselves and our lives, and constructs accounts which encompass plot, causality and conflict. This offers the potential for a nuanced model of identity which resists the temptation straightforwardly to read off identity from context, or indeed embodiment. Giddens summarises this approach to self-identity:

> 'Self-identity is not a distinctive trait, or even a collection of traits, possessed by the individual. It is the self as reflexively understood by the person in terms of her or his biography' (Giddens, 1991, p.53).

Identity therefore connects the social and the personal and involves the individual putting themselves in a collective context.

> 'A person's identity is not to be found in behaviour nor   important though this is – in the reaction of others, but in the capacity to keep a particular narrative going' (Giddens, 1991, p.54).

Jeffrey Weeks has suggested, in the context of gay liberation, that the concept of identity is like finding a map to explore a new country (Weeks, 1977). Both these metaphors connect with the idea of representation, of giving meaning, or of charting a way through, spatially or temporally. They also highlight the importance of identity for political developments: positive identity narratives are reinforced by self-organisation, and are a condition for it.

The experience of disability as a negative identity arises out of a process of socialisation, or in the context of social relations, in which impairment is the sole focus of analysis. Grief and loss are turned inwards, and suffering focuses on the self. In the absence of other socially sanctioned identities, the professional cripple role enables successful interaction with professionals, offering the benefits of sympathy and concern on the part of others. It could be conceived in terms of a tendency to 'blame the victim', to convert public issues in personal woes. As an individualised experience, the structural and cultural context is not challenged, and alternatives to the dominant biomedical paradigm are not available. Difference is either fetishised, as medical tragedy, or ignored. Assimilation is the name of the game.

The person with impairment may have an investment in their own incapacity, because it can become the rationale for their own failure. The legitimation accorded them by non-disabled people is predicated on accepting responsibility for their own incapacity, and not challenging the dominant order. Indeed, they may become token examples of the tragedy of disability, involved in consultations or wheeled out to highlight the problems.

Alternatively, various forms of denial may be involved, where a person claims to be 'really normal' and tries to minimise the importance of impairment in their lives, perhaps by concealment: in Goffman's (1968) terms, they may pass as normal. As he highlighted, this involves considerable tensions and difficulties of managing information or interaction. Other similar strategies may include religious identification with suffering – a resignation to fate or the will of God. Such quietist acceptance involves enduring the difficulties of impairment, possible in the expectation of heavenly compensation. Finally, another form of denial seeks to 'overcome' impairment. Often a strategy associated with masculine expectations, it involves a refusal to submit to reality, and an attempt to regain a normal identity through superhuman activity and endurance, for example in the case of many sporting activities.

While these various alternatives all demonstrate the use of narratives of self, I would argue that none are psychologically or socially healthy or progressive. They all involve an element of denial or failure to come to terms: they all involve a significant element of external definition, of accepting external disempowering agendas. A temporary or compromise identity may be developed, but it is frail, and ultimately has costs for personal psychological happiness and security. By focusing on the body and the individual, the disabled person is trapped in a prison not of their own devising, and cannot escape except through strategies which are ultimately self-defeating.

Disability as a positive identity is a process, to use Foucauldian language, where subjection opens up the possibility of subjectification:

> 'From popular culture to government policy, society has evidently assigned you a membership. Identity politics turns necessity to virtue' (Girlin, 1994, p.153).

This alternative to the negative identification with impairment is provided by those who resist the negative implications of the medical model and develop a response which focuses on the exclusion and injustice which characterises disability. This shift often takes the form of replacing one analytical framework (the 'medical model') with another (the 'social model') to lead to a more positive identity, often described as 'coming out'. This 'coming out' is the process of positive self-identification, rejecting the categorisation of subjection, and affirming subjectivity and collective power. It is about developing new definitions and new political forms. Frances Hasler (1993) describes it as the 'big idea' which underpinned the self-organised disabled people's movement in Britain.

While this can be a private and individual development or personal awakening, it is more likely to take place in a collective context: self-organisation itself prompts the process of identification. Even segregated institutions, such as the Le Court Cheshire home where Paul Hunt lived, can enable disabled activists to foster a response to exclusion (Hunt, 1966). Jeffrey Weeks focuses on this feeling of shared identity:

> 'Identity is about belonging, about what you have in common with some other people and what differentiates you from others. At its most basic, it gives you a sense of personal location, the stable core to your individuality' (Weeks, 1990, p. 88).

Elsewhere I have discussed the relationship between self-organisation and the development of disability as a political identity, and developed comparisons with the women's movement and the civil rights movement (Shakespeare, 1993). Critically, both self-organisation and direct action are processes with implications for identity, as well as instrumental goals: to quote a social theorist,

'The actors mobilise to regain control of their own action. They try to reclaim the right to define themselves against the criteria of identification determined by an anonymous power and systems of regulation that penetrate the area of "internal nature" ' (Melucci, 1989, p.61).

The disability movement provides the collective context for political identification; it involves processes which challenge views of disabled people as incapable, powerless and passive; and it establishes disabled people as the experts on disability and disabled people's definitions as the most appropriate approaches to disability, rather than the traditional domination of professionals.

'The move towards self-organisation has prompted increasing numbers of disabled people to adopt a shared political identity which in turn has helped to build a new mood of confidence. Disabled people no longer ask for change, but demand it. They are prepared to use a whole range of tactics in pursuit of their demands, including direct action and civil disobedience' (Bynoe, Barnes and Oliver, 1991, p. 12).

Alongside political activism, cultural forms of self-provision, otherwise known as disability arts, develop a sense of shared cultural identity which is central to these processes:

'Disability arts also provides a context in which disabled people can get together, enjoy themselves and think in some way about issues of common concern. But it goes deeper than that, as disability culture really does offer people a key to the basic process of identifying as a disabled person, because culture and identity are closely linked concepts. Simply naming the idea I think has encouraged a lot of disabled people to happily call themselves so and to be more up front and confident about themselves and that is also giving more confidence to the movement as a whole' (Sian Vasey, quoted in Lees, ed., 1992, p. 13).

Challenging stereotypes, building solidarity, recounting new stories, are all about developing a disability culture. These processes are also about new options for disability identity:

'To encourage the growth of a disability culture is no less than to begin the radical task of transforming ourselves from passive and dependent beings into active and creative agents for social change' (Morrison and Finkelstein, in Lees, ed., 1992, p.22).

I hope it has been demonstrated that the three aspects of disability identity – political, cultural and personal – are linked. By offering potential for subjectivity, for a changed self-understanding and an increased sense of personal power, self-organisation offers a way out of the traps of negative identification. From self-blame, one is enabled to blame exclusionary social processes; rather than explaining one's situation in terms of personal failure, one can justify one's identity on the basis of discrimination and prejudice. This is about embracing identity and coming to terms with one's political status in the world. What is more, it is about opening up the possibility of changing one's world.

Although I have implied that the process of positive identification is straightforward and simple, I would argue it is difficult and complex. Below, I will highlight particular issues, but here I want to suggest that positive identification should be seen as a   project, rather than a once-for-all definition or event, a project based on self-recognition and recognition by others. Calhoun argues that the politics of personal identity and the politics of collective identity are inextricably linked:

> 'Identities are often personal and political projects in which we participate, empowered to a greater or lesser extent by resources of experience and ability, culture and social organisation' (Calhoun, 1990, p. 28).

Sometimes a focus on political campaigning and political change can mask an equally urgent need to work on psychological obstacles to feeling empowered and effective. Surviving oppression can leave a legacy of distress and difficulty, and those who appear most strident and strong in the political arena can carry a burden of self-hatred and internalised oppression which makes psycho-social fulfilment precarious and problematic. There is a parallel with the arguments of the French psychoanalytical feminist group *Psych et Po*, who referred to the futility of activism without awareness of internal conflict as the danger of the 'phallus inside one's head' (Duchen, 1987, p.47ff). While Disability Studies has presented a dichotomy between the medical model and the social model, few have raised the issue of individual psychology: I would suggest that both object relations and psychoanalytical approaches offer potential benefits for those exploring disabled people's experiences, and that such analyses are long overdue.

IDENTITY PROBLEMS

Rather than propose a simple and triumphalist model of identity formation, I want to suggest there are major obstacles to developing a positive and strong disabled identity. It would not be accurate to trace a neat trajectory between being constructed as a category of otherness, and then being able to use this as a source of strength. There is nothing inevitable or determined about the process, and there are major difficulties with successfully and positively identifying as disabled. As Weeks says in the context of sexuality:

> 'Oppression does not produce an automatic response, but it does provide the conditions with which the oppressed can begin to develop their own consciousness and identity' (Weeks, 1977, p.33).

First, disabled people are socialised to think of ourselves as inferior. Within dominant discourses of subjection, as I have outlined earlier, strong messages of physical difference and personal deficit are reinforced:

> 'The messages we receive are very strong and clear and we have little access to different values which may place a more positive value on our bodies, ourselves and our lives. Our self image is thus dominated by the non-disabled world's reaction to us' (Morris, 1991, p.28).

People are socialised into thinking of disability in a medical model way. We can view this as internalised oppression. Paolo Freire analyses this:

> 'Self-depreciation is another characteristic of the oppressed, which derives from their internalisation of the opinion the oppressors hold of them. So often do they hear that they are good for nothing, know nothing, and are incapable of learning anything – that they are sick, lazy and unproductive – that in the end they become convinced of their own unfitness' (Freire, 1972, p.38).

In the case of disabled people, this is reinforced by segregated education, negative images, cultural representation, absence of positive role models, social treatment of disabled people. It parallels the experience of women in patriarchal societies. We could develop a distinction between people born with impairment, who have no alternative to viewing themselves as deficient, and people becoming impaired, who have to relinquish a non-disabled identity and accept an identity as other. Similarly,

> ' "Becoming a homosexual"; is a difficult process of "becoming the other"; or "becoming what one has learned to despise"; As such it is an individual and privatised process, the "intolerable reality", being a confrontation with oneself rather than being an open struggle with an easily located oppressor' (Gay Left Collective, 1980, p.80).

Coming out is difficult and precarious for both groups.

Second, disabled people are isolated and separated from one another, and from sources of collective support and strength.

> 'One of the most important features of our experience of prejudice is that we generally experience it as isolated individuals. Many of us spend most of our lives in the company of non-disabled people, whether in our families, with friends, in the workplace, at school and so on. Most of the people we have dealings with, including

our most intimate relationships, are not like us. It is therefore very difficult for us
to recognise and challenge the values and judgements that are applied to us and our
lives. Our ideas about disability and about ourselves are generally formed by those
who are not disabled' (Morris, 1991, p.37).

While women and black people can expect support role-models from within
the family and community, disabled people are likely to grow up in families
where there are not other disabled people, and where there is a parental
burden of guilt and shame. This highlights a difference between disability,
and race and gender, disability is more like sexuality, in the sense of familial
isolation, and the need to come out and reject the burden of difference. No
discussion of the obstacles to identifying as disabled would be complete if it
did not raise questions about the different resources, narratives and
possibilities available to different groups of disabled people, whether based
on age, impairment or other social distinctions. At this stage I will turn to
some of these questions.

Having presented a fairly schematic model of disability identity, I want to
focus on tensions and difficulties in the concept. Some of this lies in the
division between the needs of a social movement, which often deals in simple
dichotomies, and produces polemical arguments, and an academic approach,
which has a responsibility to be rigorous, which is more focused on nuance
and contradiction, and which, in the current era especially, often justifies its
existence in terms of deconstruction and elaboration. However, I think the
issues I will highlight all have major political connections, and are not merely
problems of theory or the ivory tower. What is more they are linked, and they
link disability identity into wider social theoretical debates with which
disabled people, and Disability Studies in particular, have to engage.

Jenny Morris, and other disabled feminists have highlighted difficulties in
reconciling the reality of impairment and the lived experience of disability
with the sometimes social reductionist social model. Given the other debates
consecutive with this paper, I will not engage deeply with these issues. But
certainly, the fact that people with impairments associated with ageing are
not fully represented within the disability movement points to an issue of
identity and identification. For example, looking at Jenny Morris's two most
recent books on disability, the interviewees are all under the age of sixty,
while the majority of disabled people are over the age of sixty. Some
impairments – the congenital impairments for example, or those associated

with accident or with early onset – are more likely than others to lead to individual identifying collectively and socially as disabled.

Traditional approaches to disability, highlighted above, could be considered to be essentialist. Differences, biological and sometimes psychological, separate disabled people from non-disabled people. Social approaches counter this essentialism by demonstrating how it is exclusionary policies, environmental barriers and a process of social oppression which create the category of disability. This is a social constructionist analysis. For example, it is suggested that the experience of disability varies at different times and in different cultural contexts. Political strategies focus on barrier removal. But between and within this dichotomy of essentialism and social constructionism there are debates which have been explored by feminists and queer theorists, and still await Disability Studies.

For example, despite the seeming social constructionism, there is an inherent essentialism within disability politics, and indeed in the idea of disability identity. The celebration of disability pride is the celebration of difference, and the acceptance of difference: it is about subverting negative valuation and reclaiming disability. Nietzsche suggests:

> 'A species comes to be, at type becomes fixed, in the long fight against essentially constant adverse conditions' (Nietzsche, 1990, p.199).

This means that what does not kill you, makes you strong. It also means, accepting a category created by others, revelling in abnormality, celebrating the margins. While the social model is social constructionist, the social oppression model can slide into essentialism. While the disability movement seeks inclusion and integration, it also celebrates difference. The margins are a good place to speak from, and there is a cost to coming into the mainstream. But celebrating and identifying in difference can be risky – for example, recuperating the term 'cripple':

> 'The dangerous intimacy between subjectification and subjection needs careful calibration' (Riley, 1988, p.17).

The work of Helen Liggett (1988) shows the risks of reinforcing the categorisation of disabled people as a separate group. I think there is a tension in the essentialism within the disability movement and disability studies, and it is one that parallels difficulties experienced within other identity politics: for example, problems for gay and lesbian and feminist theory and politics. Todd Girlin suggests:

'For all the talk about the social construction of knowledge, identity politics *de facto* seems to slide towards the premise that social groups have essential identities' (Girlin, 1994, p.153].

This may be an example of the opposed priorities of theory and practice. As I have suggested, theoretical sophistication may not be appropriate to the needs of social movements:

'Post-structuralism's attack on essentialism and the "decentering of the subject" came into conflict with thinking and practice rooted in the standpoint of women or the experience of gays' (Calhoun, 1990, p.15).

In practice, social constructionism may not be as politically effective as essentialism, due to a lack of rhetorical power. Some have asked why they should deconstruct their own identities when the oppressors identities are still so strong, and questioned what social constructionism can offer them:

'Social constructionism was an ambiguous ally in the attempt to oppose the devaluing of various identities' (Calhoun, 1990, p.16).

There are also contradictions internal to the political strategies, for example with the clash between the social model and the minority group notions of disability. While they are often conflated, I would argue that there are differences, and looking at the difference between British and international disability politics indicates some of these. There are in fact two, contradictory goals of disability politics: firstly, demolish the processes which disable; second defend disabled people. Carol Vance (1989) suggests that the lesbian and gay movement faces a parallel dilemma. Lesbian and gay historians have attempted to trace a history of lesbian and gay people, while social constructionist theorists have shown that there is no continuity, and that same sex activity has different meanings in different times and places. As historians begin to reconstruct the disability experience, I believe they will face similar difficulties. It is only in the late twentieth century that gayness, or disability, have been celebrated with pride.

Denise Riley has taken a similar approach to the history of the category 'woman', seemingly an essential identity, but in fact just as socially constructed as sexuality. It is a problem for feminist politics which she confronts, not just for historians: from a post-structuralist perspective, she does not have much faith in the coherence of identities:

'The impermanence of collective identities in general is a pressing problem for any emancipatory movement which launches itself on the appeal to solidarity, to the common cause of a new group being, or an ignored group identity' (Riley, 1988, p. 16).

Another example of the way these debates are relevant to disability is the debate about the role of identity after the dissolution of disabling barriers. If there are benefits to disability identity, if it is a source of strength and pride, will it persist in the utopian world where there are not barriers or oppressive processes? Is there a difference beyond oppression? Is there something about having an impairment, as opposed to being disabled, which will persist and will unite disabled people? There may be major differences here between disability, and race/ gender/ sexuality.

Crude dichotomies between social constructionism and essentialism are perhaps not particularly helpful, as Diana Fuss (1989) argues. Social constructionism can itself be quite determinist and fixed. At other times, in the rejection of biological thinking as essentialist, it can become idealist and totally decentred. Judith Butler (1990) has explored the essentialism inherent in social constructionist positions in gender, and the danger of reifying the subject. While feminists have attacked Foucault for seemingly writing out the possibilities of resistance, she develops a complex analysis which nevertheless offers some benefits to those exploring identity politics. For her, the subject is discursively constituted, but agency is possible. She describes identities as self-representations, as "fictions" that are neither fixed not stable. For example, in her view, gender centres on performativity, and she is especially interested in the marginal and transgressive actors who create themselves. Personally, I find Butler's work opaque and difficult, but I am certain it could be useful in developing beyond some of the paradoxes of disability identity (Sawicki, 1994, is a good starting point for these debates).

Let me now consider more closely this issue of difference. One of the dangers of the essentialism highlighted above, is that it provides a simplistic reductionism, an 'us and them' approach. While this is comforting and secure, it offers risks. As an example, I would suggest an article by disability activist Alan Holdsworth, in which he developed a polemic about allies and oppressors, dividing the non-disabled world into professional oppressors, liberal oppressors and allies (Holdsworth, 1993). In my view, this was unhelpful, because it reduced political agency and identity to a unilinear choice. Disabled people, by virtue of having experienced disablement, were good, and non-disabled people could only be counted as good in very specific circumstances. Now, as I have tried to outline above, it is clear that many people with impairment do not identify as disabled. Some have even been viewed as traitors to the disability community, as selling out, as tokens. For example, Bert Massie, director of RADAR, faces much opposition. So clearly not all disabled people are allies.

However, my main problem with the analysis was that it ignored the multiple identities and identity choices which people make in practice. For example, there is a danger of ignoring the fact that disabled people are also men and women, straight and gay, and come from various ethnic groups. Just as white feminists were accused by black women of ignoring the specificities of black women's experience, and even of being racist, so disabled people risk ignoring difference. It may be that black disabled people sometimes have more in common with black people than with disabled people. Sometimes the values of the disability movement – for example, autonomy, independence, choices and rights – may in fact be specifically white, western values. Perhaps an eastern or Islamic approach would want to stress family, and solidarity, and mutuality rather than what sometimes seems a very individualistic model of liberation.

Class is a particularly powerful determinant of the disability experience. It qualifies and changes the consequences of impairment, and reduces the exposure to oppressive social relations. My class and gender are better predictors of my career pattern and income than my impairment. Other people with achondroplasia would experience their disablement very differently, for example, if they had the educational opportunities which were presented to me. Often in identity politics the issue of class is obscured: both the women's movement and the gay movement have faced criticism for being too middle-class dominated, too concerned with middle-class experiences, not sufficiently attuned to the problems of poverty and exclusion. While I am not arguing that this is necessarily true of the disability movement as a whole, it is true of some in the disability movement.

Now, this is not to deny that disability is a very powerful identity, and one that has the potential to transcend other identities. I think very often it is a master/ mistress status. For example, it has the power to de-sex people, so that people are viewed as disabled, not as men or women, straight or gay. Also, I am aware that, for example, the disability movement is more open to lesbian and gay disabled people than the lesbian and gay community is open to disabled people (Shakespeare, forthcoming). But having said that, I still think it is dangerous to overlook multiple identities, and to assume that disability is the sole and significant identity.

For example, it may be necessary to move away from the unitary, essentialist disability identity and think of a variety of disability identities. Just as feminists suggested that being a black woman should not be conceived of additively, but was qualitatively a different and separate thing, so it may be for black disabled people. As Ossie Stuart suggests:

> 'The oppression that black disabled people endure is... unique... it is necessary to construct a distinct and separate black disabled identity' (Stuart, 1992, p. 94).

Thus he rejects the notion of double oppression, and instead talks of simultaneous oppression, something qualitatively different. Mark Priestley's excellent research with blind Asian people in Leeds has reinforced the need for such developments (Priestley, 1995).

Post-structuralist approaches to identity have built on this notion of difference, and the rejection of essentialism. They suggest we need a more complex, more contingent and more subtle understanding of the workings of power. Additionally, and vitally, we must be able to have 'simultaneously an account of radical historical contingency for all knowledge claims and knowing subjects' and 'a no-nonsense commitment to faithful accounts of a "real" world' (Haraway, 1988, p.579). This tightrope act contextualises my own commitment to disabled people's stories. It is for reasons such as these that Disability Studies may find post-structuralist theory useful, although the political demands of the disability movement may not allow space for seemingly irrelevant diversions.

CONCLUSION

Currently, I am engaged in researching the things that disabled people say about their sexual selves. In trying to construct a sexual politics of disability, I am interested in disabled people's ideas of identity – in terms of masculinity or femininity, being straight or gay (Shakespeare, forthcoming). I think that identity politics is both about achieving a better deal for people, but also about establishing the stories people tell about themselves, and having them listened to. A theme of this paper has been the new narratives which disability identity offers people with impairment, and an openness to the varieties, variations and differences which are available. In this sense, the theoretical complexities I have outlined have their correlation in the richness of disabled people's own stories.

Ken Plummer's book draws on literary analysis which suggests there are only five basic narratives to modern stories (Plummer, 1995, p.54). For example: the journey (a progression through stages); enduring suffering; engaging in a contest (a struggle with antagonists); pursuing consummation (achieving a goal of fulfilment); establishing a home (for example, finding a community or identity). I think these five patterns are evidenced in the identity narratives of contemporary disabled people and influence the tales we tell about ourselves. Furthermore, he suggests stories require audiences:

> 'Stories need communities to be heard, but communities themselves are also built through story tellings. Stories gather people around them: they have to attract audiences, and these audiences may then start to build a common perception, a common language, a commonality' (Plummer, 1995, p.174)

This highlights the vital importance of community and movement to disability identity, and the symbiotic relationship between individual and collective. The process of political mobilisation, the process of cultural expression, and the process of academic investigation and theorisation are equally vital to that community. Fundamental is the process of listening, which requires openness and respect.

Disability identity is about stories, having the space to tell them, and an audience which will listen. It is also about recognising differences, and isolating the significant attributes and experiences which constitute disability. Some we might choose to change, others to recuperate or celebrate. We may need to develop a nuanced attitude which incorporates ambivalence: towards our bodies, for example. Theory has a part to play in this process. But (metaphorically, if not physiologically), it all starts with having a voice. As Foucault suggests, our task is to speak the truth about ourselves.

REFERENCES

ABBERLEY, P. (1992) 'Counting us out : a discussion of the OPCS disability surveys', *Disability, Handicap and Society*, 2, 1, pp 5-21.

BUTLER, J. (1990) *Gender Trouble*, London: Routledge.

BYNOE, I., BARNES, C. and OLIVER, M. (1991) *Equal rights for Disabled People*, London: IPPR.

CALHOUN, C. (1990) *Social Theory and the Politics of Identity*, Cambridge, Massachusetts: Blackwell.

CRAWFORD, R. (1994) 'The boundaries of the self and the unhealthy other: reflections on health, culture and AIDS', *Social Science and Medicine*, 38, 10, pp. 1347-1365.

DUCHEN, C. (1987) *French Connections*, London: Hutchinson

FRIERE, P. (1972) *Pedagogy of the Oppressed*, Harmondsworth: Penguin.

FUSS, D. (1989) *Essentially Speaking*, London: Routledge.

GAY LEFT COLLECTIVE (1980) *Homosexuality: power and politics,* London: Allison and Bushy:

GIDDENS, A (1991) *Modernity and Self-Identity*, Cambridge: Polity.

GIRLIN, T. (1994) 'From universality to difference', in Calhoun, C., (ed.), *Social Theory and the Politics of Identity*, Cambridge, Massachusetts: Blackwell.

GOFFMAN, E. (1968) *Stigma*, Harmondsworth: Penguin.

HACKING, I. (1986) 'Making up people' in Helier, T.C. et al, *Reconstructing Individualism*, Stanford: Stanford University Press, pp. 222-236.

HARAWAY, D. (1988) 'Situated knowledges: the science question in feminism and the privilege of partial perspective', *Feminist Studies*, 14, 3, pp. 575-599.

HASLER, F. (1993) 'Developments in the disabled people's movement', in Swain, J. et al., (eds.) *Disabling Barriers, Enabling Environments*, London: Sage.

HINDESS, B. (1973) *The Use of Official Statistics in Sociology*, London & Basingstoke: Macmillan.

HOLDSWORTH, A. (1993) 'Our allies within', *Coalition*, June, pp. 4-10.

HUNT, P. (1966) *Stigma*, London:Geoffrey Chapman.

KITSUSE, J.I. and CICOUREL, A.V. (1963) 'A note on the use of official statistics', *Social Problems*, 11, 2, pp. 131-9.

KRITZMANN, L, (ed.) (1988) *Michel Foucault: Politics, Philosophy, Culture*, NY and London: Routledge.

LEES, S. (ed.) (1992) *Disability Arts and Culture Papers*, London: SHAPE Publications.

LIGGETT, H. (1988) 'Stars are not born: an interpretative approach to the politics of disability', *Disability, Handicap and Society*, 3, 3, pp. 263-276.

McINTOSH, M. (1968) 'The Homosexual Role', *Social Problems*, 16, 2, pp. 182-91.

MELUCCI, A. (1989) *Nomads of the Present*, London: Radius.

MORRIS, J. (1991) *Pride Against Prejudice*, London: Women's Press.

NIETZSCHE, F.W. (1990) *Beyond Good and Evil*, Harmondsworth: Penguin.

PLUMMER, K.(1995) *Telling Sexual Stories*, London: Routledge.

PRIESTLEY, M. (1995) 'Commonality and difference in the movement: an association of blind Asians in Leeds', *Disability and Society*, 10, 2, pp. 157-70.

RILEY, D. (1988) *Am I That Name?*, Basingstoke: Macmillan.

SAWICKI, J. (1994) 'Foucault, feminism, and questions of identity', in Gutting, G. (ed.) *Cambridge Companion to Foucault*, Cambridge: Cambridge University Press.

SCOTT, R.A. (1969) *The Making of Blind Men*, New York: Russell Sage Foundation.

SHAKESPEARE, T.W. (1993) 'Disabled people's self-organisation: a new social movement?', *Disability, Handicap and Society*, 8, 3, pp. 249-264.

SHAKESPEARE, T.W. (1994) 'Cultural representation of disabled people: dustbins for disavowal?', *Disability and Society*, 9, 3, pp. 283-299.

SHAKESPEARE, T.W. (1996) 'Power and prejudice: issues of gender, sexuality and disability', in Barton, L. (ed.) *Disability and Society: Some Emerging Issues*, Harlow: Longman.

SONTAG, S. (1991) *Illness as Metaphor/AIDS and its Metaphors*, London: Pelican.

STONE, D. (1985) *The Disabled State*, Basingstoke: Macmillan.

STUART, O. (1992) 'Race and disability; just a double oppression?', *Disability, Handicap and Society*, 7, 2, pp 177-188.

SUTHERLAND, A.T. (1981) *Disabled We Stand*, London: Souvenir Press.

VANCE. C. (1989) 'Social construction theory; problems in the history of sexuality', in Altman, D. et al., (eds.) *Homosexuality, Which Homosexuality?*, London: Gay Men's Press.

WEEKS, J. (1977) *Coming Out*, London: Quartet Books.

WEEKS, J. (1990) 'The value of difference', in Rutherford, J. (ed.) *Identity: Community, Culture, Difference*, London: Lawrence & Wishart.

CHAPTER 7

Identity Crisis: Mental Health user groups and the 'problem of identity'

Marian Barnes and Polly Shardlow

INTRODUCTION

One of the most fundamental objectives of user groups is to claim the right to self definition for those people whose identity and 'problems' have been defined by professionals. Reclaiming the right to define themselves and their problems is a prerequisite for attaining other objectives. Participation within such movements can demonstrate that those formerly viewed as passive and dependant recipients of welfare can be actors capable not only of controlling their own lives, but also of contributing to shaping the nature of welfare services and of achieving broader social objectives. Participation can itself contribute to a surer sense of identity.

Nevertheless, making one's identity as a user of services visible may not be easy because of the stigma attached to such a status. In the case of people whose shared identity centres around their use of mental health services there are particular problems associated not only with the status of service user, but with the fear of madness. Whilst disabled people and disabled people's movements emphasise the importance of identifying as disabled people, debates around language amongst those involved in the mental health users' movement concern the nature of the relationship with services. The question is not whether the movements should be described as 'mad people's movements' or 'mentally ill or emotionally distressed people's movements', but whether they should describe themselves as 'survivors' or 'users and ex-users' of mental health services. As well as differences within the UK user movement on this issue, the European Users' Network has been debating this question as people active in user movements across Europe have come together to campaign at an international level.

Whatever decision groups make about the description which they feel most accurately reflects their experience, it is the use or survival of services, rather than the experience of mental distress *per se* which usually provides the starting point for involvement in the movement. An exception to this is the 'Hearing Voices' movement which is becoming an increasingly important forum within which people who hear voices can seek to make sense of this experience with others who share it.

This chapter will discuss issues relating to the personal and social identity of people who have experienced mental health problems and will consider how this affects the nature of groups which seek to empower people who identify themselves as users or survivors of mental health services. It will draw on research in which the authors are engaged which has studied groups of users, as well as published accounts of individual and collective responses to mental distress.

The research in which the authors are involved is part of a much wider ESRC funded research programme which is investigating the nature of changes in the governance of public services at a local level [1] The project is looking at the development of user movements amongst disabled people and people with mental health problems and how these groups are seeking to

[1] The research on which this chapter draws was funded by the ESRC as part of its 'Local Governance Programme' - award number L311253025.

influence the purchasers and providers of health and social care services. It considers questions of civil rights, citizenship and consumerism (see Barnes, Harrison and Wistow, 1994, for a discussion of the project). Whilst the question of identity is not the prime focus for the research, the significance of individual and collective group identity has been a recurring theme within it. Similarities and differences between disabled peoples' groups and groups of people with mental health problems are considered elsewhere. In this paper we focus solely on mental health service users' groups.

PROBLEMS OF IDENTITY

We start by considering different factors which may affect the way in which someone who has experienced mental health problems feel about themselves and the way in which other people may respond to them. Unless otherwise indicated, the quotations are from interviews with people undertaken as part of the research referred to above.

1.   Personal and inter-personal factors

The nature of mental distress, which can manifest itself in many different ways, is such that it may itself undermine a person's sense of self and consequently their identity. People may experience extremes of sadness; of helplessness, hopelessness and of anxiety. At times they may feel elated and have huge amounts of energy. At other times getting out of bed or getting out of the house may feel impossible:

> 'My mood would change from day to day - you didn't know what to expect at all'
> (Ritchie et al., 1988, p. 5).

It may include experiences which are hard to make sense of and may make those who experience them afraid or confused, or which make it very difficult for them to get on with their lives:

> 'I was so paranoid. I mean I used to duck and dive in hedges, you know. I used to think the IRA were after me, or if there was a murder on the television. I thought the murderer was following me, and every time the police caught somebody I used to feel relieved for a little while.' (Ritchie et al., 1988, p. 5).

Those sorts of experiences can make relationships with other people difficult. Unpredictable behaviour can cause others to be very cautious around people they know have mental health problems. The fear of others can lead to exclusion and rejection, which in turn can result in a wish to hide distress. Thus people may be unwilling to seek help for their distress or even to acknowledge it.

There is some evidence of a gender difference here. Men may find it particularly hard to admit to themselves or to others that a problem exists. This may be a partial explanation for the gender differences in statistics relating to alcoholism and acknowledged mental health problems (Barnes and Maple, 1992).

Stigma can lead to people attempting to hide the fact they have received treatment for mental illness:

> '... in other areas I hide it I have to confess. I have a lot of friends and people who don't know... it's the stigma of it.... If you ever told people that you'd been in, then the chances are they wouldn't want to have much to do with you. And I mean I have to admit before I was involved I felt along similar lines'.[2]

Revealing a history of mental distress or breakdown can result in discrimination in the job market, in housing and in personal relationships. This in turn can result in difficult financial circumstances which further inhibit people's opportunities to become involved in activities which would enable social contact. Although as Prior (1995) has discussed, such outcomes may not be inevitable if there are social and economic benefits for 'ignoring' stigmatising labels.

The social nature of human beings means that identity is formed through interaction with others:

> 'we build a self-conception of who we are through discovering what we are and are not capable of doing, an achievement based on participation in social life' (Doyal and Gough, 1991, pp. 50-51).

Feminist psychologists have emphasised the importance of recognising the significance of relating to others in terms of individual development. They have argued that, rather than seeing a need for building an identity around relationships with significant others as a sign of immaturity which is suggested by traditional, male models of psychological development, the ability to form such relationships should be seen as a sign of strength. (Kaplan and Surrey, 1986). Thus the social isolation experienced by many of

[2] All quotations, unless attributed, in this paper are taken from our own ESRC funded research project interviews.

those with mental distress can inhibit the development of self and identity and restrict opportunities for growth.

For some people being diagnosed as 'mentally ill' is more acceptable than being labelled as 'mad' because illness is less stigmatising than madness. However, others reject the notion of mental illness as being incompatible with their experience and they may find themselves being regarded as lacking insight as a result. If your own understandings of the nature of your experiences are denied by powerful others this can further undermine confidence in self:

> 'But a lot of people who have mental health problems, they think they're not being believed and that's sad really. Because they know how they feel'.

Unlike physical impairment, mental distress may be a temporary or intermittent experience. The sense that this is an experience from which people hope that they might recover may mean that some people do not want to accept it as an identity which will determine a commitment to devote themselves to the user movement. However, many people who have experienced mental distress describe a fragility in their recovery. One said: 'You never know when you stop being a user'. The effects of the experience stay with you for a long time; there is a fear that the mental distress will return and the experience of being admitted to hospital and all that that involves has a lasting effect on many people's lives. Unlike a spent criminal conviction, a record as a psychiatric patient can affect people's prospects throughout their lives and consequently their social relationships:

> 'Mind you it can always come back, even with a depression and breakdown... they fear they are labelled for life'.

These factors suggest that personal experience of mental distress may not only make it difficult for people to become activists within the movement, but also that the movement must respond to the personal as well as political aspects of the experience of mental distress and of receiving services. Some of the most powerful expressions of what it is like to be on the receiving end of psychiatric services which have inspired the development of user groups both in this country and elsewhere, have been very personal statements of the way in which individual experiences and the responses of others can challenge and undermine a belief in yourself and who you are. Judi Chamberlin (1988) and Kate Millet (1991) have published accounts of such experiences, but they are also to be heard whenever users speak on conference platforms and demand that the voices of those who have experienced emotional distress should be heard and respected.

2.   Structural factors

There are a number of different structural factors which are significant in considering the status of people with mental health problems and which thus have consequences for their personal and social identity. Here we briefly consider the relevance of class; race; gender and age. We also discuss the power of mental health professionals in this context.

There is substantial research evidence of the relationship between mental health problems and social class, although whether being working class is more likely to lead to mental ill-health, or whether mental ill-health results in people 'drifting' down to the working class is still debated (Warner, 1994). Warner argues that, whilst the political economy is clearly a significant factor affecting both the incidence of mental health problems and their outcomes, the relationship is not unidimensional. What is not in dispute is that mental health problems are clearly associated with socio-economic disadvantage which, together with the stress associated with material hardship, results in reduction of opportunities for social interaction and loss of self esteem with consequences for a person's identity:

> '... because once you've been say, branded as having been in one of those places realistically there is very little hope of getting a job no matter how well qualified you are..'

> 'I was now pushed into a situation while I was at (bed and breakfast hotel) where I was in absolute poverty. I didn't even have enough to live on. I had to go back to my parents with my hands out... after I'd supposedly broken away and become independent and learned how to manage for myself. It wasn't very dignifying' (Ritchie et al., 1988, p. 8).

Race is an important determinant of identity as well as affecting a person's social status and the likelihood that they will find themselves identified as mentally ill. There is evidence of difference in the use of mental health services by different ethnic groups, with black people of African or Caribbean origin most likely to find themselves subject to the controlling powers of mental health legislation (Barnes et al., 1990; Bowl and Barnes, 1990). Fernando (1991) has discussed the imperialism of Western psychiatry which has devalued explanations of experience and behaviour based in different notions of the person. He has considered how black people may find their cultural beliefs misunderstood and pathologised.

Few black people were involved in the three groups we studied in our research. Early in the project we made contact with the National Black Mental Health Association and heard of the difficulties the group was having in establishing a presence for black people within the mental health user movement. There are black user groups, but responses from people we spoke to during our project suggest that the user movement is currently primarily a white movement which may be unable to speak to the experiences of black mental health service users.

Gender is another structural variable which has substantial significance in relation to people's experience of the mental health system. Again, not only is it a question of unequal representation as users of mental health services, but the way in which mental distress is identified is affected by gender, as is the response of mental health professionals to those experiencing such distress (Barnes and Maple, 1992; Ussher, 1991). The 'diagnosis' of mental disorder (in particular personality disorder) is affected by a perceived lack of conformity to stereotypes of female behaviour, whilst many constructs of mental distress are clearly gendered in nature: 'hysteria' is an obvious example, whilst the category 'housewives syndrome' has not long been erased from psychiatric textbooks and still lurks within the thinking of some practising psychiatrists. Sexual abuse has been acknowledged to be an experience which is a significant factor in the lives of many women who are admitted to psychiatric hospitals (e.g. Bryer et al., 1987) and provides a potent example of the way in which the oppression women experience in their everyday lives may translate into diagnoses of mental disorder and result in treatment within the mental health system. Not being believed by clinicians when speaking of experiences of sexual abuse can further contribute to the abuse of women's sense of self within what is meant to be a healing environment. Women's identity as users of mental health services may thus be experienced in different ways from men's experiences and this needs to be acknowledged within the user movement.

Mental health problems can be experienced throughout the life span. There are ever-increasing numbers of older people within the population. 15% of people over the age of 65 are affected by depression severe enough to need treatment and 1 in 4 people aged over 85 experience dementia. For older people emotional distress may be associated with experiences of loss - loss of role; loss of physical health or loss of loved partners. These factors may make it more difficult to participate in valued activities and people may lose their motivation to do so. Losing a role as a worker; as a mother; as a lover can undermine older people's sense of themselves. For those who experience dementia the fragmentation of the self may be almost complete (Bernlef, 1988) and for the older partners of those with dementia the loss of a known personality even whilst they are still together physically may be one of the hardest things to bear. For some becoming old in an ageist society can be an experience of losing a sense of value and a sense of self.

The power of mental health professionals to define what is 'mental illness' can be considered another structural feature affecting the identifies of those experiencing mental health problems. In his study of a large asylum in Northern Ireland, Lindsay Prior (1993) has demonstrated the way in which mental disorder can be seen to be constructed by the way in which mental health services are organised by professional groups. There are shifting and permeable boundaries around what is considered to constitute mental disorder which may have more to do with policy imperatives and inter-professional rivalry than with the personal experience of people with mental health problems. At any one time, the 'management' of people experiencing emotional distress requires categorisation to fit the ordering of the service system:

> '..no two users suffer from exactly the same illness and all of those illnesses are categorised into different segments and they say this is what you're suffering from and they put a label on you: "you suffer from affective disorder; you suffer from schizophrenia; you suffer from one of the depressive illness; you're an alcoholic; you're a drug user". Everybody is labelled'.

Because people in distress are scared of losing any sort of help, or because they themselves are confused by or scared of what is happening to them they may go along with the explanation they are given of what is wrong with them. If later they come to question professional authority to define their problems, either individually or collectively, they may find themselves patronised, or worse, treated as unreasonable upstarts (Barnes and Wistow, 1994).

The above demonstrates that whilst the experience and impact of mental illness is very personal, there is considerable evidence concerning the structural factors associated with the identification and experience of mental distress, and that these can contribute to the 'problem' of identity for people experiencing such distress. However, whilst social/ psychological; political/ economic; and environmental explanations of mental distress have been advanced by professionals as well as from within the user movement (e.g. Davey, 1994), there is little evidence that the mental health user movement bases its strategies on a 'social model of mental illness' comparable with the social model of disability. We return to this issue in the conclusion.

3.   Citizenship status

People with mental distress may experience similar 'object' status in relation to professionals as do disabled people, and they also share experiences of poverty and exclusion. However, there are particular exclusions from the status of citizenship which do not apply to other disabled people (although they do in some circumstances to people defined as 'mentally impaired').

Being defined as 'mentally incapacitated' can result in individuals being denied the status and identity of citizens in important respects. The civil rights of those who do not pass the legal test of capacity are constrained. For example, those considered incapable of managing their property or affairs may find that they have to apply to the Court of Protection before they can spend money belonging to them; contracts entered into by those subsequently considered to be mentally incapacitated at the time the contract was entered into may be declared invalid. Whilst such measures are designed to protect people from exploitation, they also clearly represent a significant constraint on basic citizenship rights. Such constraints are even more evident in the ineligibility of mentally incapacitated adults for jury service, and to vote. Decisions about the latter are made by the returning officer (Law Commission, 1995).

People diagnosed with a physical illness cannot be legally forced to enter hospital, nor to receive treatment in the interests of their health, unless it is required in an emergency to save their lives. Those diagnosed as mentally disordered can be both forced to enter hospital and to receive treatment against their will. The potential for compulsory detention; for forced medical treatment; and supervision following discharge from hospital are all experiences which are particular to people considered to be mentally disordered. This has direct effects for those subject to the provisions of the

Mental Health Act, and has a knock on effect for those who fear the possibility of being detained. Thus, not only can mental disorder affect people's personal and social identity, it can also affect people's identity as citizens.

HOW DO MENTAL HEALTH USER GROUPS RESPOND TO THE ISSUE OF IDENTITY?

In this section we consider the ways in which user groups may seek to respond to these different problems associated with the identity of people experiencing mental distress.

The three groups that we have worked with in our research illustrate some of the diversity amongst groups of people experiencing mental distress. We will describe them very briefly.

Group One is a long established organisation which aims 'to promote the interests of users and ex-users of the psychiatric services (town)'. It is an umbrella group for a number of other groups, has a well developed advocacy service and is a broad church in terms of its response to specific issues. It has developed and continues to develop a relationship with both service providers and with users and ex-users, and aims to influence service provision both locally and nationally. It works on democratic lines, although formal membership is not necessary for people to participate within it. The group starts from people's own understandings of their mental health problems and does not adopt a 'party line'. For example, if individuals want help to ensure that they receive a particular form of medication advocates will take that on. Personal experiences of distress and of service use provide the focus for wider action through collective advocacy in relation to services. The group has substantial contact with and involvement in local service planning forums. Personal support and empowerment of members through action within the group is a significant part of their purpose, although the group was not seen by activists primarily as a support group. The rights of the individual to exercise choice over their use of mental health services are considered important and the group will provide advocates to support people in appealing against compulsory hospital admission. Different projects have developed under the umbrella of this group including one which focuses on the empowerment of people within society as a whole, rather than as users of mental health services.

Group Two is a small campaigning group of users and ex-users who work within the local MIND organisation. There is no membership as such, but the campaign group attempts to keep in contact with users of services through providing an information and advice line and through seeking views and involving people in specific campaigns in which they become engaged. An advocacy project based in a local hospital has been developed under this group's umbrella. Choice and individual rights are seen to be important, but the group does not provide collective support and empowerment through membership of the group itself. The group has had involvement in service planning, but at the time of our last contact some concern was being expressed about the effectiveness of relationships with health and social services.

Group Three is first and foremost a service run democratically by users, for users. The group campaigns only on an informal and individual level. It provides a drop-in facility aimed primarily at younger people with mental health problems. It offers an alternative place to go for those who have found statutory services unsympathetic. Within this largely unstructured environment different activities are organised depending on the skills and interests of the users at the time. If people want simply to come to have a coffee and be quiet they can do so, but if people want support and help in dealing with things like housing or benefit problems other users will help out with this. If people want to take on a particular role in managing the centre or organising activities they are encouraged to do so. One part of the building is designated as a women's space and women users organise their own activities as well as taking part in running the overall centre. The group accepts people at whatever stage they are at - people can come to the centre without becoming active within it, although there are rules about behaviour within the centre and there have been instances in which people have been asked to leave. There is a reluctance to become involved with statutory service providers or planners.

The three are very different examples of mental health user groups and provide different examples of the way in which the mental health user movement may help in addressing the problems of identity amongst people experiencing mental distress.

1.   Personal and inter-personal

Why do people become involved and what do they get out of being part of individual groups and, in some cases, the wider user movement?

By involving themselves in these groups a user or ex-user has to 'come out' as someone who has experienced mental distress. Through their involvement, individuals have to be prepared to identify themselves in this way, even if only within the group itself. People also have to find value in being with other users of mental health services.

In this study we have been focusing on those who have become activists within the groups. For this group of activists the often negative experiences of mental distress and of service use have become a source of expertise and understanding which can confer credibility when representing that experience to service providers and planners, and which can enable them to provide support to users who may still be finding it difficult to speak up on their own behalf:

> 'I think you've got an understanding, you know, if you have been through it yourself, you can help other people because you can understand what they feel like. If they're nervous you know why they're nervous and you give them time, you don't pass any judgements, make any comment on it'.

Whilst not all those we spoke to were happy to identify themselves as service users in all situations, in circumstances where they felt it was appropriate to help people identify with someone who has been through the same situation they will make public statements identifying themselves in this way.

In different ways the groups provide 'safe environments' in which sometimes fragile identities can be supported, and confidence and skills can be developed and applied outside the group when the individual feels safe to do so. We heard many testimonies of the way in which involvement in the group had built personal confidence and which had enabled people to turn damaging experiences into a positive outcome:

> 'In some ways it turned out to be a positive step for me. It changed my life around from something that was killing me, virtually, to something that I finally got some kind of reward in'.

> '..it's given me a life and without it I wouldn't have dreamed of doing half the things I do now. It's given me confidence, assurance... I get up now and speak at a conference quite happily. A few years ago I would have no more done that than fly! So really we are here for ourselves as well as other people'.

For them, accepting an identity as a user or ex-user of mental health services and working with others who shared similar experiences had enabled them not only to provide valued support for others, but to find a valued sense of themselves:

> 'It makes you feel good... I mean everybody is accepted'.

Rather than being 'ghettoised' in the user movement, the movement had enabled them to discover their own strengths. They also recognised the same process taking place for others:

> '... there's quite a few that have come here and when they came they wouldn't say boo to a goose. They've been here a bit, you can't shut them up - which is what we want to hear'!

Participation within a group quite literally gives people a 'voice' and as confidence develops people are often able to play a role in organising the group, in planning forums involving service purchasers and providers, and in representing the group at conferences and seminars. Acquiring new skills can provide a further boost to confidence and self-esteem and can also be a springboard to potential opportunities outside the movement:

> 'I believe in 3,4,5 years time maybe.... that will give me a chance then as an individual to join the mental health service as a professional, and I'll be able to take my experience forward with me'.

The groups accept the difference and sometimes difficult identities amongst those who become involved. For example, Group 3 was described as a 'family' which allowed people 'to be', rather than forcing them 'to do'.

Others emphasised the 'normality' of mental distress and the people who experience it and they saw a wider acceptance of this view as a role for the group:

> '... a vicar's wife once said "what if I invite these people into my home? How would they be?" And I said "well they'll be like you, they'll have two eyes, a nose and a mouth and two ears". You know, they think they're going to see something weird and they don't know that perhaps they'll have a nervous breakdown and start with a mental illness'.

Nevertheless, whilst they are accepting of unusual behaviour which they recognise as a result of mental health difficulties, groups have rules about behaviour, for example in terms of the use of racist and sexist language, to ensure that positive rather than destructive inter-personal relationships can be encouraged.

User groups recognise that it may take some time for members to become active, and that some will never want to take on active roles. There is also a recognition that advocacy is based on acceptance of people's own understandings of their needs and that this may make it difficult for the group as a whole to adopt a particular stance on issues such as the use of particular forms of medication. This does not mean that they cannot advocate at a collective level for users to receive information which will enable them to make informed choices over what form of treatment they should receive.

2. Structural

Addressing the structural inequalities which affect the identities of people with mental health problems is more problematic. User movements are more about agency than structure and there is little evidence of groups allying themselves with class based movements. The poverty experienced by many people with mental health problems can be addressed in part by individual advocacy in relation to welfare benefits entitlements, but none of the three groups we looked at were involved in broad ranging campaigns in this area. They may perhaps be better understood as examples of 'new social movements' whose objectives are cultural and ideological rather than structural and material (Melucci, 1985). This was most evident in the work that had developed under the umbrella of Group 1 which was making links between environmental concerns and mental health issues and which sought to relate activity to improve the quality of life of people with mental health problems to broader issues of community and economic development.

One of the three groups we have been studying had tried unsuccessfully to engage with black groups but none had adopted an explicit race perspective within their work. On the other hand two had addressed the gender dimension within mental health: one by providing a separate women's space within the centre and one by very active participation in MIND's 'Stress on Women' campaign. Within this group challenging people's perceptions of themselves and placing their difficulties within a wider context of societal expectations and economic circumstances was encouraged:

> 'You see women, they're walking in here everyday of the week, you know, they're struggling with 3 kids at home, single parents and so on, and they think they've failed, you know, I mean, what man in a similar situation would succeed....'.

None of the groups had focused on the concerns of older people who had experienced mental health difficulties and indeed Group 3 was specifically aimed at younger people.

But it is also relevant to consider the role user movements play in addressing structural issues from a rather different perspective. Not only does the movement provide an opportunity for the collective empowerment of users through working together to address issues which are common to their experiences, participation in two of our groups illustrates very convincingly that people who have experienced mental distress are capable of participating in decision making structures with service providers:

> 'One of the major roles that we can play is actually to say, we are users, we can participate at this level, we can articulate, we can challenge, we can negotiate, we can write papers, we can do this, instead of [being] some bumbling idiot that doesn't know what they are doing'.

Whilst none would claim that this has resulted in a fundamental shift in the balance of power within the mental health system, it has provided a challenge to the prevailing system and has forced those in existing positions of power to look at things in a different way. It has, in some circumstances, changed the nature of the relationship between providers and recipients of health and social care services, and has enabled users of those services to play a part in their definition and construction.

On a wider level, the groups that we have studied demonstrate that people who have used mental health services can be active agents, not only in controlling their own lives, but also in providing services to each other, and as participants within decision making networks, and this provides a challenge to public perceptions of people with mental health problems as incapable of rational thought or action. By running awareness raising campaigns which point to the commonality of mental distress and its links with the day to day experiences of large numbers of people, the casting of people experiencing mental distress as 'other' becomes more difficult.

3.   Citizenship

We were surprised that civil rights issues did not feature highly on the agendas of these three groups. Involvement in campaigning for anti-discrimination legislation was not a high profile activity as it was in the case of disabled people's groups we studied. Nor was there much evidence of engagement in relation to the specific limitations on citizenship deriving from 'mental incapacity'. Individuals were given support in making complaints and in appealing against detention under the Mental Health Act, but there was no evidence of active campaigning against the use of restrictive powers at a local level. Such issues are being taken up at a national and international level and it was suggested by some of those we spoke to that there was little point in attempting local action in response to issues which derive from legislation or national policy. Only a minority of users of mental health services are directly subject to the Mental Health Act or to restrictions arising from mental incapacity and thus it is likely that such issues are not such a high priority as concerns relating to services being received on a day to day basis. It may also be that the personal experiences of distress are so much more immediate than concern with more abstract notions of citizenship.

Nevertheless, a more general concern with individuals' rights to receive the services they need, and with issues of social justice in relation to people's lives as a whole were important aspects of the work in which the groups were engaged:

> 'We are all unanimous that we want to have people with mental health problems to have much more say in their life in general, where they live, what medication - it's just the right to do as other people that are sound in mind, limb and body want, we want the same for people, you know, all of us'.

In some instances the motivation to become involved in user groups came from personal experiences of injustice or from having witnessed bad treatment of others within psychiatric hospitals. Advocacy was the method most often used to seek to achieve individual rights to services, whilst awareness raising amongst the general public were seen to be important ways of overcoming stigma and discrimination.

CONCLUSION

The anti-psychiatry movement of the 1960's suggested that mental illness was whatever those with authority to pronounce on 'normal' or 'deviant' behaviour might choose to make of it. Whilst the ideas of Szasz, Laing and others associated with anti-psychiatry provided an important challenge to the medical model of mental illness and opened up the possibility of other ways of understanding behaviour defined as symptomatic of illness, those ideas have not been developed into an alternative model (equivalent to the social model of disability) which can provide the basis for both understanding the origin and nature of distress and providing enabling and empowering assistance to those experiencing such distress. The anti-psychiatry movement was never a direct expression of the experience of those with mental health problems, but was an analysis provided by intellectuals and professionals who would have been uncomfortable with the notion that their authority to define the origin and nature of problems might be challenged by those who were the subjects of their analysis. The only user group to share a similar stance to that of the anti-psychiatrists has been CAPO - the Campaign Against Psychiatric Oppression, whose membership has always been tiny (Rogers and Pilgrim, 1991).

There has been some attention from sociologists to the experience of mental health service users. For example, Rogers et al (1993) undertook a large scale survey of users' experiences; Prior (1995) has drawn on the work of Goffman to reassess the impact of institutionalisation on the identity of psychiatric patients; whilst Joan Busfield (1982) and Agnes Miles (1988) have brought a sociological perspective to bear on the issue of women's experience of distress and of the mental health system. But there has been little attempt to develop a 'sociology of mental health' to equate with Mike Oliver's 'sociology of disablement' (Oliver, 1990) and which draws on both the experiential knowledge of mental health service users as well as theoretical insights from within sociology.

A potentially useful sociological perspective which we are starting to apply in the context of the research on which this article is based is that of new social movement (NSM) theory (see e.g. Dalton and Kuechler, 1990; Scott, 1990; Touraine, 1985). Disability theorists (e.g. Oliver, 1990, Shakespeare, 1993) have applied NSM theory to disabled people's movements, but with the exception of Rogers and Pilgrim (1991) there has been little use of this body of work in relation to the mental health user movement.

Our research suggests that the factors which provide the strongest motivation to participate in mental health user groups are the shared experiences of distress and of being a recipient of mental health services - of being a 'patient'. For many the values attached to participation are as much about the personal support and growth which can come from participation as about political or service developmental outcomes which can be achieved from collective action. In starting to apply NSM theories to the study of mental health user groups we have found it necessary to distinguish between movements based on commitment to a cause, for example environmentalism, and those based on a shared identity, such as that of a user of mental health services. Identity based groups are concerned with personal experiences and responses to stigma, exclusion and disadvantage; with valuing devalued identities and experiences; and with building those personal experiences into a basis for collective action.

Thus it is important to understand and to theorise personal responses to mental distress in order to make the link between such experiences and collective action. The work of feminist psychologists, sociologists and political scientists can assist in this, but it may also be valuable, as Prior (1995) does, to draw on other theories of identity construction.

Since our research was not designed directly to address the relationship between personal identity and collective action, we can only speculate on this at this stage. Clearly, identity is important to those active in mental health user groups in all the dimensions discussed in this paper. Participation has provided a route through which the identity of passive recipient of services can be transformed into that of an active contributor to service development. Working with others with similar experiences has enabled activists to challenge the assumption of incompetence which often follows a diagnosis of mental illness, and to challenge the exclusions which can result from this. By no means all those involved in user groups reject the notion of 'mental illness' or are totally opposed to the provision of medical treatment. The objectives of those who do consider mental illness to be a reality are to ensure truly 'informed consent' to such treatment and to enable access to the information which will enable them to make choices about alternative types of treatment and to decide when and if to continue with what they are receiving. They also argue that being 'mentally ill' does not mean that people are abnormal or even different - mental illness is something which anyone could experience at some stage of their lives and should be regarded as one aspect of the normal experience of being human. Thus the social, economic and civil rights of those experiencing mental distress should not be affected. However, they have not developed a strategic approach to addressing the structural and legal factors which do, in practice, mean that the position of people with mental health problems as citizens is affected.

Others do suggest that the concept of 'illness' is wrongly or too widely applied. This leads to actions intended to secure alternative opportunities for rebuilding self confidence and self esteem, and for developing positive identities as citizens participating in the lives of their communities in ways that make sense to them. In some instances that also leads to an analysis of the social, economic and environmental conditions necessary to support mental health for all.

At this stage in their history user groups still have to develop ways of ensuring that differences associated with gender, age, race and sexuality can be positively embraced within the movement. No-one we spoke to claimed that their experience of mental distress defined their total identity, nor would want it to, however much they valued the affirmation of themselves provided by working with others who had similar experiences.

The area in which the user movement has been most successful is in supporting the participation of people with mental health problems as active agents, capable not only of determining their own personal histories, but also in determining future directions for mental health services and in achieving broader cultural goals. In order to achieve this, user groups will need to continue to recognise the importance of responding to people's personal experiences of distress and of service use, alongside the development of collective strategies for achieving change.

REFERENCES

BARNES, M. and MAPLE, N. (1992) *Women and Mental Health: Challenging the Stereotypes,* Birmingham: Venture Press.

BARNES, M. and WISTOW, G. (1994) 'Learning to Hear Voices: listening to users of mental health services', *Journal of Mental Health*, 3, pp. 525-540.

BARNES, M., BOWL, R. and FISHER, M. (1990) *Sectioned: Social Services and the 1983 Mental Health Act,* London: Routledge.

BARNES, M., HARRISON, S. and WISTOW, G. (1994) *Consumerism and Citizenship amongst Users of Health and Social Care Services,* Working Paper, Department of Sociological Studies, University of Sheffield, & Nuffield Institute of Health, University of Leeds.

BERNLEF, J. (1988) *Out of Mind*, London: Faber and Faber.

BOWL, R. and BARNES, M. (1990) 'Race, Racism and Mental Health Social Work: implications for local authority policy and training', *Research, Policy and Planning*, 8, 2, pp 12-18.

BRYER, J. B., NELSON, B. A., MILLER, J. B. and KROL, P. A. (1987) 'Childhood sexual and physical abuse as factors in adult psychiatric illness', *American Journal of Psychiatry*, 144, 11, pp. 1426-1431.

BUSFIELD, J. (1982) *Managing Madness: Changing Ideas and Practices*, London: Hutchinson.

CHAMBERLIN, J. (1988) *On Our Own. Patient controlled alternatives to the mental health system*, London: MIND.

DALTON, R. J. and KUECHLER, M. (eds.) (1990) *Challenging the Political Order. New Social and Political Movements in Western Democracies*, Cambridge: Polity Press.

DAVEY, B. (1994) *Empowerment Through Holistic Development: A Framework for Egalitarianism in the Ecological Age*, Nottingham: Nottingham Advisory Group/ Ecoworks.

DOYAL, L. and GOUGH, I. (1991) *A Theory of Human Need*, Basingstoke: Macmillan.

FERNANDO, S. (1991) *Mental Health, Race and Culture*, Basingstoke: Macmillan.

KAPLAN, A. G. and SURREY, J. L. (1986) 'The relational self in women: developmental theory and public policy', in Walker, L. E. (ed.) *Women and Mental Health Policy*, Beverley Hills and London: Sage Publications.

LAW COMMISSION (1995) *Mental Incapacity*, Law Com no. 231, London: HMSO.

MELUCCI, A. (1985) 'The symbolic challenge of contemporary movements', *Social Research*, 52, 4, pp. 789-816.

MILES, A. (1988) *Women and Mental Illness*, Brighton: Harvester Wheatsheaf.

MILLETT, K. (1991) *The Looney Bin Trip*, London: Virago.

OLIVER, M. (1990) *The Politics of Disablement*, Basingstoke: Macmillan.

PRIOR, L. (1993) *The Social Organisation of Mental Illness*, London: Sage.

PRIOR, P. M. (1995) 'Surviving psychiatric institutionalisation: a case study', *Sociology of Health and Illness*, 17, 5, pp. 651-667.

RITCHIE, J., MORRISSEY, C. and WARD, K. (1988) *Keeping in Touch with the Talking: The Community Care Needs of People with Mental Illness*, Birmingham Community Care Special Action Project/Social and Community Planning Research.

ROGERS, A. and PILGRIM, D. (1991) ' "Pulling down churches": accounting for the British mental Health Users Movement', *Sociology of Health and Illness*, 13, 2, pp. 129-148.

ROGERS, A., PILGRIM, D. and LACEY, R. (1993) *Experiencing Psychiatry, Users' Views of Services*, Basingstoke: Macmillan.

SCOTT, A. (1990) *Ideology and the new social movements*, London: Unwin Hyman.

SHAKESPEARE, T. (1993) 'Disabled people's self organisation: a new social movement?', *Disability, Handicap and Society*, 8, 3, pp. 249-264.

TOURAINE, A. (1985) 'An introduction to the study of social movements', *Social Research*, 52, 4, pp. 749-787.

USSHER, J. (1991) *Women's Madness: Misogyny or Mental Illness*, London: Harvester Wheatsheaf.

WARNER, A. (1994) *Recovery from Schizophrenia.   Psychiatry and Political Economy*, London: Routledge.

CHAPTER 8

Sick-but-Fit or Fit-but-Sick? Ambiguity and identity at the workplace

Ruth Pinder

A PROLEGOMENON

> 'I think arthritis is, in some ways, unique, in that it's a crossover between disability and illness, whereas other disabilities aren't like that. I think that people with arthritis tend to have more time off through illness than other disabled people because of this crossover, and perhaps that puts them in a more difficult situation than other disabled people. It is difficult ... (She hesitated, and then resolved the ambiguity) ... No, disability and illness are separate things'.

This is how one informant, Lucy[1], wrestled with the problem of how to equate her understandings about disability with the refractory demands of her body which fitted less neatly with established ways of perceiving the world. My questions are, firstly, what implications do Lucy's comments have for

[1] I have used pseudonyms for interviewees throughout the text.

disabled people trying to integrate into a tight labour force, and for the policies which might better facilitate this? And secondly, what does this 'crossover' tell us about the way disability is currently represented by, and the future goals of, the Disability Movement?

A basic human urge is to impose order upon the world, to search for clear-cut lines and concepts. As Murphy (1987) notes:

> '.. it is an empirical fact that the mind seeks to impose systems of some kind of order upon all it surveys. It is a property of all peoples and all cultures ... We look for order because it makes predictability possible, and we see predictability to avoid danger in an essentially perilous world' (p. 29).

The quest for clarity and simplicity find expression in our social institutions, reflected, for example, in employment policies that require employees to be either sick or fit, and is mirrored in the rules governing receipt of invalidity benefit: therapeutic earnings apart, claimants cannot be partly well.

Experience at the margins which fails to tally with our known ways of classifying the world, is especially problematic. As Douglas (1966) argues:

> 'Danger lies in transitional states, simply because transition is neither one state nor the next, it is undefinable. The person who must pass from one to another is himself in danger and emanates danger to others'(p.97).

THE SOCIAL MODEL OF DISABILITY: TAKING A BROADER VIEW

One such evolving cultural system, the social model of disability, is viewed as the definitive way of representing the lived reality of disabled people as they struggle for social as well as political rights. It has become the means of explaining why disabled people fare so disproportionately poorly in the labour market, as in other areas of social life, such as education and housing (Oliver, 1990; Morris, 1991; Higgins, 1992; Swain et al., 1993). Firstly, disability is a problem of society, difficulties resulting from a disabling environment rather than from the defects or deficiencies of disabled people as individuals; and the term 'disablism' has been coined to give voice to the marginalisation, if not exclusion, of disabled people from mainstream society. Secondly, as society has 'manufactured' the problems in the first place, disability theorists argue, the onus is on society to change: impairment is, at most, a minor issue.

With a husband disabled by Multiple Sclerosis, I have considerable sympathy with these views: at one level I know what they mean. Collectively they represent an attempt to move away from representations of disability as defective body parts and disabled people as tragedies, focusing instead on the oppressive practices which disabled people feel stifle their chances to participate in society. The Leeds Conference[2] showed the profound unease which exists within the Disability Movement to the idea of re-introducing impairment into the debate, and its implications for returning to a 'medical model' of disability against which it has campaigned so vigorously over the past three decades (Oliver, 1996). It would create an anomaly, and anomalies, as Douglas (1970) and Bauman (1991) argue, are often defined as dangerous and polluting.

However, to rely primarily on the 'barriers and facilitators' approach which is promoted provides only a limited understanding. As Bury (1996, chapter 2 of this volume) notes, 'Without a working definition of disability linked to impairment, the strong form of relativism in the "social oppression" approach threatens to overwhelm any form of enquiry'. The reification of 'disabling environments' is as partial as the previous exclusive concentration on bodies-to-be-rehabilitated neglected the social structure. Whilst focusing on those common external structures which deny access to disabled people has proved to be a powerful unifying political force, such a focus represents only part of a much more complex, multi-layered picture.

Although a few disability writers such as French (1993) and Crow (1996) have given impairment an airing, neither adequately grapples with the relational aspects of disability and impairment in the context of wider economic and socio-cultural contexts. It is not simply a question of 'a bit more impairment'. The body is embedded in a wider nexus of structures which render a view of disability as social oppression alone over-simplistic. We need to address the age-old problem of the relationship between agency and structure, or, as Freund (1988) puts it:

> '... the interpenetration of the biological and the social in order to avoid the rarefied idealist bias that pervades it... In actual, concrete existence ... (mind, body and society) ... are in process and are "mutually determining" and "interpenetrate" each other' (p. 860).

[2] 'Accounting for Illness and Disability: Exploring the Divide', organised by the Disability Research Unit, School of Sociology and Social Policy, University of Leeds, 19-21 April, 1995.

The very elusiveness of this interaction renders the focus on 'oppressive environments', characteristic of much contemporary writing on disability so compelling – and at the same time so incomplete.

GOING SICK AT WORK

The tensions inherent in over-emphasising the social model of disability are highlighted when we consider the situation of people with long-term deteriorating conditions, such as rheumatoid arthritis, as they attempt to 'make it' at work. Arthritis often involves periods of unwellness as well as disability, and sickness at work is often a focal point of unease for disabled people. However, as Douglas (1966) notes, 'anomalies are good to think with'. The sick record cannot be discounted in the way those with a stable condition are able to claim highly dependable work attendance records.

The problem of determining whether disabled people are sick enough to warrant exemption from work or not, or too sick to merit continued employment, is fraught with uncertainty and contradictions. A balance has to be carefully gauged. Yet it is not just an individual decision. As Bellaby (1989) makes clear, '... what constitutes acceptable absence' from work or not 'is secured only by the evolution of conventions' (p.424), which are themselves framed by fellow employees, employers, medical practitioners, and close relatives in the context of particular economic and historical circumstances. Taking time off, he concludes:

> '...is a structured social process which is reducible neither to morbidity nor to individual reasoning in isolation from other people and from conventions of conduct' (p.437).

Moreover, the way in which time taken off sick in the past is construed as an indicator of future performance is also embedded in a set of meanings as to what sickness 'is', and what disability at the workplace may entail in terms of productivity and reliability of performance in the workplace.

Going sick thus involves a particular set of economic and socio-cultural relationships which illustrate the difficulties involved in despatching impairment and disability into neat, watertight compartments. A useful framework for exploring the dialectic between them may be found in Scheper-Hughes and Lock's (1987) interplay between the 'three bodies': first, the individual body, or the body as self; second, the social body, or the body as a natural symbol, whereby a healthy body represents organic wholeness and the body in sickness offers a model of disharmony and conflict; and third – and the most dynamic of the three – the <u>political body</u> which refers both to the control of bodies in times of crisis, and the reproduction and socialisation of the kinds of bodies society needs.

Using such a typology, this chapter explores some of the ambiguities of going sick at work for people disabled with arthritis, illustrating the way personal, social and cultural identity is both reflected in, and itself shapes, disabled peoples' working lives. Firstly, it argues that a proper understanding of disability at work means bringing impairment back into the equation. Secondly, the chapter demonstrates that we cannot understand the experience of disability at work, particularly for those with long-term deteriorating conditions, without taking the mutually constitutive nature of bodies, selves and society into account. Thirdly, if the Disability Movement is to be fully universal in the way envisaged by Zola (1989), this chapter argues that the social model of disability needs to be painted with a broader brush. Feminists have become increasingly aware of the dangers of presupposing some underlying sameness to women. As Moore (1988) notes:

> '...it has often seemed as if the existence of a shared feminine identity, the commonality of gender, has somehow transcended the existence of other forms of difference' (p. 189).

Similarly, the experiences and needs of disabled people have all too often been assumed to be universal. As this chapter shows, the meanings of disability are multi-vocal. If unacknowledged, that powerful single voice which has been the stuff of successful political activism may be in danger of re-producing the very inflexibility of a wider ablist society the Disability Movement so rightly perceives as unfeeling and unresponsive to its needs.

These aims will be accomplished through the narrative accounts of two informants disabled by arthritis, Phillip and Lucy, who formed part of a wider qualitative study on employment commissioned by the charity Arthritis Care[3]. After the onset of rheumatoid arthritis at the age of thirty-four, Phillip lost his dearly won place in the police force, and found himself trapped in his attempts to pursue a satisfying career elsewhere: he was fit-

[3] The study was part funded by Arthritis Care 1993-1994. My thanks go to Ronnie Frankenberg and Sally French for their comments on an earlier draft of this paper, but the author alone is responsible for its remaining inadequacies.

but-sick. Over her short working career, Lucy's psoriatic arthritis had necessitated periodic times off sick, resulting in many difficulties with her various employers. However, in her new post as co-ordinator in a local disability organisation, she was now challenging her line manager to take a less hostile stance: she was sick-but-fit.

Philip's dismissal

Phillip had set his heart on being a policeman ever since he could remember. Securing a place as a probationer had taken some perseverance on his part, as his first application had failed the Final Board. A second attempt had been rejected owing to a freeze on recruitment. With his third successful application, the probationary period had initially taxed him to the limits because of what he described as 'difficulties with the bookwork'. That hurdle surmounted, the onset of rheumatoid arthritis towards the end of his probation was a severe blow. Events telescoped in his mind:

> 'I've always wanted to do it. And I got there, and I made it. And then I got arthritis. That all went out of the window, and that really hurt'.

The story gradually unfolded:

> 'I got called into the office and I was told I was finished because I had this arthritis. And because of the nature of the disease, there's no cure so you're never going to get over it, you're never going to be fit enough to remain as a policeman... It was all cut and dried before I knew anything about it. Basically the Medical Officer said that I wasn't fit and so that was it'.

The finality of the decision had profoundly affected his sense of self. Even his considerable personal skills – he talked with fluency and good humour at the interview and at the Arthritis Care group meeting where I first met him – had been to no avail: there was evidently little room for manoeuvre. Particularly galling was his consultant's letter, giving a fairly encouraging picture of his prognosis, – 'they had caught it early' – to the Police Federation Medical Officer, which had subsequently been overturned. He expostulated: 'This was a consultant. The Force's Medical Officer is only a GP, but he disregarded this report. He worked on the "if you've got arthritis, you're not capable. Out" '. Phillip found that medicine was, at best, an uneasy ally in his struggles to sustain a role within the Force.

Reflecting on the anomaly Phillip felt that, on the one hand, he understood their predicament:

> 'I can understand their view because arthritis is obviously something you can't guarantee the future. You've immediately got a disadvantage, if you like. Anyone could walk under a bus. But if you've got arthritis, you're already half way there, aren't you! So why take the risk? You can get rid of him for nothing, rather than risking ... You never know, in five years' time I might be incapable of doing the job anyway. You can't tell, that's the trouble with this arthritis, isn't it, because there's no routine, no set pattern'.

The very ambiguities of the illness and its likely future course which, in one context gave rise to some optimism, in another setting worked against him. He was trapped both in the inconsistencies of his own body and in the contradictory response to it from others: rheumatoid arthritis was evidently in a different league from spinal cord injury where tolerably reliable predictions could be made: the future was highly uncertain.

On the other hand, Phillip was irked by the fact that his dismissal came at a time when, after a short period of sick leave, he was once more holding his own on daily patrols. He wrestled with the anomaly of being simultaneously fit as he saw it, but sick in the eyes of others, a contradiction to which he continually returned in the interview:

> 'It was a shock, because what really got me is that they pulled me off the streets to tell me I wasn't capable of doing it! And I knew I was capable of doing it, because I'd been doing it for the last three months. I mean I can do ninety-eight per cent of what I could do before I had it. And that two per cent is really so small that it might restrict me a little bit, but not to the extent that I would call myself disabled. You see even that two per cent which prevented me from staying in the police force wasn't something I couldn't do, because I was doing it. It was something that might happen. I think that's the percentage that kicked me out'.

> RP: 'So they were making decisions about possibilities, not probabilities?'

> 'Oh yes, possibilities. It was all what might happen. Nobody knows to this day what will happen with arthritis, because it's such a varying thing. Everyone's different. Oh yes, definitely a case of better safe than sorry. I said this to the recruiting officer and he said "well, you could be right". And that's all he could say, but obviously he wasn't going to commit himself one way or the other. But I got the impression that I'd hit it smack on the nail. That's what's so annoying'.

That crucial 'two per cent' – it was such a small anomaly – and the inconclusive nature of his future prognosis cost him dearly: he was fit-but-sick.

Efforts to negotiate an extension of his probationary period for twelve months 'just to see if I could manage', or to find a desk job in the police force, proved fruitless. Moreover, the failure of the Force to compromise on the ambiguities of employing a probationer ninety-eight but not one hundred per cent fit had important consequences. Future career prospects in an area already hit hard by the recession were bleak. Discharged with a 'record', how was he to explain his departure from the police force to prospective employers? And how should he account for his impairment now? Phillip felt cornered:

> 'What do you put? If I put I got fed up with them (the police) then it doesn't look good, does it. If I put I was sacked that looks even worse, so the only thing I can put is I was discharged medically and "will explain in detail on interview". On application forms it always says "do you suffer from any physical disability?" and I've always put "no". As far as I'm concerned, I can do everything I could before, although I might be in a bit of pain now and again, but I can do it'.

The awkwardness of knowing how to classify himself in a way that would not jeopardise his career prospects dogged his efforts to obtain another post. The complexities of his bodily experience were at variance with the black and white requirements of administrative reasoning. Neither could he circumvent standard selection procedures in order to demonstrate his competence on a face-to-face basis:

> 'If you got to the interview, you could p'raps talk your way through it and explain the situation. You'd stand a chance. But you've got to get shortlisted, and that's the bit. I had one month sick when I initially had it. I've worked for years without time off. When I was a driving instructor, six or seven years, I probably had two half days. Since I've had arthritis, apart from that initial month, I haven't had any time off at all. I put "no time off sick since then" on the form. As far as future employers are concerned, you're going to be a pain in the neck. You're always going to be off ill, so they don't bother shortlisting you. That might be how people feel'.

The possibility of being seriously disabled in the future was only one of the problems Phillip had to contend with. His sickness record was affected by a host of other considerations, not least his lack of paper qualifications:

> 'You see there's nothing on paper, and at the end of the day, the majority of interviews are done on paper, aren't they. I mean you get shortlisted and it's what you're taking with you on paper. I've got seven CSEs, and that's it. I mean I'm capable of doing a lot more than what I do, but it's getting there in the first place. You see the problem is not knowing whether it's the arthritis or not that's causing it.

His previous career in the Army where he had been a small arms instructor and, eventually, a tank commander had ill equipped him for Civvy Street. Able to turn his hand to 'all manner of tasks', his application lacked the solid weight of educational qualifications. He was already disadvantaged in the labour market prior to the onset of disability. The frustration lay in not knowing what to attribute to his impairment and what to his lack of formal qualifications.

Matters did not end there. With a young family of three to support, how was he to retrain when:

> 'You've got to be unemployed for twelve months before joining. So what am I to do? Not work for twelve months so I can get on the course, and hope I'll get a decent job at the end of it? It's a joke. Just impossible'.

He was forced to turn down an offer to join the Ambulance Service, which would have been a satisfying alternative for him:

> 'Because there's the money side of things. I mean the Ambulance Service pays about £8,000 a year and I've been on £15,000 and you've got to live as well, and these three kids cost a fortune'.

Thus the problems arising from Phillip's current, or future, impairment were embedded in a web of other social and economic structures making a concentration on 'oppressive environments' alone as an explanation for his predicament oversimplistic. He was disadvantaged in a host of other ways relating to his comparative lack of educational qualifications, and his role as the major breadwinner in a young family. He was also a young man of his time: the high unemployment rate locally, where he was competing with an unknown army of able-bodied applicants, only compounded matters.

DOING NORMAL SICKNESS: LUCY'S STORY

Lucy knew the contours of her impairment in a way that Phillip was only dimly beginning to discern. Now aged 32, she has had psoriatic arthritis since her early teens, but it was only when she started work that 'things started to accelerate'. Her first job as a printing assistant in a small local firm ended abruptly. The running sore with her employer over the question of her regular hospital appointments was aggravated by his refusal to grant her paid leave to attend her grandmother's funeral. Diffident by nature, she nonetheless lost her temper:

> 'Eventually I just blew my lid and went absolutely potty and told him all the things I'd been really unhappy about, and then said, " I'm leaving at the end of the week". It was good I was upset. I didn't really care what he thought'.

With a second job as a camera operator in a large corporation, her future seemed more settled when it transpired that her new manager also had arthritis. An immediate bond was established between them. 'I was very lucky' she acknowledged. 'I think if he hadn't had arthritis, I don't think I'd have got the job to be perfectly honest'. Initial apprehensions from her co-workers that she would not be able to pull her weight soon melted away, and despite periods of unwellness, Lucy was not unhappy.

However, with the arrival of a new manager, trouble brewed once more over the question of her sick leave:

> 'I had to have a day off every three months to hospital, and at one point several of the joints in my feet had dislocated, and my toes were quite badly mis-shapen, and it was difficult to get shoes that were comfortable. The shoes used to rub on the top of my toes. I got a really bad ulcer, and I was actually off work for about eight weeks, because I couldn't wear anything on my feet, and of course he wasn't very happy about that at all. He made it very difficult'.

Mistrust and animosity between the two escalated, and Lucy's numerous hospital appointments became the focus of his hostility:

> 'With my type of arthritis I've got a skin complaint as well. Although it's one particular disease, they don't treat it as a whole thing. You have to go to a dermatologist and a rheumatologist, and if you've got a problem with your stomach you have to have medical checks with a gastro-enterologist. So I'd have to have three days off at a time. That made it even worse. It was, "you went to the hospital last week, you can't be going again", sort of thing'.

The complexities of her impairment strained the limits of tolerance. Being disabled was one thing, but multiple impairments, requiring a series of hospital visits, raised serious questions in her employer's mind about the genuineness of her sick leave.

As in Phillip's case, Lucy enlisted the help of her doctor in the hope of calming the troubled waters, but her consultant's intervention only inflamed the situation. She explained what happened:

> 'I spoke to my rheumatologist about the difficulties I had in being able to come up to hospital and she wanted to know why. And she wrote a letter to the Personnel Department and the Manager saying that I'd got this particular illness and it was necessary for me to come to the hospital, and she gave an outline of how many times she thought it was likely I'd need to come a year. I presented him with this letter, and also presented it to his superior and the manager of personnel, and he completely changed, and he said to me "Why have you done this? It wasn't necessary". And I said "Well, because you were questioning my hospital appointments". And he said, "Well, I don't know where you got that impression from, it just wasn't necessary to do this". In a way it probably aggravated him even more. It made the situation worse because he was annoyed'.

Her consultant, although anxious to help, proved to be an equivocal ally in negotiating credibility at the workplace. Later Lucy reflected upon how little by way of careful negotiation had taken place between the hospital and her employer: it had evidently been a matter-of-fact, no-nonsense approach to the dilemma[4].

Illness at work does not exist in isolation from the wider contexts in which disabled people live out their lives. Lucy's situation was complicated by the nurturing and caring role she performed for her parents and grandparents. Yet the close-knit family ties from which she too drew support and sustenance were taken away from her at a time when she most needed them.

> 'I had a lot of problems in my personal life. My father died suddenly in 1991 and I became ill because of that. I was off work for three months, something like that. And I developed a stomach ulcer which I think is related to the drugs which I'd been taking over the years for arthritis'.

Absenteeism was difficult enough to justify to her new manager on the basis of her impairments. When overlaid with the emotional and physical problems of bereavement, her credibility was seriously jeopardised. Returning to work on a part-time basis, her efforts to negotiate a return to full-time employment were unsuccessful, and she was reluctant to risk further endangering a tricky position by 'making a fuss'. The arrangement nonetheless had some advantages: she was able to spend the afternoons at home caring for her mother, now increasingly incapacitated. But the situation was too volatile. Shortly afterwards she was called down to the Personnel Office and, despite the obvious availability of work, was formally made redundant.

After a period of low morale and dwindling job prospects, a vacancy for a co-ordinator arose in a local disability organisation and, with the help of the (then) Disability Resettlement Officer, Lucy was given the job. Yet the continuing need to take time off for family as well as for medical reasons soon led to difficulties with her able-bodied line manager.

> ' I've been there two years or so, and in that time, a lot's happened. I had to go into hospital and have an operation on my other foot for three months – there were complications, – and in the summer my mother died. I've had quite a lot of time off and it's made it difficult with the line manager. She's saying that that amount of time off is not acceptable. She's happy with my work, but she's not happy about the amount of time I'm taking off. The committee of (disabled) people are supportive and on my side, but this particular person is powerful and she can be quite manipulative, so there's a bit of confrontation going on there at the moment'.

---

[4] The consultant rheumatologist who referred me to some information in the study herself commented on the inadequate attention given to occupational medicine as a speciality.

RP: 'So the sick record doesn't go away, does it?'

'No, it always seems to be the sticking point, promoting policies for disabled people when disabled people are ill. I don't quite know how to handle that'.

At her previous monthly supervision meeting, Lucy had been presented with the ultimatum:

'... to have the whole of November without having any time off! Which is impossible, whether you're disabled or non-disabled. I don't think it's possible for anyone to say, "oh yes, I'll definitely do that"...'.

At interview, Lucy was planning to challenge the line manager at her next monthly meeting. I telephoned Lucy shortly afterwards to find out how matters stood. The challenge had evidently been successful:

' It's a good outcome. She's been told that if people are off sick, it's not their fault. She's stopped hassling me. I'm much happier now about the sick record. I feel I've got the support of other people'.

Her sickness was 'normal', like everyone else's. She had gained a temporary reprieve, and with it the possibility of re-framing the disability and sickness dilemma which opened this chapter. She was sick-but-fit.

WHO AM I NOW THAT THIS HAS HAPPENED?: QUESTIONS OF IDENTITY

The way that both informants crafted a sense of identity for themselves was continuously being shaped and re-shaped in response to events that befell them, with differing implications for their respective work lives. Phillip had been propelled into a sick role which accorded ill with his perceptions of his body and his job competence, leaving him profoundly at odds with himself. His experiences raised in sharp form the question of identity: was he disabled, ill or sick, or a mixture of all three? Phillip tussled with the dilemma:

'That's a difficult one. I don't know that I felt disabled as such, or just ill. To me, if you're disabled, you can't do something because something is missing. You've lost a hand, something like that. As far as I was concerned, I temporarily couldn't do something, but it's something temporary that could be controlled with the drugs. I never got to the situation where I couldn't walk and knew I wouldn't be able to walk. That's what I would call disabled ... I suppose temporarily I was disabled when I couldn't get up and do things, but I've tended to look at it more as an illness'.

Phillip no longer felt confident about how to classify his new two per cent differentness: he fitted into no neat pigeonhole. The image of disability as the loss of a hand or the inability to walk, although temporarily relevant, did not beckon as a source of identity. The strain was towards identifying with able-bodied norms, but key figures in his able-bodied world had rejected him. I wondered how far he had felt discriminated against. The question irritated him:

> 'Aaah (sighed). That's some word is discrimination. I think it's used much too often to be honest'.

And he proceeded to give a spirited example of how he felt the term had been overused at his local school where he had a seat on the Board of Governors. Nevertheless, he acknowledged that he had little direct experience of the difficulties of his more visibly impaired acquaintances, first encountered at the Arthritis Care meeting: this was unknown territory. Although encouraged by their evident ability to 'cope', he had been shaken by the extent of their impairment and what this might entail for his own future. Summing up his resistance to being categorised one way or the other he concluded:

> 'I want to continue on with my life and just work with this arthritis. Yes I've got it, but it doesn't mean I've got to have a label stuck on my head'.

Lucy, on the other hand, was finding her new job as disability co-ordinator stimulating and fulfilling, and her identity as a disabled person was becoming more secure. Nevertheless, despite her deepening involvement with the disabled community, the question of sickness still troubled her, interfering periodically with the image she wished to present of herself to the world. I encouraged her to reflect anew on the contradictions raised at the beginning of this chapter.

> 'Disability is a separate thing to illness. But certain types of disability can be responsible for subsequent illnesses, so it is difficult to separate the two. It's very complex. I don't quite know how to go about it! It goes back to the illness bit of it really. And very often with a disabled person, their disability is static. It doesn't change. But with arthritis, it changes from day to day. It's difficult to lump everything together and say "this is how it is for disabled people"'.

> RP: 'I got the feeling when I first met you that you felt that illness is somehow letting the side down?'

'I did, but I don't so much now. People think of disabled people as sick but that isn't necessarily the case'.

Prior to starting her new post, she had exemplified the very stereotype she most wanted to challenge. However, since the confrontation with her line manager, the ambiguities of her situation seem to have been, at least temporarily, resolved. She had succeeded in re-writing the script, and, for the moment, her career prospects were more settled. Only time would tell whether her stand could be sustained.

However, her new allegiance was not entirely without reservations. She reflected again on the question of physical difference:

'If I was offered a cure tomorrow, I'd definitely take it. Some disabled people say that if they were offered an alternative of being "normal", if you like, they wouldn't take it. I can't really understand that myself. If I was in a room with disabled people and I said that, a lot of them would feel very unhappy about it. I don't know why, I can't understand why disabled people wouldn't want to take a cure if that was possible'.

Whilst much of Lucy's experience resonated with the philosophy of the Disability Movement, the correspondence was not an exact fit. Nevertheless, her challenge at work had crystallised her determination to be a disabled person in her own right:

'No matter what people say, I know that on the whole, I can do most things that I want to try and do, and certainly the belief in myself as a disabled person to challenge other people is much stronger. I am much more confident than I was'.

Phillip had just embarked on a journey, the outlines of which he could only dimly envisage as applying to himself. His brush with the disabled world had been fleeting: he was in the process of becoming a disabled person, with all its painful searchings and oscillations between able-bodied and disabled cultures. Lucy, on the other hand, already had a fund of experience of being disabled and, occasional disquiet apart, was fully involved with, and committed to, the social model of disability: the disabled community was her world. Where Phillip's and Lucy's interests coalesced lay in the fact that both were intent on putting the obduracy of their bodies as central markers of their identity to one side.

CONCLUSIONS: MAKING WIDER CONNECTIONS

This paper has explored the particular experiences of two informants with arthritis, one at the margins of disability and the other who, whilst thoroughly committed to a disabled identity, nonetheless cannot entirely integrate her experience into a social model of disability. A picture of overlapping categories has emerged. Different though Lucy's and Phillip's stories are in detail, their stories illustrate the difficulties of confining the lived experience of arthritis to one discrete domain or the other. It is not simply that the insistence on minimising the impact of impairment gives a lopsided view: their narratives indicate how deeply the body (and the self) are implicated in wider social, economic and political structures. Reducing the difficulties disabled people encounter in forging viable work lives for themselves almost entirely to a question of external environments is misleading. As Lock and Scheper-Hughes (1990) note:

> 'The individual body should be seen as the most immediate, proximate terrain where social truths and social contradictions are played out, as well as a locus of personal and social resistance, creativity and struggle' (p. 71).

A successful employment policy needs to address the complexity and ambiguity of disabled peoples' experiences, as well as draw upon the common threads which underpin their struggle to compete economically in an ablist society.

We have already seen how Phillip's position was constrained by his lack of formal educational qualifications, his family commitments and the particular employment difficulties of a small Midlands town hard pressed by recession. Lucy's situation was equally compromised by what Rosaldo (1974, p.35) refers to as 'the structural opposition between domestic and public domains of activity' which characterise many women's lives in contemporary Western society (Dalley 1988). Returning to the questions raised at the beginning of this chapter, this concluding section will firstly draw out some wider implications of the interplay between the individual, social and political bodies; and secondly, explore how experience at the margins might inform a more holistic approach to disability as the Movement gathers momentum to face the challenges of the twenty-first century.

(i) The embodied self: Despite having similar impairments, Lucy and Phillip positioned themselves differently, with differing implications for their future work lives. As we have seen, Lucy now firmly allied herself with the disabled community, although the contradiction which opened this chapter was only partly resolved, and in one respect – the possibility of a cure – her former able-bodied self still beckoned. Phillip, with minimal impairment, regarded himself primarily as able-bodied, although he could no longer dismiss the uneasy question mark which hung over his future. To an extent both were partly ' "betwixt and between" … the recognised fixed points in space-time of structural classification' (Turner, 1967, p.96), although Phillip's position was more precarious than that of Lucy, who was able to draw on the strengths of a collective discourse to reframe her situation. Had the complex realities of their experiences been more neatly resolvable, Phillip's unceremonious ejection from the Police Force, and Lucy's earlier struggles to present a morally competent version of herself despite sickness might have been more readily addressed.

Thus we are dealing not just with the discomfort which still exists between disabled people and the wider able-bodied, or 'Temporarily Able-Bodied' society (Zola, 1989, p.406), but between disabled people, wider society, and those with partial impairments who may occupy a liminal status between these worlds. Turner (1967, p.97) has argued that '…what is unclear and contradictory (from the perspective of social definition) tends to be regarded as (ritually) unclean. The unclear is unclean'. As Shakespeare (1996) recognises, both disabled and chronically ill peoples' identities are multifaceted, challenging the assumption that disability is everywhere constituted the same way. Lucy's recent bid for acceptance as 'normally sick' reassures us that multiple renderings of disability can provide an important critical challenge to the orthodoxy of a healthist workforce.

(ii) The social body: Questions of identity are intimately implicated in the way the body and the self are symbolic of the wider social order. If, as Higgins (1992, pp. 30-31) argues, disability is associated with moral blameworthiness, then the two narratives presented here indicate that the additional presence of sickness may carry more disturbing connotations. Phillip's 'two per cent that might happen' was, in William James' (1901/2, p.2) celebrated phrase 'matter out of place'. Douglas (1970, p.93) has drawn attention to the way in which the ailing or disabled body is a metaphor for the social system:

'The social body constrains the way the physical body is perceived. The physical experience of the body, always modified by the social categories through which it is known, sustains a particular view of society'.

Bodies which are flawed, or, as in Lucy's case, conspicuously sick convey powerful symbolic messages concerning social order and disorder. As Williams (1983) and Pinder (1995) have argued, attempts to sanitise disability, to present it as something mechanical distinct from fundamental cultural beliefs about the representation of health as a virtue and illness as sinful, may not ultimately be helpful. If only intuitively, we recognise how intimately they are bound together. However, in trying to reframe a healthist model of the labour force which constrains both disabled and able-bodied people, we need to draw on our common strengths and vulnerabilities: sickness in the workplace is likely to affect us all. If employment policies are to capitalise on the rich potential disabled people have to offer, they need to reflect this ambiguity rather than negate it.

(iii) The political body: The relationships between individual and social bodies are intimately woven into the political domain, raising important questions about power and control. Neither Lucy's nor Phillip's struggles were trivial: they attest to the multitude of ways in which chronically ill and disabled people assert an alternative view of their bodies. Although both informants found their everyday lives difficult and frustrating at times, their struggles with the able-bodied world contain an important critical standpoint. Three issues are important here.

First, the question of genuineness ran like an invisible thread through the two informants' attempts to sustain a viable work role. Much as they wished to discount the significance of their physical differentness, it structured their relationships to the world of work in a new and problematic way. On the one hand, prior to her attempt to redefine her absences as 'normal sickness', Lucy's working career had been characterised by a continuous struggle to legitimise herself as sick-but-fit. On the other, Phillip had failed in his attempts to persuade an inflexible police bureaucracy to take a chance on his future work capabilities as fit-but-sick. Both had continuously overstepped the 'limits of tolerance'.

Dodier (1985) notes that, 'Moral judgements made at work can be decisive for a career', as both informants discovered to their cost. Phillip's dismissal and Lucy's earlier redundancy were not simply straightforward practical decisions concerning their respective physical capabilities: they were laced with moral connotations, which were themselves embedded in wider shifting structural relationships. In the contemporary economic climate of heightened uncertainty and job insecurity, both informants were caught in what Lock and Scheper-Hughes (1990) refer to as 'a nervous vigilance about exits and entries', where anxieties about maintaining existing body boundaries and body purity may be exacerbated.

Second, in trying to negotiate credible versions of themselves, both informants became entangled in the ambiguous relationship which exists between medicine and capitalism. As Bellaby (1990) notes:

> 'Medicine, as an institutional complex, sits uneasily between employer and employee. It is not an unequivocal ally of capital in the social control and reproduction of the labour force ... but neither is it necessarily the worker's friend, whatever the attitudes of the individual medical practitioner may be' (p. 60).

Both informants' search for credibility brought them face to face with the differing imperatives of the medical profession, with its stress on mind-body dualism, and the labour market, which emphasises productivity and performance. A morally adequate explanation of what to expect of arthritis in the formalised setting of the hospital clinic carried little credence in the specific context of Lucy's and Phillip's respective workplaces. The discipline of occupational medicine is still in its infancy. Stronger links between trade unions, disability employment advisers, the medical profession and the disabled community are vital if the careful assessment and negotiation of options for re-deployment, so integral to responsible work practices for disabled people, are to be fully considered.

Third, events fan outwards. Once 'on the books', the sick record itself became an invisible form of discipline, blocking Phillip's career advancement and seriously jeopardising Lucy's earlier credibility. As a means of classifying illness behaviour and making unambiguous decisions about sickness or fitness, it was a symbol of unpredictability and unreliability. Foucault (1977, p.190) has alerted us to the way in which records represent:

> 'the fixing, at once ritual and "scientific" of individual differences ... (they are) a process by which an individual is linked by his status to the features, the measurements, the gaps, the "marks" that characterise him and make him "a case" '.

For both informants in this chapter, the record had functioned as a 'thing out there', constraining and shaping perceptions and future possibilities. Yet, as we have seen, it would be mistaken to characterise either Lucy or Phillip as victims: both wrestled actively with their respective situations.

Thus, to focus almost exclusively on a model of disability which fails to take into account the way the body and the self are inextricably tied to a wider web of economic, social and cultural relationships gives a misleading picture. The validity of Lucy's and Phillip's narratives will be strained unless we pay attention to the interplay between them: herein lie the seeds of creativity and change. As disabled people grow in confidence, the dialectic between agency and structure is constantly shifting.

My final observations concern the implications of these findings for the Disability Movement's continuing exploration of its own identity, and the development of policies which may strengthen its message. Douglas (1966) notes that cultural categories:

> '...cannot neglect the challenge of aberrant forms. Any given system of classification must give rise to anomalies, and any given culture must confront events which seem to defy its assumptions. It cannot ignore the anomalies which its scheme produces, except at the risk of forfeiting confidence' (p. 40).

For reasons grounded historically in its own struggles, the Movement is ill at ease with ambiguity. Chronic illness is still seen as 'medical' and therefore falling outside its provenance. The voices of those who, like Phillip, may weave in and out of disability, have so far been comparatively muted.

Yet, the two stories presented here have shown that the contradictions inherent in relying primarily on a social model of disability to explain the difficulties chronically ill and disabled people face at work cannot be ignored. As Bauman (1991, p.73) notes, 'Ambivalence cannot be wished out of existence'. Phillip's narrative has as much to tell us about what it means to be able-bodied with physical limitations as Lucy's more conventional story alerts us to the pressures of being disabled. If the Movement is to adequately reflect the lived reality of their work lives, the experience of difference-within-difference needs to be acknowledged too. Feminists have already paved the way in this respect: 'The differences between women are important' writes Moore (1988):

> 'and they need to be acknowledged because it cannot be part of feminist politics for one group of women to speak for and on behalf of another' (p. 198).

It would be tragic if, in sifting the 'proper' from the 'improper', the Disability Movement failed to gather under its wing the many elderly and chronically ill people who may have difficulty in relating to a social oppression model of disability, but who nonetheless share similar inequities of treatment. As Williams (1996) argues, there is a danger that unless the Movement confronts its own ambiguities and speaks to the many other injustices (age, class, gender, and race) that plague our society, it may cut itself off from more general issues of public policy. If the particular problems of disabled women – and increasingly women from ethnic communities – are now well established in disability theory, Phillip's story alerts us to the importance of attending to the other 'variables' and their interdependence. However understandable in a young political movement still flexing its wings, efforts to tame variety can only restrict its influence. A more holistic definition of disability, of the way in which disability is intimately linked to other structural relationships which differentially disadvantage social actors, is the hallmark of a Disability Movement which has truly come of age.

Before his untimely death in 1994, the disabled sociologist Irving Zola urged the Disability Movement to embrace a universal approach. He wrote:

> 'Only when we acknowledge the near universality of disability and that all of its dimensions (including the biomedical) are part of the social process by which the meanings of disability are negotiated will it be possible fully to appreciate how general public policy can affect this issue' (1989, p. 420).

The dilemma for disability theorists is whether, in bringing into the fold 'experience at the margins', the political momentum can be sustained. I believe it can only be strengthened and enriched. If Lucy's and Phillip's narratives have highlighted the more complex questions which will need to be faced now that the 1995 Disability Discrimination Act (however inadequate) is on the statute books, this chapter will have made a modest contribution to that debate.

REFERENCES

BAUMAN, Z. (1991) *Modernity and ambivalence*, Cambridge: Polity Press.

BARNES, C. (1991) *Disabled People in Britain and Discrimination: A case for Anti-Discrimination legislation*, London: Hurst.

BELLABY, P. (1989) 'The social meanings of time off work: a case study from a pottery factory', *Annals of Occupational Hygiene*, 33, 3, 423-438.

BELLABY, P. (1990) 'What is genuine sickness? The relation between work discipline and the sick role in a pottery factory', *Sociology of Health and Illness*, 12, 1, 47-68.

BURY, M. (1996) 'Defining and researching disability: challenges and responses', in C. Barnes and G. Mercer, eds., *Exploring the Divide: Illness and Disability*, Leeds: Disability Press, ch.2.

CROW, L. (1996) 'Including all our lives: renewing the social model of disability' in C. Barnes and G. Mercer, (eds), *Exploring the Divide: Illness and Disability*, Leeds: Disability Press, ch.4.

DALLEY, G. (1988) *Ideologies of Caring: Rethinking Community and Collectivism*, Basingstoke: Macmillan.

DODIER, N. (1985) 'Social uses of illness at the workplace: sick leave and moral evaluation', *Social Science and Medicine*, 20, 2, 123-128.

DOUGLAS, M. (1966) *Purity and Danger: An Analysis of the Concepts of Pollution and Taboo*, London: Routledge.

DOUGLAS, M. (1970) *Natural Symbols: Explorations in Cosmology*, London: Barrie and Jenkins.

FOUCAULT, M. (1977) *Discipline and Punish: The Birth of the Prison*, Harmondsworth: Penguin.

FRENCH, S. (1993) 'Disability, impairment or something in between?', in Swain J. et al., (eds.) *Disabling Barriers – Enabling Environments*, London: Sage.

FREUND, P. E. S. (1988) 'Bringing society into the body: understanding socialized human nature', *Theory and Society*, 17, 839-864.

HIGGINS, P.C. (1992) *Making Disability: Exploring the Social Transformation of Human Variation*, Springfield: Illinois: Charles C. Thomas.

JAMES, W. (1902) *The Varieties of Religious Experience*, London: Longmans.

LOCK, M. and SCHEPER-HUGHES, N. (1990) 'A critical-interpretive approach in medical anthropology: rituals and routines of discipline and dissent', in Johnson, T. M. and Sargent, C. F. (eds.) *Medical Anthropology: A Handbook of Theory and Method*, New York: Greenwood Press.

LONSDALE, S. (1990) *Women and Disability: The Experience of Physical Disability Among Women*, Basingstoke: Macmillan.

MOORE, H. L. (1988) *Feminism and Anthropology*, Cambridge: Polity Press.

MORRIS, J. (1991) *Pride Against Prejudice: Transforming Attitudes to Disability*, London: The Women's Press.

MURPHY, R. (1987) *The Body Silent,* London: J. M.. Dent.

OLIVER, M. (1990) *The Politics of Disablement*, Basingstoke: Macmillan.

OLIVER, M. (1996) 'Impairment and Disability: definitional issues', in C. Barnes and G. Mercer, (eds), *Exploring the Divide: Illness and Disability*, Leeds: Disability Press, ch.3.

PINDER, R. (1995) 'Bringing back the body without the blame? The experience of ill and disabled people at work', *Sociology of Health and Illness*, 17, 5, 605-631.

ROSALDO, M. Z. (1974) 'A theoretical overview', in Rosaldo, M. and Lamphere, L. (eds.) *Women, Culture and Society*, Stanford, USA: Stanford University Press.

SCHEPER-HUGHES N. and LOCK, M. (1987) 'The mindful body: a prolegomenon to future work in medical anthropology', *Medical Anthropology Quarterly*, 1, 6-41.

SHAKESPEARE, T. (1996) 'Disability, Identity, Difference', in C. Barnes and G. Mercer, (eds), *Exploring the Divide: Illness and Disability*, Leeds: Disability Press, ch.6.

SWAIN, J., FINKELSTEIN, V., FRENCH, S., and OLIVER, M. (1993) (eds.) *Disabling Barriers – Enabling Environments*, London: Sage.

TURNER, V. (1967) *The Forest of Symbols: Aspects of Ndembu Ritual*, London: Cornell University Press.

WILLIAMS, G. (1983) 'The Movement for Independent Living: an evaluation and a critique', *Social Science and Medicine*, 17, 15, 1003-1010.

WILLIAMS, G. (1996) 'Disability and the Environment: Some questions of phenomenology and politics', in C. Barnes and G. Mercer, (eds), *Exploring the Divide: Illness and Disability*, Leeds: Disability Press, ch.11.

ZOLA, I. (1989) 'Toward the necessary universalizing of disability policy', *Milbank Memorial Quarterly*, 67 (Suppl. 2), 401-428.

CHAPTER 9

General Practitioners' Role in Shaping Disabled Women's Lives

Nasa Begum

INTRODUCTION

Environment can be defined as embracing most aspects of the society people live in, such as physical features, political/economic structures and the social climate within which people function. Alternatively, the term environment may be used to identify particular features of the world, this is perhaps most commonly done when describing the physical composition of the world people live in. In order to explore the divide between illness and disability I will adopt a broad definition of environment, but primarily focus on the interaction between disabled women and GPs.

RELATIONSHIP BETWEEN MEDICINE AND THE ENVIRONMENT

Studies on women's health have revealed concerns about the social control aspects of medicine. Feminists have documented how the medical profession controls the lives of women and defines what is acceptable and unacceptable conduct. Helen Roberts explains:

> '... women and doctors (even if those doctors are women) don't just have subtly different viewpoints about health, they inhabit different worlds. Doctors have the power to define what is, and what is not, illness, what is and what is not appropriate behaviour in a patient; and what is to go on in the consulting room' (Roberts, 1985, p. 2).

Feminists have argued that exploring the different ingredients that influence women's health is crucial to understanding sexist ideology. Notions of 'normality' and male superiority verses female inferiority are all based on theories and philosophies about the human body. Therefore examining the relationship between disabled women and GPs (General Practitioners or Family Doctors) is a useful mechanism for not only exploring the divide between illness and disability, but also assessing how the medical world can determine the environment disabled women live in.

The medical model of disability which equates disability with illness, has been used extensively to organise and control the lives of disabled people. Focusing on an individualistic approach to disability, pathologising disabled people as problems, rather than recognising the structural oppression disabled people face, has blurred the distinction between illness and impairment. Consequently, on the one hand disabled people are having to challenge the relevance of a medical model of disability and advocate an understanding of disability based on attitudinal, environmental and institutional barriers; whilst on the other hand disabled people are also struggling to access appropriate health services.

In the past, disabled people have fought so hard to challenge the medicalisation of disability that anxieties about health needs have tended to be minimised. Concerns about the oppressive nature of medical treatment, and the fear of disability being construed as a catalogue of medical problems, has made disabled people wary of putting health issues on the public and/ or academic agenda. Whilst this may be an understandable response to the intrusive and often interventionist nature of the medical world there can be little doubt that disabled people, whether as a result of impairment, or as a consequence of everyday illnesses, are consumers of health services.

Margaret Lloyd (1992) points out:

> '.. the narrow defining of disability as clinical conditions results in an all-pervasiveness of doctors' power over disabled people's lives, of which the power to make decisions about fitness for work and entitlement to welfare benefits are but examples. This does not necessarily mean, however, that the medical aspects of their lives are unimportant for disabled people' (p. 211).

The authority and control the medical profession exercises over the lives of disabled people, inevitably has a profound impact on both disabled men and disabled women. Nevertheless disabled people are not a homogenous group, factors such as race, class, age, sexuality, sex and gender also often play a significant role in shaping disabled people's experiences of health services. For example many Black disabled people have drawn attention to the way perceptions of people with Sickle Cell being 'drug addicts' often prevents access to health services. Similarly disabled women have raised concerns about the way rehabilitation programmes place an emphasis on 'cultivating competitive attitudes' and addressing concerns about male sexuality, therefore whilst enabling men to aspire to dominant notions of masculinity, the needs of disabled women are ignored or left on the periphery (Morris 1989; Matthews, 1983).

Although the glory of the medical world does not shine in a local doctor's surgery, a GP can often act as the passport to a whole range of services and support. The response received by a GP significantly influences the lives of disabled women. GPs are not only the first point of contact when health matters need dealing with but they potentially exert a great deal of authority over other aspects of disabled women's lives. The medical model of disability means that GPs are often required to have an input on matters which many people would argue should not be in the domain of the medical profession.

In this paper, I will draw upon a small illustrative study of disabled women's experience of GP's, using qualitative material to suggest that the way GPs respond to the needs of disabled women can be disabling, and the division between illness and impairment is much more complex than both medical sociologists and disabled theorists have previously thought.

The paper will start by outlining the methodology and sample characteristics. Next it will discuss some of the reasons why disabled women have contact with GPs. It will then go on to highlight how GP's respond to disabled women's impairments and experience of illness. Finally the paper will conclude that whilst the relationship between illness and impairment is not as clear cut as we might like to think, care needs to be taken not to throw the baby out with the bath water.

RESEARCH METHODOLOGY

Initially, the research I aimed to carry out focused on in-depth interviews with a small number of women in order to establish the nature of disabled women's relationships with their general practitioners. Advertisements were placed in the disability press, inviting women to contact me if they were willing to take part in the study by completing a questionnaire or participating in a face-to-face interview. It was envisaged that a very short questionnaire with a series of open ended questions could be designed to obtain an idea of the types of issues that concerned disabled women. This would be followed with a small number of qualitative interviews.

The response to the advertisements was overwhelming. Over 100 women throughout the country responded and 3 organisations asked for multiple copies of the questionnaire. The telephone discussions and letters received about the research clearly showed that disabled women's experience of GPs was a major area of concern for them.

In order to utilise the experience of all the women who expressed an interest in the research, a decision was made to develop the questionnaire further, so that it could be circulated to everyone, and to use it as a postal questionnaire. Women who could not fill in the questionnaire were offered the opportunity to take part in a telephone discussion, have a face-to-face interview or receive practical support to fill it in.

The questionnaire was designed to incorporate quantitative and qualitative information. Its primary aim was to explore the experiences of disabled women rather than investigate the characteristics of the GP or the GP's practice. It included open ended questions about current and previous GPs. A total of 80 completed questionnaires were returned by the deadline set.

LIMITATIONS OF THE RESEARCH

Most empirical research has its limitations; either because of the methodology used, or by the very nature of the subject matter itself, and sometimes a range of other unexpected factors. This research was no exception. Although it was not meant to be a representative study, the mere fact it relied on self selection built an inherent bias into the sample, as it inevitably attracted disabled women who wanted to share their experience of GPs. Also, relying on questionnaires as the main tool of the research excluded some disabled women, particularly women for whom written English is not their preferred method of communication. If this work is developed further it would be important to use, what Mike Oliver calls, an emancipatory research paradigm (Oliver, 1992) with a particular emphasis on group discussions and semi-structured interviews to target disabled women who are not properly represented at this stage.

The emphasis of the research was on setting an agenda from the perspective of disabled women, and there is therefore very little information about the women's GPs, the type of practice they work in, frequency of contact and so on. In retrospect it may have been useful to explore further information about the characteristics of GPs. Nevertheless the material elicited from the research provides a useful starting point for highlighting a neglected area of experiences.

Finally, the study does not incorporate any comparative work with non-disabled women or disabled men. It is clear that many of the issues raised are not unique to disabled women. However the central thrust of this research is to demonstrate the extent to which GPs can shape the lives of disabled women, and to highlight the urgent need to include them in the discussions about women's health, primary health care and disabled people's use of health services.

CHARACTERISTICS OF THE SAMPLE

The women who responded were fairly well distributed geographically with 43% living in a city, 33% in a town and 20% in a village. Almost a third of the sample lived alone. Thirty percent lived with a partner, 14% with a partner and children, 7% lived with their children and another 7% lived with other family members. Only 1 person stated that she lived in a residential home so this is one group who are clearly under-represented in this study.

Only 4% of the sample did not identify their sexuality. The other 96% comprised 5% lesbians, 9% bi-sexual women and 82% heterosexual women. Given that it is estimated that 1 in 10 of the population are not heterosexual, the research appears to encompass a fairly representative proportion of lesbian and bi-sexual women.

Just over half (52%) of the women had children. This figure includes those whose children were grown up and had left home, as well as those whose children were still living with them.

African Caribbean women formed 5% of the sample, Asian women 2%, and UK European women 84%. It is difficult to know the proportion of Black disabled women in the population. Although their representation in this study may seem reasonable in theoretical terms, it has not ensured Black disabled women are a significant proportion of the sample.

Approximately two-thirds of the women were between the ages of 21 and 49 years, while only 14% were between the ages of 50 and 59 and another 14% over 60. The government's survey of disabled people indicated that the largest proportion of disabled women are over the age of 60 (OPCS, 1988). In contrast, this sample appears to mainly represent women whose impairments to a large extent are not part of the ageing process.

Twenty-nine percent of the women were born with an impairment, another 17% became disabled before the age of 22, while the remainder acquired their impairment later in adult life.

The majority of women described their impairment as a physical condition with multiple sclerosis accounting for 20%, back/ spinal injuries experienced by 12% and arthritis/ osteoarthritis by 11%. Deaf women only formed 3% of the sample and blind women totalled 5%, although 22% indicated that their impairment affected their sight.

DISABLED WOMEN'S CONTACT WITH GPS

Disabled women will present to their GPs for a whole host of reasons, ranging from a request for support with everyday illnesses such as flu, or gaining access to other health services, to obtaining specific advice around women's health issues like maternity services, or dealing with issues relating to their impairments.

In the research study the most common reason cited for contacting a GP was to obtain repeat prescriptions, or issues relating to one's impairments. A breakdown of the reasons why disabled women referred to their GPs showed that contact relating to women's health matters, such as screening services, menopause, children's health and contraception appeared to be relatively low, given that two thirds of the sample was between the ages of 21 and 49 years. On the other hand contact with a GP for medical reports and authorisation for other services appeared to be rather high. Whilst one may consider it appropriate for GPs to provide medical reports sometimes, concerns are inevitably raised about the excessive reliance on a medical model of disability which requires GPs to involve themselves in different spheres of disabled people' lives.

GPs are used extensively as the passport to other non-medical resources or activities. The pervasiveness of the medical model of disability is so extensive that access to employment, and leisure facilities can be dependent upon a GP's recommendation. The GP's response is often based on what s/he believes to be the ability and competence of the disabled person based on their functional impairment, rather than a recognition of how external factors, such as access to the right equipment, or how the availability of sign language interpreters at a work place, will effect them.

The personal views and prejudices of GPs play an important role in determining the type of support that will be provided to enable disabled people to live their lives. This is problematical as expectations of disabled people are often very low, as one disabled woman explains:

> 'previously I had a female GP, but she had a very naff attitude towards disability. Every visit for cold or flu I used to be told to stop working, I shouldn't bother to work due to my disability. Always assumed that I wouldn't be working at every visit, even though I had told her I work a number of times'.

Another woman talked about the difficulties she faced:

> ' It's like they fob me off because I am disabled ... They do not think I should have a life and being disabled expect to (be in) bed all time'.

Jenny talks about how her GP's opinion about women taking up benefits affected her Department of Social Security (DSS) application.

> 'She refused to give me a sick note, although when DSS phoned her she said I will never work, but she thought women who do not work should not get benefits. She even told DSS I did not need the benefit... I did not know if I should go without or maybe find another doctor'.

There may be specific values and beliefs held about certain groups of disabled women, like disabled lesbians, Black disabled women or women with learning difficulties. One woman with learning difficulties points out:

> 'GPs have the power to either allow people with learning difficulties to fully participate in society... My GP has abused his power. I had to stand up and advocate my ability to participate in student holidays, jobs and travel abroad. My GP was going to take my rights away from me because of his assumptions of people with learning difficulties'.

GPs shape the environment disabled women live in through their ability to enforce a medical model of disability. The individualistic approach to disability where substantial power is vested in GPs (and other health professionals) is a major source of contention for disabled people. The pervasiveness of the medical model of disability is a major barrier for disabled people. Maggie explains:

> 'I find difficult the extent to which my doctor is given control over my life. In the last year she has had to confirm that I can travel abroad, need the adaptations in my house, can have alcoholic drinks and give a full medical for a second mortgage... I have to pay for these services. She did not design the system and would like it to be different, nevertheless it does affect our relationship'.

Given that there are increasing demands upon GPs, and discussions about the most effective way of organising primary health care services are rife, this debate, exploring the divide between illness and disability, is very timely.

RELATIONSHIP BETWEEN ILLNESS AND IMPAIRMENT

It is not my intention to define illness, impairment and disability here as this has been done elsewhere in this volume (see chapter three). Nevertheless I will point out that the term impairment is used to describe a person's physical, emotional, sensory or learning difficulty condition, whereas illness refers to everyday ailments and other biological, physical, psychological issues that people would not define as 'normal' for them.

In the research study, disabled women described their general health as reasonably good, Lucy points out that 'having excellent general health, contact with GP is very limited'. But 8% of the women felt that their health was either fairly poor or very poor.

A common perception is one of disabled people being 'sick' or 'unwell'. Therefore it is quite possible that in an attempt to challenge popular beliefs (particularly within the medical profession) disabled women may have subconsciously decided not to identify with the general ailments associated with everyday living. For example one woman explained that she 'refused to give in to illness'. The very fact she uses the term 'give in' suggests that illness is perceived as a weakness.

Some disabled women appear to be fighting the 'sick role' concept by asserting a positive identity and either managing everyday health concerns (like flu or stomach upsets) without going to a GP, or ignoring them until they become more serious.

> 'I am less affected by other illnesses and tend to ignore them which has led to the development of some serious illnesses due to neglect'.

Equally some disabled women were taking positive steps to ensure their general health was well maintained by taking vitamin tablets, changing their diet, trying to avoid stress and so on. On the whole disabled women were no more susceptible to illness than any other women.

For some disabled women illness and impairment were two totally separate issues, Victoria points out:

> '... any illness I have is not related to my disability (referring to impairment)'.

Nevertheless for other disabled women the very nature of a woman's impairment or the practical affects of an illness can have other repercussions. More than half (58%) of the women felt that their impairment affected their experience of illness. Sometimes illness had very practical repercussions:

> 'Flu affects mobility including sitting down, turning in bed, getting into car, keeping comfortably warm. Coughs and colds affect ears and balance... Skin slower to heal with cuts'.

> 'My normal independence is very curtailed, I need to find a friend to make sure I have lots of drink and easy food, and try to get more "Care Hours" (external help) if I have a stomach bug'.

In other situations too, impairment and illness seemed to become inextricably linked.

> 'Vulnerable to infections, poor appetite and stomach problems. Also gynaecological problems'.

> 'Immunity system not so good, also monthly periods give rise to more arthritic pain, if coupled with a cold unable to do much'.

Wislocka explains how although her experience of illness is linked to her impairment sometimes, the perception at work is that the two things are synonymous with each other:

> 'I cannot keep fit and am more susceptible to flu, ear infections and chest infections.... but what is worse is that people at work do not see a difference between an impairment and illness, and perceive me as being "ill" and "weak" and taking a lot of time off work - whereas I have only had 14 days total sickness in 2 years'.

The relationship between illness and impairment is a complex one. On the one hand, impairments do not constitute a 'medical problem' but are merely a fact of life that disabled women live with. On the other hand, some disabled women may be more vulnerable to illnesses because of an impairment, or the affects of an illness on an impairment.

Regardless of where disabled women's experience of impairment and/or illness falls in terms of a continuum of interaction between illness and impairment, there will be additional concerns arising from the specific health needs of disabled women as women. These can not be described as an illness or impairment, but are simply an integral part of women's health care needs. Again for some disabled women biological processes such as menstruation, child birth and menopause will not be affected by impairment, but for other disabled women the two may sometimes become linked. The challenge for GPs is whether they can manage the triangle of illness, impairment and women's health care needs.

GP'S RESPONSE TO DISABLED WOMEN

The way GPs responded to disabled women's impairment varied greatly. Sally points out how her GP attributes any health problems to her impairment, she explains:

> 'Everything from sore throat to heavy periods is blamed on my "impairment".... he says you must expect these things in your circumstances'.

Sometimes the pure fact a disabled woman had an impairment was a source of curiosity and enthusiasm, particularly if it was something that the GP had not come across before in their everyday work. Several disabled women talked about how they had to deal with the GP's fascination with their impairment, when visiting for something else.

'They were usually more interested in my main impairment than the problem I was asking for help with, which some of the time had nothing to do with Muscular Dystrophy, i.e. it might have been a bump on the head or a rash'.

'My current GP is often more interested in my disability than in the reason for my visit. I have visited my GP for contraception only to be questioned about my lack of sight'.

For many disabled women the biggest problem they encountered was the reluctance of GPs to believe and support them in the diagnosis or treatment of their impairment.

'My current GP along with previous staff in the medical profession have insisted that my spinal problems are non-existent despite the findings and opinions of chiropodist and others dealing with spinal difficulties. Current GP insists that my being overweight is the cause despite the fact that I had the same difficulty standing when I was four years of age and weighed two stone'.

Disabled women who were not believed or diagnosed inappropriately encountered substantial problems.

'I was told that my disability was psychosomatic and the GP refused to contact exam boards when I was in severe pain during one of my "A" level exams. The GP was paid for each appointment he attended, so I would miss endless classes to attend appointments. If I didn't turn up, the necessary painkillers and other medication was stopped and it was a major task to try and re-initiate them'.

Judith explains:

'Over-riding problem I have is I don't have my input recognised or believed... If I don't get well they say it's psychological (hypochondria etc.). If it's psychological it's not real/ "genuine" (apparently). If it's not real, it doesn't need treatment, it's a sign I just need to "pull myself together". If I argue/ disagree/ don't comply it's proof of these theories. It's a no-win situation regardless of whether it's physical or psychological. They know almost nothing about my situation and seem to feel that's my inadequacy!' .

The labelling of women's behaviour as psychosomatic, 'neurotic', 'hysterical' and so on was not an uncommon experience. This often led to a misunderstanding about disabled women's needs and inappropriate intervention.

'... she tried to get me admitted to the psychiatric hospital twice on the grounds that I was a hysteric/ suicide case. I was having an arthritis flare-up on both occasions...'.

'As a child tinnitus and it's upsetting effects were ignored. I even had a spurious diagnosis of schizophrenia made due to the assumption that I was "backward" I would not know the difference between a noise or a voice in my ears'.

The experiences of women with learning difficulties and/or women with impairments which are not immediately physically visible, suggests that there are profound difficulties with the way GPs react. Women with learning difficulties are rarely recognised as able to manage their affairs (with support of their choice), therefore GPs are more likely to accept the views and opinions of parents or other 'professionals'.

One disabled woman talked about how her GP refused to deal with her directly:

> 'Even though he knew I was going to university he still treated me like a child. Once when I was undressing prior to an examination I shouted answers over the screen to questions directed at my mother, which should have been directed at me. I was accused of being cheeky'.

GPs inability to tackle their own negative attitudes towards disabled people, can have massive repercussions for disabled people who have no alternative, but to rely on their GP for access to essential resources. Sally spoke of how difficult it was for her as a young disabled woman with her family doctor:

> 'I tried to cope secretly with incontinence - no support at all from GP. When I asked for (after support of other spinal cord injured women I met), told to obtain continence supplies "out of town" - to avoid bringing shame to family'.

Sometimes judgements about the nature of women's impairment influenced the way a GP responded. Alicia explains:

> 'My occupation of dancer/actress during my 20s/ early 30s caused many GPs to blame my profession for many movement problems, and my nomadic existence for my fluctuating menstrual cycle'.

The fact GPs can define women's experience, and behaviour in such judgmental terms, is indicative of the way the medical world has used sexist ideology to label and control women's behaviour.

Disabled women seemed to receive mixed messages about their roles as women. On the one hand disabled women's concerns have primarily been perceived in the context of their roles as 'baby making machines' and fulfilling their husbands needs:

> 'I realise that things are not always easy to diagnose but felt he was totally unco-operative. He suggested I see a psychologist (I refused). When my husband went to discuss with him how worried he was about me, he asked him if he was more worried about his lack of sex life which was not the case'.

'The relief doctor came to see me and he got hold of my hand and my thumb and began twisting them, then said "oh it's rheumatics, have a baby every year, that will keep it at bay", it came back twice as bad as soon as I had the babies, but it is them that has kept me going all these years'.

On the other hand GPs were reluctant to acknowledge disabled women's need for health services specific to their requirements as women. Sharon had difficulty in getting her needs as a woman properly recognised. She explains:

'I feel that in general my GPs have viewed me firstly as a blind woman rather than a woman. This has meant that they have not given me the information I have often needed'.

She goes on to highlight the lengths her GP went to exert influence over what was 'acceptable' or 'unacceptable' for a disabled woman. The over-riding message being that a disabled women should not have children:

'When I was pregnant with my first son I received a letter from the hospital asking me to attend the out patients clinic. I had no idea what it was about, but assumed it was a check-up of some sort. When I arrived I was told that a letter had been sent by someone (whose name could not be divulged), who had suggested that I should be offered an abortion'.

Disabled women's right to have children has been attacked from many quarters. Feminist debates about genetic 'engineering' or abortion have rarely taken on board the reality disabled women have to confront when the only option presented to them is sterilisation or abortion.

'GP refused to refer me to gynaecologist when I wanted to marry. Refused to prescribe the pill - advised me to obtain sterilisation privately - which I did - reluctantly. Feel very bitter as other women with my impairment have had support and encouragement to have children. Did not know I had the right to change doctor then or had any other choices'.

Sterilisation has been used extensively to control the sexual activities of women with learning difficulties. The emphasis with women with learning difficulties has predominately been on preventing reproduction rather than supporting women to make more informed decisions and choices about their sex lives, this is probably as much a recognition of the fact women with learning difficulties are vulnerable to abuse, as it is a concern to control sexual behaviour, or prevent women with learning difficulties from having children.

Occasionally a GP was supportive in terms of enabling a disabled woman to choose whether or not to become a mother. Wislocka explains:

'Despite my back injury I am desperate to have a child. Everyone said I was crazy but my GP looked at it from both sides saying that there may be problems but if I was happy with being a mother I would feel less stressed and may feel less pain. She suggested a referral to someone who does couple counselling about fertility issues and also referred my husband for reversal of vasectomy'.

How a GP views and responds to a disabled woman's needs will not only have a crucial impact on the disabled woman's health care, but will have much wider ramifications for the way she is able to live her life.

GPS AND THE SOCIAL MODEL OF DISABILITY

A crucial question for GPs (and other health professionals) in responding to the needs of disabled women is whether or not the social model of disability is relevant to their work. Therefore it is useful to briefly explore what the social model may mean for GPs, other health professionals and even medical sociologists.

The social model of disability suggests that attitudinal, institutional and environmental barriers are the root cause of disabled people's oppression. Arguably the case is fairly clear cut, it is not people's impairments that exclude them from society, and render them subject to prejudice and discrimination, but rather the prevailing ideologies and structures within our society that prevents disabled people participating as full and equal members of society.

The common perception is that the social model of disability renders impairment redundant in any analysis of disability. Although the emphasis to date may have been on the structural barriers identified within a social model of disability, there is nothing to suggest that impairments are totally irrelevant. The social model of disability acknowledges impairment as one part of an equation, but accepted it as a given fact, just as the colour of a black person's skin in an analysis of racism. To counteract the heavy emphasis given to impairment within the medical model of disability, in the past disabled people have focused attention away from impairment.

A GP who can recognise the importance of these structural factors shaping disabled women's lives is more likely to work in a way which empowers disabled women.

'My current GP has a number of spinal cord injured women in her practice, she is honest enough to admit we know more about our requirements than she does and if she can help us access other services she will do her best to do so'.

Another woman explained:

'On the positive side he has been interested in my purchase of a powered wheelchair seeing it (rightly) as an extension of my freedom and independence rather than as a symbol of having given up (the reaction of some of my friends)'.

As far as many disabled women are concerned a GP's ability to adopt a broader approach to their work and acknowledge how attitudinal, environmental and institutional barriers will effect them, does not negate the medical practitioner's role in managing their impairment, and general health needs, but rather enhances it.

A GP or any other person in the field of medicine who accepts and supports disabled women in tackling disabling barriers, and managing rather than 'curing' impairments will be much more effective in fulfilling their role and obligations within their profession. Judith speaks for a lot of disabled women when she says that what she wants most from her GP is to be listened to, have her experience and expertise acknowledged, and the GP's lack of experience and expertise acknowledged. Judith explains:

'I'm not asking for cure... I'm asking for support in managing my situation. This might mean acknowledging it's tough, helping me access resources, helping me plan health management and learn relevant skills'.

So where does that leave disabled theorists and medical sociologists?

CONCLUSION

I would like to suggest, as a conclusion to this debate, that the divide between illness and impairment is, perhaps, not as much of a massive gulf, as we may have thought before. Clearly, there are distinctions, depending on whether an individualistic or structural emphasis is adopted. However, there is also an awful lot of muddy marshland in between, where perhaps the distinctions are not quite as clear, and there may be scope for much more collaborative work between disabled people and those in the field of medicine.

This paper has highlighted how the medical world can control the environment disabled people live in, by drawing specific attention to the way GPs respond to the needs of disabled women. It has also demonstrated that the relationship between disabled women's experience of illness, impairment and health needs as women is sometimes totally separate, and at other times intricately woven with each other. Therefore whilst there is a lot of concern about the pervasiveness of the medical model, there is a clear need for people in the field of medicine to work with disabled people to enable them to manage their impairments and illnesses in a way which is defined as being appropriate by the disabled person.

Finally the social model of disability is not irrelevant to GPs, medical practitioners and academics, as it provides a framework for recognising both individual factors (that is impairment) and external barriers. The challenge now is for disabled people and medical sociologists to work together to find out how we can wade through the muddy marshland, without having to throw out the important work that has been done to reach an understanding of illness and disability.

REFERENCES

LLOYD, M. (1992) 'Does She Boil Eggs? Towards a feminist model of disability', *Disability Handicap and Society*, Vol. 7, No 3, pp. 207-221.

MATTHEWS, G. F. (1983) *Voices from the Shadows*, Ontario, Canada: The Women's Press.

MORRIS, J. (1994) 'Gender and disability' in French, S. (ed.) *On Equal Terms: working with disabled people*, Butterworth-Heinemann: London.

MORRIS, J, (ed.) (1989) *Able Lives: women's experience of paralysis*, London: The Women's Press.

OLIVER, M. (1992) 'Changing the social relations of research production?', *Disability Handicap and Society*, Vol. 7, No.2, pp. 101-11.

ROBERTS, H. (1985) *The Patient Patients*, London: Pandora Press.

(This chapter is based on 'Doctor, Doctor... Disabled Women's experience of general practitioners', in: Morris, J., ed. (1996) *Encounters with Strangers: Feminism and Disability*, London: The Women's Press.)

CHAPTER 10

Breaking Down Barriers

Judith Emanuel and David Ackroyd

INTRODUCTION

In July 1995, the North West Regional Health Authority (NWRHA) published *Breaking Down Barriers: Guidelines for Purchasers of Health Services for Disabled Adults aged 16-64 with physical and sensory impairments* (NWRHA, 1995a). The development of these Guidelines took over 18 months and this chapter aims to describe that process and discuss some of the issues raised.

Breaking Down Barriers is a short document, the main part of which comprises 12 Guidelines, brief comments, and actions that purchasers should take. The Guidelines are backed up with a Companion Volume which includes more detailed comments, an extensive bibliography, information from the initial consultation, and details of the members of the strategy group. The Guidelines are targeted at health service purchasers, that is, Health Authorities and GP Fundholders.

The Guidelines were developed by a strategy group and edited by ourselves. Members of the strategy group included disabled people, some of whom came from disabled people's organisations and some of whom were purchasers and providers of services, and a group of non-disabled people who were providers and purchasers of services for disabled people. The chairperson of the strategy group was David Ackroyd who was Project Manager (Community Care) for the North West Regional Health Authority and also the Project Leader. Judith Emanuel was the co-ordinator of the project, working for the Regional Health Authority on a freelance basis.

The work on the guidelines started in 1993. It was an initiative which began under the auspices of the then North Western Regional Health Authority which covered the area of Lancashire and Greater Manchester. In April 1994 the Regional Health Authorities were re-organised and the North Western and Mersey Regional Health Authorities merged. The resulting North West Regional Health Authority was the organisation which published the Guidelines and was responsible for monitoring their implementation although any ongoing monitoring or development work has, from April 1996, fallen to the NHS Executive, North West Office.

BACKGROUND TO DEVELOPING THE GUIDELINES

The impetus for developing Guidelines came from national directives. The Department of Health issued Guidance to Health Authorities which identified overall objectives but did not assist purchasers to think about the actions they needed to take to meet them. In 1992 the National Audit Office gave guidance on targets for some services which have been built into planning guidance and corporate contracts. Officers at the Regional Health Authority had noticed, however, that the information returned in corporate contracts indicated that these issues were not being adequately addressed by purchasers. The development of Regional Guidelines was an attempt, therefore, to give purchasers support to address these issues.

The brief given to the consultant was refreshingly unusual. There were few preconceptions about what the Guidelines would eventually look like. The concern was about process so that an important part of the outcome would be as wide an ownership of the Guidelines as possible. From the outset it was recognised that while the Regional Health Authority could put some pressure on purchasers and providers to address the issues, the impact would be substantially increased if the pressures were also coming from other directions. So one of the purposes of the consultation was to develop awareness amongst disabled people about how the purchasing process works in the hope that they would then feel more able to influence it.

The design of the process for developing the Guidelines was influenced by people from disabled people's organisations from the very beginning. The project leader and officers from Greater Manchester Coalition of Disabled People (GMCDP) discussed it prior to the recruitment of the consultant and they were offered the opportunity to tender for the work through their consultancy agency but decided this was inappropriate.

The initial discussions with GMCDP were influential. The project leader initially proposed that the consultation should ask disabled people, their carers, service providers and purchasers about what they thought of services as one group. GMCDP suggested that disabled people should be consulted separately from the other groups and drew attention to the power imbalance between the various interest groups. As a result it was decided that the consultation should be with three separate groups; disabled people as users of services, purchasers of services, and providers of services.

The other major impact that the early discussions with officers and the chairperson of GMCDP had on the design of the project was around our thinking about carers issues in the Guidelines. Over recent years the role of unpaid carers has received considerable public attention. Pressure groups have vigorously campaigned for carers needs to be recognised, social scientists have published research about carers (for example, Finch and Groves, 1983), and government policy has encouraged health and social services departments to consider the needs of carers when providing or purchasing services.

Originally the Guidelines were to address the needs of disabled people and their carers. The GMCDP representatives were very concerned that the needs of disabled people and carers should be considered separately. Our lack of knowledge of the disabled people's movement perspective on carers may reflect the way carers needs have been highlighted by campaigns, research and policy when compared with the absence of publicity given to the independent living movement promoted by disabled people. However, we have become very aware that amongst many academics and professionals there is an absence of awareness or lack of willingness to be aware of this perspective. We think it is, therefore, worthwhile to go through the discussions which we had so that all readers can understand how we reached the decisions which we adopted. (See Morris, 1993, ch. 3.)

We understood from our discussions that the disabled people's movement reject the commonly held view of carers because it is based on people being dependent. They do not consider that independence is based on the tasks people can do but by the degree to which people have control over their own lives. We were told that people in the disabled people's movement think that the high profile of carers can be explained because non-disabled people are more likely to perceive their situation as similar to carers than to disabled people. Furthermore even if the concept of carers was accepted, it neglects the fact that many disabled people are also carers as parents, partners, children and friends.

These ideas were new to us and made a lot of sense. We realised that we had been influenced by a policy agenda which grouped disabled people and carers together and a research agenda which is concerned about the autonomy of a disadvantaged group, carers, who are mostly women. This helped us to recognise the potential conflict of interest between carers and disabled people and that the assumption that they were both users of services for disabled people was patronising towards disabled people. A member of GMCDP likened it to consulting men about women's health services.

At the same time it is well recognised that while the majority of health service care is carried out by unpaid carers these same people have increasingly been acknowledged as having health and social care needs as users or consumers. This emphasis on carers as consumers of care is central to the philosophy of the National Health Service and Community Care Act, 1990.

It became increasingly clear to us that, with the advent of the split between purchasers and providers of services, unpaid carers need to be viewed as providers. This is not to diminish in any way the parallel acknowledgement that carers, like health service staff, have personal needs of their own which also require to be addressed by purchasers. However, as this was not the prime purpose of this project we made the decision to consult the carers as providers.

THE INITIAL CONSULTATION

As the project began under the auspices of the former North Western Regional Health Authority the initial consultation took place in Greater

Manchester and Lancashire with five separate groups. The method of consultation was individually negotiated to ensure that it was most appropriate to the particular circumstances of each group.

- A contract was agreed with GMCDP jointly to organise and run a consultation day with the project co-ordinator. The day was targeted at disabled people from the Greater Manchester area, which included, but not exclusively, GMCDP members.

- West Lancashire Association of Disabled People (WLAD) have a research project looking at the impact of the Community Care Act. They are interviewing a number of disabled people at set time intervals to measure this. It appeared most appropriate to commission a report from WLAD based on the research rather than organise a separate event.

- The project co-ordinator worked with members of Ethnic Disabled Group Emerging (EDGE), a Manchester based black disabled people's group, to develop consultation meetings for members of the group.

- A meeting was held for purchasers which included people from health service commissioning agencies and social services. Attempts to involve GP fundholders were unsuccessful.

- Two meetings of providers were held which included providers from voluntary and statutory agencies, unpaid carers and people from pressure groups. The pressure groups, which included Community Health Councils and voluntary organisations run by non-disabled people, were somewhat anomalous among providers. We were concerned that they should not speak for disabled people but neither were they providers. By running separate workshops within the provider strand we felt we could accommodate them most appropriately within this group.

The model for consultation presented us with the opportunity to target specific questions to the three groups. We wanted to know from disabled people what they saw as their health needs. The purchasers were asked what influenced their decision making. If we understood the forces driving the purchasers we hoped we could link these to the needs identified by disabled people and make it easier for purchasers to act. From providers we wanted to know what made them responsive to purchasers so that we could frame the Guidelines in ways that would make the contracting process effective in influencing change where this was necessary.

Representatives from pressure groups were asked what they could offer disabled people and purchasers in order to get a sense of their potential role. Unpaid carers were asked about their own health needs related to their roles as carers. While the carers welcomed this, having identified carers as providers this was not, in hindsight, the appropriate question to ask them. To be consistent we should have asked them what would have made them responsive to purchasers and providers as by that time it was clear that if carers needs were to be addressed this should be done separately. Although there was a carer on the strategy group, issues from a carers perspective were not further developed after the initial consultation.

At the end of the consultation period we had information: from disabled people's organisations on the needs of disabled people; from purchasers about the driving forces in their decision making; and from providers that might help us to understand how they respond to purchaser's directives. There is insufficient space to give a detailed account here but it is available in the Companion Volume to the Guidelines (NWRHA, 1995b, ch.3).

We were particularly pleased with the consultation process because it did mean that we were only asking disabled people about their needs and we were asking purchasers and providers how best to make the system work to meet people's needs. This seemed to be what consultation should be about but rarely is. Certainly many of the providers and purchasers were surprised at the nature of our questions and had to think a lot about how to answer them.

THE MEMBERSHIP OF THE STRATEGY GROUP

In the initial design of the project it was decided that at least 50% of the membership of the strategy group should be disabled people. This was seen as reaffirming our commitment to the principle that disabled people should have the central role in developing the Guidelines. We were also keen that there should be a fairly even distribution between the number of people involved as purchasers, providers, and disabled people who were users or potential users of services. Care was taken to select members who came from different geographical areas and who represented as wide a range of interests as possible.

Each of the disabled people's organisations involved in the initial consultation was invited to select two people to be members of the strategy group - a responsibility for which they would be paid. Other disabled people involved included a Health Authority member, an officer of a purchasing authority and a member of staff from a provider organisation, the National Centre for Mental Health and Deafness. A comment on the subject of payment to participating disabled people is important. While it is acknowledged that there is a place for voluntary involvement in the health service, a principle behind this project was that the expertise of each participant should be equally valued. Since most members of the group participated as part of their regular (paid) employment, it was essential that disabled people who were not there in a capacity for which they were paid should also have their contribution recognised financially.

Other members of the strategy group included a Chief Executive from a Family Health Service Authority, a GP fundholder, a Consultant Physician in Rehabilitative Medicine, a Carer, a purchaser from Social Services, a Community Care Co-ordinator in a Trust who was also an occupational therapist, a community physiotherapist, and an officer from a voluntary organisation.

One of the issues that emerged early on, not surprisingly, was whether purchasers would be able or willing to find the financial resources necessary to deliver what we recommended. Whilst no assurances could be given it was significant that the strategy group believed that much of what needed to be done had little or no financial implications. There were two main reasons for this. First, it was felt that some resources were currently being wasted on services or equipment that were not what disabled people needed or wanted. Second, it was argued that so much depended on the attitudes of health service staff which, if addressed through training and other in-service means, could make a radical difference to access to services. The need for all members of the strategy group to believe that they could make a difference was critical to what followed.

DEFINITIONS AND TERMINOLOGY

The first task of the strategy group was to attempt to reach a consensus about definitions and terminology. It may not be surprising to readers of this book that this was by far the most contentious and most difficult task of the whole project. We naively assumed that definitions would be agreed at the first meeting. While we were certain from the start that the Guidelines should have a social model perspective we were unprepared for the variety of interpretations of both the medical model and the social model which were presented by a group of 18 people, albeit representing different interests.

The discussions did not include reflections on the relationship between impairment and disability - as explored in Liz Crow's chapter (four) in this volume. This subject did come up, however, when the group were working on a definition of health. The definition agreed was 'health is a state of physical, mental, psychological, and spiritual well-being free from unacceptable (unnecessary) pain or stress' (NWRHA, 1995b, p. 3, expanding on the well-known definition promulgated by the World Health Organisation). For some members of the group, however, it was crucial that the definition of disability related exclusively to social issues. This was understandable given their agenda to secure recognition of the way in which the structure and organisation of the health service disables people who have impairments, an issue that has hardly been addressed.

There were two main starting points. They were the definitions agreed by the British Council of Organisations of Disabled People (BCODP) and those agreed by the World Health Organisation (WHO) and used in the International Classification of Impairments, Disabilities and Handicaps (WHO, 1980). It will be clear from other chapters of this book that there are people who will argue that both of these definitions reflect a social model. Our experience was that the professionals on the strategy group were not as attached to the WHO definition as some of the medical sociologists who have contributed to this book. Conversely, the GMCDP representatives in particular were completely committed to the BCODP definition of disability.

The disability theorists reject the World Health Organisation definition as a social model. They argue that the World Health Organisation definition of the word 'disability' focuses on the individual as being problematic, requiring change to or by the person. In contrast the definition of the word 'disability' which has evolved from the disability movement focuses on society's approach to enabling people to participate in an equal way. Therefore, the decision about definitions was crucial. The Guidelines were to advise purchasers of services for disabled people. The definition would determine what the Guidelines should address. The principle was accepted by the strategy group that the definition should be one that was acceptable to the disabled people in the group.

Terminology was an equally important and contentious issue. The words we use make us think about meaning and the impact of our actions on, and our attitudes to, other people. There were two groups of disabled people on the strategy group who could not agree with each other on terminology. While people from GMCDP preferred to use the term 'impairment - where part of an organ or mechanism of the body is unable to function fully', the profoundly deaf members of the group felt the word 'impairment' has a negative meaning and should be rejected. They preferred to talk in terms of 'difference'. They emphasised cultural and language differences rather than the existence of an impairment. However, 'difference' was unacceptable to the GMCDP members because it was regarded as too general and did not classify the functional range which is the basis on which oppressive societal and individual attitudes are formed. As no consensus could be reached, it was agreed to use the word 'impairment' but to include a statement outlining the deaf member's perspective.

The following definitions were agreed:

> **Impairment:** occurs where part of an organ or mechanism of the body is unable to function fully (while recognising deaf member's preference for the term 'difference'.)
>
> **Disability:** occurs where society is structured or organised in such a way as to prevent or restrict activities being undertaken or potentially being realised because of an impairment.
>
> A **Disabled Person** is someone who has a physical, sensory or mental impairment (or difference) and who is as a result prevented from undertaking a range of activities because of environmental or attitudinal constraints imposed by societies or individuals.
>
> **Access** was defined as referring to a fully accessible society. This included addressing all barriers which could be physical/ structural/ environmental; emotional/ psychological; communication/ information; and financial.

One consequence of adopting these definitions was to confirm that the Guidelines would be addressed to the totality of health provision and not exclusively to that part of the service which is concerned with a person's impairment. The Guidelines also highlighted the needs of disabled people for using health facilities as parents, relatives, or friends of other users, as well as the needs of disabled staff.

Controversy about terminology continued throughout the project both inside and outside the strategy group, including objections from a local MP to some of the terms used during the final consultation.

THE GUIDELINES

Twelve guidelines were identified and each included actions that should be undertaken by purchasers to meet them.

1.   Adopt the definition of disability and impairment.
a)   Adopt this definition as a basis for all purchasing decisions by Health Authorities and GP fundholders.

The members of the strategy group all felt that purchasers in the Region should adopt the definitions that we had identified. The reasons for this varied from the positive, that they were the best consensus that could be reached, to the negative, nobody wanted to go through the lengthy process of agreeing new definitions! However, it has to be acknowledged that the process of arriving at a set of definitions was itself very constructive, if difficult.

2.   Assign lead responsibility for action on purchasing of services for disabled people to a single senior manager.
a)   Assign lead responsibility to a senior manager.
b)   Establish a monitoring group of disabled people whose first task should be to set achievable targets.
c)   Establish arrangements for reviewing and monitoring contracts.
d)   Ensure that details of the targets are written in future purchasing plans and   corporate contracts.
e)   Liaise with GP fundholders to develop a corporate contract.

Although a number of health authorities who commented had some concerns about how this would fit with their organisational structure, we could not come up with a satisfactory alternative which would ensure that responsibility would be clearly allocated. This guideline does however indicate the commitment to involving disabled people in the purchasing process.

3.   Endorse the principle which places the individual disabled person at the centre of service planning.

a)   Approve these principles as a basis for all Purchasing decisions.

b)   Seek agreement with providers to include commitment to the principles in all contracts.

The principles underpinning the guidelines borrow heavily from the 'Living Options' principles (Fieldler and Twitchin, 1992, p.2) and concern choice, consultation, information, participation, recognition and autonomy (see NWRHA, 1995b, p. 11). The principles are significant in informing the philosophy and process underlying the development and delivery of services. It was therefore important to the strategy group that, just as purchasers were expected to use the agreed definitions, so they should work with these principles and use them to improve provider practice through the contracting process.

4.   Involving disabled people from disabled people's groups in influencing strategy and decision making at all levels.

a)   Establish links with local disabled people's groups including black disabled people, disabled women and disabled lesbians and gay men on action that would be relevant to ensure that services are more appropriate to their needs.

b)   Encourage participation in influencing strategy and decision making by publicising the process for involvement e.g. through Local Voices.

c)   Ensure that the practical arrangements for involvement are inclusive in terms of access arrangements, valuing people's time etc.

d)   Jointly with disabled people identify and develop contracts for a minimum   of three services by April 1996.

A number of issues should be addressed by taking these actions. It establishes the heterogeneity of disabled people and that links with different groups within the disabled community need to be established if all the needs are to be identified. It also establishes that disabled people are part of the wider community and should be encouraged to participate in broader consultation initiatives. 'Local Voices' is a strategy for consultation with the whole population of a District (NHS Management Executive, 1992).

The third action concerns making participation practical. A considerable amount has been written about the importance of encouraging consultation and how to do it, both of populations in general (see, for example, Guideline 7) and disabled people in particular (Bewley and Glendinning, 1994; and Lindow and Morris, 1995) but there has been little guidance on how to put the product of consultation into action. The fourth action aims to encourage practical action based on consultation and was inspired by the Greenwich Empowerment Project (Morris, 1994) which involved disabled people in identifying four services for which they would like to recommend service specifications. Disabled people then worked alongside the commissioning agency and the Trust to develop the specifications.

5.   Ensure that all disabled people have the same access to health services as non-disabled people.

a)   Agree a five year programme of audit and inspection of premises and other facilities to identify disabling features.

b)   Negotiate with other organisations to participate in the audits.

c)   Negotiate a programme of action with all the providers and include this in their contract.

Despite the fact that a definition of access had been agreed which included information communication, emotional and psychological access as well as physical access, this guideline was worded to mean access in rather a narrow sense. It is appropriate, however, that the initial guidelines are largely concerned with ensuring that the services provided are what disabled people want and that this guideline is about guaranteeing that they can physically use services. This should cover their own requirements as health service users, as well as in all the many other ways that people need physical access to health services - for example, as workers, visitors and to support friends and family using the services.

6.   Require provision of relevant and appropriate information about services in written and aural formats which are accessible.

a)   Decide what information needs to be made available directly from purchasers and through providers.

b)   Develop information on who is responsible for providing specific services for providers and disabled people.

c)   Agree a strategy for information dissemination which covers sources, formats and content.

This guideline is concerned with a second aspect of access within its broader sense.

7   Contracts should ensure that different professions within the health service and across agencies co-ordinate effectively.

a)   Ensure that *Health of the Nation* (DoH, 1992) initiatives address the needs of disabled people so that they can fully participate if they wish.

b)   Identify priorities with disabled people for areas where appropriate multi-disciplinary arrangements are unsatisfactory and reach agreement with Statutory and Voluntary Agencies about how they can be addressed.

c)   Ensure contracts and/ or service specifications specify the need for multi-disciplinary assessments where appropriate.

d)   Ensure monitoring covers effective co-ordination and working across organisations.

This guideline is written in 'professional speak' but does attempt to address issues which cause great frustration to service users. Whose responsibility is it to provide which service? Do the service providers work co-operatively and in support of the service user or competitively and often with only secondary consideration to what the service user wants?

The processes involved in the actions here continue to encourage the consideration of the needs of disabled people within the context of implementation of policy targeted at the whole population (Health of the Nation, DoH, 1992), as well as policy targeted more particularly at provision for disabled people (Community Care).

8.   Require a programme of staff training to develop awareness and action on disability issues among Purchasers and Providers.

a)   Involve local disabled people who are accountable to organisations of disabled people who will participate in the design and delivery of disability awareness and action training programmes.

b)   Identify specialist courses and elements that should be included in other programmes.

c)   Arrange for all purchaser staff to participate in disability awareness and action training and monitor the identified actions.

d)   Negotiate with providers a programme of awareness and action training to cover all employees, incorporate this in contracts and monitor the identified actions.

e)   Adopt a policy of positive action towards the recruitment of disabled people and negotiate similar arrangements for providers.

This guideline proposes actions to involve the widest range of staff in purchaser and provider organisations. The objective was that disability issues do not become the exclusive concern of people with specific responsibilities but of everyone within the organisation. It clearly states that local disabled people should have a central role in the design and delivery of training and that positive action should involve recruitment throughout the work organisation. Thorough implementation of this guideline could lead to the development and implementation of a large number of action plans throughout all sectors of health service organisations.

9.   Provide appropriate and accessible health services to black and minority ethnic disabled people.

a)   Obtain local information on the types and incidence of relevant diseases and health related needs.

b)   Ensure that training programmes for purchasers and providers include awareness of the needs of black disabled people.

c)   Ensure that counselling and advocacy services which are acceptable and accessible to black and minority ethnic disabled people are available, as well as to deaf people who are culturally deaf.

The representatives from EDGE, the black disabled group who participated in developing the strategy were very clear that they wanted a separate guideline to consider the needs of black disabled people. The group expressed concern that the needs of black people become marginalised when they are combined with the needs of other multiply oppressed groups. The guideline reflects the fact that EDGE has less concern about social and medical models and over-riding concern that whatever is provided for white people is made appropriate for black and disabled people as well. The deaf people involved identify themselves as culturally deaf and therefore part of a minority ethnic group with similar needs to other minority ethnic groups. They were therefore keen to see their needs addressed here.

10.   Ensure that there are effective arrangements to provide appropriate services for people moving from children's to adult services.

a)   Identify, in conjunction with other agencies, those young people reaching the transition period in each year.

b)   Establish a formal review mechanism to assess the ongoing needs of each person with the primary objective of removing as many as possible of the disabling features of health provision.

c)   Negotiate contracts with providers that specifically refer to the needs of young people at the transition period.

Guidelines 10 and 11 are driven primarily by the professional agenda and the agenda of pressure groups run by non-disabled people. The emphasis, however on implementation should be centred around support for young people to take responsibility for themselves and the use of mainstream services.

11.   Assess disabled people's medical need for services in relation to their impairment and determine how appropriate services should be provided to meet these needs.

a)   Negotiate arrangements with relevant providers to ensure a social model of service delivery which includes putting the disabled person at the centre of those services and the planning for them.

b)   Estimate the need for medical services which relate specifically to impairments within the District.

c)   Review provision and the way it is provided in consultation with disabled people and providers. Identify priorities to improve appropriateness of services.

d)   Negotiate with other purchasers where it is apparent that it will not be
      economic to provide the services on a single District basis.
This guideline is particularly significant in terms of what it does and does not
address and how. It is clear that the role of medical services for a person's
impairment should be very specific and clearly delineated and that the
majority of the health needs of disabled people should be met through
mainstream services.

    If the guidelines had been more concerned with function, for example the
way impairment was defined, then it is likely that this would have been one
of the first guidelines and the other guidelines would have concentrated on
medical issues and come from the standpoint of professionals. For example,
the concern about access might have been about rehabilitation and there
would have been greater concentration about the medical needs of particular
groups of disabled people with impairments, for example, the need for
services for people who are brain injured.

**12.   Make arrangements to ensure that the intended outcomes from
the purchasing strategy and the action taken on this Guidance
actually do occur and that they remain relevant to disabled people.**
a)   Use clinical audit structures, protocols, research and development,
      national initiatives and biennial reviews of the purchasers role in
      implementing these Guidelines.
b)   Ensure that the network of disabled people and their organisations
      play an active part in these reviews.
c)   Ensure that all parties are able to engage in a critical appraisal of
      progress and relevance by employing an external facilitator to oversee
      the review.
Again this guideline illustrates the integration of the involvement of disabled
people while using the existing organisational framework.

COMPARISON WITH OTHER STRATEGIES

We were interested to see what differences there were between the
Guidelines published by the NWRHA and elsewhere and to analyse the
factors which might have influenced the differences. Three elements of the
guidelines were analysed; definitions used, membership of the groups who

produced the guidelines, and the issues prioritised. In particular we were interested to see the degree to which the totality of health provision was addressed and whether or how carers needs were taken into account.

Five different documents were analysed. Two were from Regional Health Authorities - South East Thames (1991) and Northern (1993); two were from Joint Planning Groups, St Helens & Knowsley (1995), and Southern Derbyshire (1987); and the other was from the British Society of Rehabilitation Medicine (BSRM, 1993). 'Furthering Abilities', a strategy which was recently produced in St Helens & Knowsley (1995) used the definitions proposed in *Breaking Down Barriers*. All the others used WHO definitions including the British Society of Rehabilitation Medicine (BSRM, 1993) in its 'Advice to Purchasers: Setting NHS Contracts for Rehabilitation Medicine',

Details on who developed the documents vary. Southern Derbyshire Joint Planning Group produced their strategy in 1987. There were 18 members of the group most of whom were from the Health Authority. It also included members from the local authorities and voluntary sector including one person from the Derbyshire Coalition of Disabled People and one person from the Derbyshire Centre for Integrated Living. There are no specific details about the membership of the St Helens and Knowsley Group but it does state there were people from the Health Authority, several local authority departments, the Community Health Council, the Local Medical Committee, service providers and a local Action Group. There are no details at all about who wrote the South East Thames Regional Health Authority Document, but the Northern Region document was written by three public health doctors, a social scientist, an epidemiologist and a Health Needs Assessor. Two consultants wrote the British Society of Rehabilitation Medicine document, one in Rehabilitation Medicine and one in Acute Services Planning.

It would appear that there is a range of people who may be identifying the needs of disabled people. While all the documents are concerned to promote independence of disabled people in principle, most of the guidance produced by the two Regions and the British Society for Rehabilitative Medicine concentrates heavily on provision to 'restore and maintain physical and psychological function' (SETRHA, 1992, p.64). In contrast the documents from Southern Derbyshire and St Helens & Knowsley encompass a very wide variety of issues reflecting their production by a range of agencies.

The key issues identified by the St Helens and Knowsley document are information, transition, access, supporting independence, equality and joint commissioning, both for disabled people themselves and their carers. The South Derbyshire document is valuable because it brings together a very wide range of interests. It includes personal assistance and access issues which are likely to be high on the agenda of disabled people's organisations. It also includes carers needs in the form of respite care and training and the more professionally led needs such as rehabilitation.

Guidelines or strategy documents, provided they receive support from the agencies on behalf of which they are produced, will inevitably be a compromise of the interests of the people who develop them. Disabled people's organisations had a relatively strong influence in the development of *Breaking Down Barriers* compared with the other documents considered here. The disabled people's organisations main priorities were, firstly, to agree a definition of disability which was based on the way society is structured and organised and secondly, to develop Guidelines which would improve the way health services are structured and organised in the interests of disabled people. We believe that it is this emphasis that has led to *Breaking Down Barriers* being a fundamentally different type of strategy document to others that we examined.

CONCLUSIONS

The Guidelines received considerable support notably from both disabled people's organisations and the Department of Health as well as purchasers and provider organisations. David Pilgrim (1996) has provided a useful analysis of where the agendas of social movements and public service commissioners meet in the current political situation. He describes how commissioners need alliances with consumers against the old professional elites. These alliances take the form of user involvement and participation. New social movements, of which the disabled people's movement is one, focus strongly on the role of personal experience and identity which fits relatively easily with this role. He explains that some of the interests of service commissioners and disabled people converge. This would appear to explain why it was possible to develop the Guidelines with the definitions that were agreed and the proposed actions and achieve support from both commissioners and disabled people's organisations. Where there was criticism or concern about where the Guidelines were heading it came, not surprisingly, from some clinicians. The review of guidelines developed elsewhere as well as the way *Breaking Down Barriers* was received indicates that purchasers are open to a wide range of influences in terms of the development of services for disabled people at this time.

There were several points at which the project could have failed to progress. First, it was a much larger project than had been originally envisaged and the extra resources that were required might not have been available. This included the availability of the consultant to carry through the work to its conclusion. This 'largeness' of the project had two dimensions. It was very much more complex than originally envisaged and it took a great deal more chronological time (i.e. from start to finish). Undoubtedly getting a group of professionals together would have made it simpler and shorter. However, it would not have contained, either within the process or the output, anything of the richness we believe emerged from a genuine effort to hear what the recipients of services actually thought and needed. We did not want tokenism but real participation and this proved costly in terms of both time and money. We are convinced, having completed this work, that the real cost of effective participation is usually underestimated by purchasers and providers alike.

A second reason why the project might have failed was because the strategy group made very slow progress for a considerable time. This was partly because of the time it took to agree the definitions and therefore to be able to develop a sense of what the Guidelines would be about, partly because of our reticence to stop consulting about every detail and begin to commit ourselves to paper with draft documents, and partly because of the dynamics of the strategy group. The diversity of the group made all this essential because everyone concerned had to feel secure and to believe that this was a genuine partnership with a commitment to an outcome that had the potential to make changes to practice within the Health Service.

The methodology used for developing the Guidelines enabled the following to happen. A disabled people's organisation, GMCDP, played a key role in identifying that users, providers and purchasers should be consulted in separate groups. This meant the needs could be identified by disabled people and the focus of the consultation with providers and purchasers was how to use contracting to meet those needs. GMCDP's influence also ensured that disabled people were seen as the service users, and carers were seen as providers. The central role of disabled people on the strategy group led to definitions and terminology being agreed which were strongly influenced by their views. This played a key part in ensuring that the issues addressed were predominantly about access in its widest sense to all health services and that the 'divide' explored throughout this book was at least partially bridged in *Breaking Down Barriers*. We believe that, if purchasers and providers enter into real dialogue with local disabled people, the Guidelines can form a foundation on which to build better and more appropriate services in many cases with little or no additional ongoing cost.

REFERENCES

BEWLEY, C. and GLENDINNING, C. (1994) *Involving Disabled People in Community Care Planning*, York: Joseph Rowntree Foundation.

BRITISH SOCIETY OF REHABILITATION MEDICINE (1993) *Setting NHS Contracts for Rehabilitation*, London: BSRM.

DEPARTMENT OF HEALTH (1992) *The Health of the Nation*, London: HMSO.

FIELDER, B. and TWITCHIN, D. (1992) *Achieving User Participation, Planning Services for People with Severe Physical and Sensory Disabilities*, London: Living Options in Practice Project Paper No. 3 Prince of Wales Advisory Group on Disability/Kings Fund Centre.

FINCH, J. and GROVES, D. A. (1983) *Labour of Love: Women, Work and Caring*, London: Routledge, Kegan and Paul.

LINDOW, V. and MORRIS, J. (1995) *Service User Involvement: Synthesis of Findings and Experience in the Field of Community Care*, York: Joseph Rowntree Foundation.

MORRIS, J. (1994) *Greenwich Empowerment Project*, London, *Unpublished*.

MORRIS, J. (1993) *Independent Lives? Community Care and Disabled People*, London: Macmillan.

NHS MANAGEMENT EXECUTIVE (1992) *Local Voices: The views of local people in purchasing for health*, London: Department of Health.

NORTHERN REGIONAL PHYSICAL DISABILITY NEEDS ASSESSMENT GROUP (1993) *Adults with Physical Disability: A Handbook for health needs Assessment*: Newcastle: Northern Regional Health Authority.

NORTH WEST REGIONAL HEALTH AUTHORITY (1995a) *Breaking Down Barriers: Guidelines for Purchasers of Services for Disabled Adults aged 16-64 with Physical and Sensory Impairments*, Manchester: NWRHA.

NORTH WEST REGIONAL HEALTH AUTHORITY (1995b) *Breaking Down Barriers: Companion Volume*, Manchester: NWRHA.

PILGRIM, D. (1996) *Accounting for Disability: Customer Feedback or Citizen Complaints?* (In Press).

SOUTH EAST THAMES REGIONAL HEALTH AUTHORITY (1991) *Draft Guidance - Commissioning Services for Adults with Physical Disability*, London: SETRHA.

SOUTHERN DERBYSHIRE JOINT PLANNING GROUP FOR YOUNGER DISABLED PEOPLE (1987) *The Right To Be Able - A Strategy For Services For Younger Disabled People*, Derby: Disabled People.

ST. HELENS AND KNOWSLEY HEALTH (1995) *Furthering Abilities - A strategy for services for Younger Physically Disabled People*, St.Helens: St Helens and Knowsley Health Authority.

CHAPTER 11

Representing Disability: some questions of phenomenology and politics

Gareth Williams

INTRODUCTION

The business of writing about disability has become a hotly contested terrain in recent years. Parallel discourses have developed with scarcely any cross-fertilisation of ideas. There are many reasons for this absence of dialogue. There are long-standing differences in the terms people use for describing disability. Indeed, language of disability itself has become the object of political analysis and dispute, and it is increasingly difficult to use terms to describe chronic illness and disability innocently (Zola, 1993).

There is, therefore, no neutral language with which to begin the process of discussing chronic illness and disability, and language itself is central to any discussion of how we approach the problem of dealing with 'disability'. In short, disability is fundamentally a problem of 'representation'. It is a problem of representation in the sense that there is no language to talk about it that is untainted. It is a problem of representation in that the language and categories we use influence both the definition of the problem and the size of the problem as an epidemiological phenomenon. And it is a problem of representation in the sense that there is continuing dispute about who are the legitimate representatives of the experience and reality of disability in the modern world.

At the heart of the dispute over representation lies the question of how one construes the relationship between the experience of 'impairment' and the 'environment' that constitutes the reality of the experience of chronic illness and disability. The relationship between the environment and impairment is a core issue in much of the work that has been undertaken in disability theory, sociology, and rehabilitation. However, the nature and direction of the relationship has been approached very differently within these fields. Within rehabilitation, the environment has been defined for the most part as a physical phenomenon, a set of discrete obstacles or barriers, which add to and amplify the problems of impairment afflicting individuals. Within disability theory, the environment is regarded as the expression of power, a universe of discrimination and oppression within which disability is created. The sociological study of chronic illness and disability has tended to define the environment as something arising out of the symbolic and social interaction that takes place between individuals and their worlds as they negotiate their everyday lives.

These varying conceptualisations of the relationship between disability and the environment lie at the heart of the disputes that have arisen between people working in these different fields. Focusing too much on the impairments is seen to deflect attention from the systematic way in which the environment excludes people from participation in civil society. Placing too much emphasis on the politics of exclusion may be regarded as a way of underplaying the real effects of different impairments and the complex, 'negotiated' aspects of everyday life, thereby creating a spurious homogeneity. Focusing on interaction and the negotiation of identity can lead the investigator to be sucked into a bottomless pit of phenomenological analysis where the structures which underpin or destroy identity are lost from sight. As well as reflecting the organisation of different interests in the disability field, these varying approaches also reflect diverse perspectives on the nature of social science and the relationship between social science and political action.

The dilemmas posed by these different definitions of the situation have been spiced by the current ferment in the movement for the civil rights of disabled people. For those who are on the front line of the political battle currently taking place, the niceties of sociological analysis may seem an undesirable luxury or an irritating irrelevance. However, using the work of the American sociologist and disability activist Irving Zola as an example, I will argue that it is possible to be politically committed without being sociologically one-dimensional and that a multidimensional understanding of 'the environment' is required if ways are to be found of making civil society less oppressive and more homely.

IMPAIRMENT AND REHABILITATION

The medical model that informs traditional approaches to disability takes the biological reality of impairment as its fundamental starting point. The focus of the analysis and the intervention is on the functional limitations which an individual 'has' and the effect of these on activities of daily living. Although rehabilitation practitioners may make reference to the way in which disability affects the 'whole person' or 'all aspects of an individuals life', the nature of this wider context is rarely built systematically into analysis or recommendations for intervention (Gloag, 1985; College Committee on Disability, 1986). There is a recognition of the crucial role of 'the environment', but little if any attempt to develop a phenomenological or political analysis of the constitution of the forces which make up the environment for the individual or groups of people who 'have' the impairment or 'live with' the disability. The environment is something added, almost as an afterthought, to the basic project of dealing with the impairment.

From the early 1970s onwards, those professionally engaged in the rehabilitation world recognised the need to move away from the highly reductive conceptions of functional limitations focusing on deficits in limbs and organs which had traditionally characterised physical medicine and physical therapy. This new 'holism' was enshrined in official reports, with the promulgation of broader definitions of rehabilitation as 'the restoration of patients to their fullest physical, mental, and social capability' (Mair, 1972; Tunbridge, 1972).

Increasingly, broader definitions of health status in patients with chronic illness and disability were used for two main reasons (Williams, 1987). First, to assess needs for treatment, therapy, services, or benefits; and secondly, to provide a baseline from which to perform more realistic evaluations of change in the health and functional status of patient, both informally and as part of research. The focus of these evaluations was still very much on the individual, but with a recognition that it was the person who could or could not perform certain kinds of activities rather than the organ, the limb, or the body conceived abstractly as a bundle of capacities and incapacities.

The most common type of descriptor consists of assessments of performances in daily living stressing those activities which are purportedly carried out habitually and universally (Williams, 1987). There is no doubt that measuring directly a range of daily activities is an improvement on the conventional clinical measures of 'functional capacity'. However, the fact that they are deemed to be universal rather than context-bound implies that they can be used across multiple settings without any substantial reconsideration of their validity, and without consideration being given to the meaning of the items for the person with the impairment. The Barthel Index, for example, asks only whether a person can walk 50 yards on level ground regardless of whether he or she wants to, needs to, or has anywhere to go (Granger et al., 1979).

In other words, such traditional assessments provide a picture of 'activities of daily living' devoid of any phenomenological grasp of the individual's own experience and any political analysis of the structures and contexts within which the activity takes place. In line with the positivistic underpinnings of medical science the emphasis of traditional assessments is on some universal definition and measure that can be applied by appropriately qualified people without reference to the disabled person's own perspective, the roles they occupy, the relationships in which they are embedded, the circumstances of their milieux, or the wider political context of barriers, attitudes, and power.

In research on rehabilitation within this perspective, the environment and the experience of the individual may exacerbate the consequences of impairment, but the focus remains very much on the impairment:

'Lower-limb amputation represents a formidable handicap whatever its cause. The young man who loses a leg following a road traffic accident becomes impaired at a time when occupational and financial responsibilities may be heavy....The social problems experienced by the disabled are generally slow to resolve, and current health and social services policies fail to recognise these difficulties (Thompson and Haran, 1983, p. 165).

Both medical sociology and disability studies have in different ways attempted to develop a critique of such traditional models of the relationships between disability and the environment, in the context of the experience of individuals in relation to their milieux and the wider structures. In that sense they are both a critique of positivism, but they vary in the emphasis which they give to subjectivity and structures.

SYMPTOMS AND SITUATIONS

'The numbness in my hand is getting very trying...The Baby puts the lid on it all. Can't you see the sordid picture? I can and it haunts me. To be paralysed with a wife and child and no money - ugh!' (Barbellion, 1984, p. 253).

Sociological research on chronic illness and disability has focused on the meaning of illness in its context. The depth of the exploration of meaning varies depending partly on the extent to which the analysis focuses on one or other of two senses of meaning identified by Bury (1991). Bury argues that the meaning of an illness can be defined in terms of its 'consequences', which refers to the impact it has on practical aspects of the person's roles and relationships in everyday life; or in terms of its 'significance', which relates to the cultural connotations, the symbols and significations, surrounding different sorts of illness and disability.

Both these forms of analysis of the meaning of chronic illness and disability have the notion of embodied experience at their centre, but rather than attempting to define functional incapacity or activity restriction in biomedical terms, they explore the ramifications of the experience from the point of view of the person affected. In other words, while the biomedical model has disease or dysfunction at the centre of its picture, the sociological perspective focuses on illness as something whose meaning and reality vary depending on the biography of a particular individual and the circumstances in which they find themselves.

W.N.P.Barbellion, the pseudonymous nineteenth century diarist (who the 'experts' believe had what would nowadays be diagnosed as multiple sclerosis), illustrates very nicely how important both senses of meaning are in understanding the experience of chronic illness, and how they interact. The numbness in his hand is upsetting for him because of what it might signify about him; and what it might signify about him is dependent upon his circumstances - a new father with financial responsibilities in the context of British society prior to the development of a health service and a welfare state. Taken together these represent a 'sordid picture' in his own mind. Regardless of the fact that his symptoms at the time he was writing were limited in the sense that he was not restricted in most activities of daily living, from his point of view and situation the symptoms were highly significant and consequential.

The attempt to understand the meaning of experience by looking at it in its context lies at the heart of the medical sociological project. The focus on chronic illness and the experience of disability associated with it can be seen as an attempt to move away from the rehabilitation models which were rather static, in addition to their being reductive and focused on the mechanics of functional limitations and activity restriction. While the experience of 'adaptation' to a limb amputation or some other trauma-induced impairment clearly has its own dynamics, influenced by personal, situational and treatment factors, chronic illness adds a new dimension of enormous variability and unpredictability (Bury, 1982; Strauss and Glaser, 1984). Moreover, the experience of different chronic illnesses is - to tempt tautology - clearly a very different experience. While disability might have certain common features, sociologists have been interested in both subjective variation in responses to the 'same' illness and impairment and variation in the meaning (in the second of Bury's senses) of different kinds of symptoms in society. Explorations of breathlessness, raging skin, inflamed joints, heart problems, end-stage renal failure and many others have allowed sociologists and anthropologists to explore the seemingly infinite permutations of the experience of being physically different in a highly normalising society (Anderson and Bury, 1988; Strauss and Glaser, 1984).

Some of these sociological analyses are phenomenologically 'deep' or 'thick', others are more inclined to skate over the surfaces of meaning, but nevertheless deal with the interaction between symptoms and situations.

The hallmarks of this kind of work are, therefore, its focus on the symbolic and material interaction between the individual and society, and the interpretative processes whereby individuals construct meaning from their experiences. The environment focused upon is that which emerges in the meaning-giving processes of interaction between the individual, their milieux, and the wider society. It therefore follows from this that disability (or 'handicap') in the World Health Organisation's (1980) sense is the product of complex processes of interaction between an individual with an impairment and the discriminating, disadvantaging, stigmatising and prejudiced wider society. It is neither 'in' the individual nor 'outside' the individual 'in' society:

> 'The extent to which functional limitations and activity restrictions constitute a problem, or are otherwise handicapping, is not only variable historically and culturally but is also somewhat dependent upon more immediate contexts; their meaning is not the same across different social and environmental settings' (Locker, 1983, p.5).

The point for Locker, therefore, is that 'disability' or 'handicap' as a social reality of people's experiences is caused by neither the externalities of the environment, nor by any 'facts' of biological trauma or deterioration. This kind of analysis is primarily concerned with meaning as consequences rather than meaning as significance, though it may - as Locker does - explore at some level the 'significance' of symptoms to individuals in terms of some notion of 'felt stigma' (Scambler, 1989).

With this shift in focus from the individual with an impairment to the meaning-giving nature of interaction there comes a shift in the nature of the intervention that may be appropriate. If the problem is not the need of the individual to adapt to the impairment, but rather the complex process of negotiating the interactions out of which daily life is created, then the role of professional experts as people who do things to the impaired body is clearly limited. Much more important may be a supportive milieux of lay people who can help the individual renegotiate their place in the world (Williams and Wood, 1988).

The notion of re-establishing a place in the world is at the heart of some of the more phenomenologically deep analyses of the meaning of chronic illness and disability. These too may concentrate on the interactions within the mundane world, but there is a sense in which the purpose of these interactions can be interpreted as having rather more transmundane qualities. Such analyses lead us away from the empirical features of the impaired individual's interaction with the material world back into the individual's 'self' and 'body'. The focus of the problems shifts from interactionism to the exploration of the lived body, the body incarnate, drawing its theoretical inspiration less from symbolic interactionism and more from philosophical phenomenology.

In some of the work of Charmaz for example, she talks of the process of 'immersion in illness' which 'means experiencing the vulnerability of one's body' (Charmaz, 1991, p. 80). The process of living with chronic illness becomes so highly personalised that it leads us further and further away from any sense of the society in which the anguish of experience is embedded; and, as a consequence, the processes through which the response to chronic illness and disability emerge become less and less social and collective and more and more rooted in the psychological, cognitive and existential world of the individual. There is less exploration of the interaction between the person and the 'environment' in the presence of the disruptive effects of chronic illness, and more searching the constitution of the self in the presence of a disordered body.

Some of the most powerful phenomenological analyses come from individuals, usually middle class and often academics or writers themselves, who have tried to explore autobiographically the depths of their own experiences of cancer, neurological disease, heart attack or whatever else (Murphy 1987; Frank 1991). The best of this work gives pre-eminence to the ill person's perspective, emphasising the 'illness' (the social experience) above the 'disease' (the physiological processes). However, the aim within this project to attempt '...to consider illness stories as embodied also deconstructs the distinction: the illness experience is an experience in and of a diseased body' (Frank 1995, p. 187).

In much of this work the storied or narrative nature of illness and disability is emphasised. The exploration of the experience of illness becomes a vehicle for exploring basic questions about the nature of the self in the world, the fundamental meaning structures in a person's life. The concept of a narrative is a powerful framework for analysing the experience of chronic illness for a number of reasons: it provides a vehicle for exploring the temporal nature of illness; it describes a life as both a sequence of events and as unified around some purpose or purposes; and it moves back and forth between the subjective experience and the world in which the experience is lived out. If the chronic illness and disability can be seen as experiences which disrupt 'biography', making problematic the relationship between the individual and the environment, it makes sense to regard the experience of having a chronic illness or disability as part of a process of 'narrative reconstruction' (Williams, 1984).

There are now too many examinations of narratives of chronic illness and disability to do justice to the range and complexity of such work here. It is a body of work which has many origins. It is partly to do with a growing interest in narratives, across a range of disciplines and beyond the specific issues of illness and disability (MacIntyre, 1981; Ricoeur, 1991). It is also a form of discourse about illness which has been given a high public profile by the history of HIV and AIDS where the intersections of personal identity and the history of a societal response to disease, disability and death have, of course, been particularly sharply defined. While some of this work emphasises the materiality and the historicity of such narratives - the political economy of illness (Radley, 1993) - other research engages more and more deeply with the subjectivity of the experience - the negotiation and renegotiation of identity through talk, the rediscovery of self in the chaos of illness and so on (Sacks 1985). Some have explored with great skill and empathy the different kinds of narratives which can be constructed about the experience of chronic - often terminal - illnesses (Frank, 1995; Mathieson and Stam, 1995).

In the end, however, the danger in much of this work is that it loses sight altogether of the structures which make the experience take the shape it does. History and even biography are dissolved in ever deeper phenomenological penetration into the interstices of self and world. What started out as a sociological analysis becomes part of a quasi-religious or spiritual quest for the truth which illness is supposed to reveal. So profound is the truth of illness that even the person experiencing the illness is merely a vehicle for allowing the body to speak of its suffering. This is truly the body incarnate:

> 'The body is not mute, but it is inarticulate; it does not use speech yet begets it. The speech that the body begets includes illness stories; the problem of hearing these stories is to hear the body/ speaking in them' (Frank, 1995, p. 27).

While Christian theology and the learning of other world religions certainly provide rich languages for exploring questions of ultimate concern: life and death, suffering, guilt and redemption, they can also - if we are not very careful - reduce the individual to a body, and limit the experience of illness and disability as a personal quest for meaning and truth. The politics and history of illness and disability become marginalised. The realities of health and social care become forgotten. All that is left is the individual engaged in some abstract process of overcoming bodily 'failure' and 'coming back' to normality:

> 'Coming back is the process of returning to a satisfactory way of life, within the physical/ mental limitations imposed by a disabling condition .... To come back is a very personal experience. Although others can provide assistance, only the individual can come back' (Corbin and Strauss 1991, pp. 138-139).

While it is certainly not the intention of this sociological analysis to produce a prescription for what is to be done that denudes the situation of its politics and material basis, it does show how difficult it is to explore the experiences of individuals while remaining alive to the politics of the situation.

THE POLITICS OF DISABILITY

Against this background, it is not surprising that those working from within the movement for the rights of disabled people should want to distance themselves from sociological contributions to the study of chronic illness. It is not my intention to review the work of disability theorists and activists in any detail (they are well represented in this volume and can speak for themselves). Let me just provide enough of a commentary on their work to provide a clear counterpoint with what has gone before.

I have tried to show how sociologists have responded to the limitations of traditional rehabilitation perspectives on chronic illness and disability. They have done this by emphasising the need to move away from professional definitions of impairment and disability in order to explore the ways in which people with chronic illness and disability defined the relationship between their symptoms and situations. Using various forms of qualitative method they have attempted to reconstruct from people's own accounts of their experiences the reality of chronic illness and disability as something which emerges out of the relationship between the person and the environment.

The World Health Organisation's Classification (1980) illustrates at a conceptual level what most of these studies attempt to accomplish at an empirical level. The concept of 'handicap' is used to describe a reality which is relational or interactional, and most of the studies of chronic illness and disability within sociology echo that conceptualisation.

However, I have also indicated how the relational can at times slip into a phenomenological analysis in which the individual or even the body returns to the centre of attention, albeit constructed in a discourse somewhat different from that employed within rehabilitation medicine. While explorations of the lived body can illuminate experiences of extreme situations, once detached from the political economy and history of disability and its relationship to State and society, they can become an unhelpful form of self-analysis. The consequence of this is that what began as an attempt to see chronic illness and disability as the product of the complex relationships between individuals, milieux and social structures becomes a picture in which the illness is portrayed as something which causes certain social consequences.

This is in stark contrast to the work of many disability theorists in Britain and elsewhere for whom the prime mover in causal terms is most certainly not the illness, nor the individual in a state of tragic adaptive 'failure', but the oppressive society in which disabled people live. If disability is seen as a personal tragedy, disabled people are treated as the victims of circumstance. If disability is defined as social oppression, disabled people can be seen as the collective victims of an uncaring, discriminatory society (Oliver, 1990). This fundamental position is that which underpins most of the writing by disability theorists in Britain. It is a line which leads to a very different picture of, for example, the nature of dependency. Let me contrast two quotations in order to give a flavour of the difference between some medical sociology and the work of disability theorists:

> 'Certainly physical dependency, if not also social and economic dependency, can result from illness' (Charmaz, 1991, p.80).

> 'Dependency is created amongst disabled people, not because of the effects of functional limitations on their capacities for self-care, but because their lives are shaped by a variety of economic, political and social forces which produce it' (Oliver, 1990, p. 94).

The problem to be overcome is not anything within the individual's body, mind or soul. There is no personal road to redemption and salvation. It is, as

I indicated in looking at the work of sociologists like David Locker, to do with the resources in society. However, in this case, the relationship between the individual and society is much more clearly stated: disability and dependency are caused by society. On this analysis '...hostile environments and disabling barriers - institutional discrimination' are seen as the 'primary cause of the problem' (Barnes, 1992, p. 20). Proponents of this 'social model' of disability argue that disability is caused by society, and if you change society you can eliminate disability.

The causal relation is reversed and, as a consequence, the traditional models and practices of those engaged in rehabilitation come to be seen as part of the problem. If the dominant ideology of the medical model informing rehabilitation defines the focus as what has happened to an individual and what can be done 'for the patient', attention is distracted from the primary structural causes; and the medical profession and those working alongside them become key figures in the perpetuation of oppression. Sociologists who concede any primary role to the bodily disorder or impairment are seen to be participating in an oppressive ideological practice, and the WHO classification which (as far as I can judge) was put forward to socialise and collectivise our understanding of 'disablement' becomes transformed into an extension of the medical model. Sociological analysis of what disability is like, from the point of view of someone with an impairment or disability - the phenomenological or interactionist exploration of the construction of reality - becomes another ideological justification for the oppression of disabled people.

My arguments against this position are well known (Williams, 1983; 1988; 1991). It seems to me that the oppressive quality of everyday life for many disabled people is without question, and the origins of much of this oppression lie in the hostile environments and disabling barriers which society (politicians, architects, social workers, doctors and others) erect. However, the processes whereby discrimination takes place are often extraordinarily subtle, for three reasons. First, most disability in modern societies emerges from chronic illness, and illness, unlike ethnicity or gender, emerges slowly over time. Secondly, someone who is able-bodied is only temporarily so. Disability is therefore a category theoretically open to everyone, and as populations age, one that becomes a more likely end-point for any given individual. Thirdly, disability is, at some level, undeniably to do with the pain or discomfort of bodies, and this is a dimension of the oppressive quality of chronic illness and disability for large numbers of people. While civil rights movements are therefore a powerful response to some aspects of the oppression of disability, they are not the whole story.

In the final section I examine briefly the work of one of the very few social scientists, also an activist, who managed to retain a phenomenological and interactionist analysis of disability within a collectivist framework.

REPRESENTING DISABILITY

Irving Zola was one of the key participants in the self-help and disability rights movements in the USA. He was also a medical sociologist who had written extensively on the relationship between culture and illness and the nature of medical power. Zola had experienced polio as a young child and a serious road traffic accident in his teens. These experiences had made him aware of his body, the extent to which he was treated differently, and the roles and activities of professional experts. Although Zola had a long-standing involvement in politics and had written penetratingly about the dangers of medical power (1972), he did not apply these twin concerns to his own experience of disability and the reality of life for disabled people until he was well into his career. These experiences have been written about by Zola with considerable autobiographical insight (Zola, 1982; 1983), and much of his writing was a blend of the personal and the political:

> 'What I have produced might well be called a socio-autobiography, a personal and social odyssey that chronicles not only my beginning acknowledgement of the impact of my physical differences on my life but also my growing awareness of the ways in which society invalidates people with a chronic disability' (Zola, 1982, pp. 6-7).

Zola was concerned to represent the interests of people with disabilities, and to explore new ways in which those interests could be represented. He preferred to talk about 'people with disabilities', putting people first, but he emphasised that in choosing certain terms he was '...not arguing for any "politically correct" usage but rather examining the political advantages and disadvantages of each' (Zola, 1993, p. 171) and, in Zola's view there was no single, unequivocal authentic voice of disabled people (Zola, 1988a), nor is there any set of definitions of the universe of disability which can or should be adopted as some kind of secular gospel.

Zola's writing on disability has a number of different aspects. His early work drew on his own personal experiences and his involvement in the self-help movement in order to develop a critique of the rehabilitation system and its models of adjustment and adaptation. Along with many other activists Zola was concerned with two interrelated problems: first, that the rehabilitation process was not producing the kind of 'adjustments' that actually enable disabled people to live independently in society. Secondly, that even with good rehabilitation, the determinants of independence for disabled people were more to do with the organisation of the physical and social environment than with any professionally managed adaptation process.

During the early 1980s, Zola recognised that while his politics had to be unwavering in the articulation of demands for independence and an end to discrimination, there was more to a sociological analysis of disabled people's oppression than an empirical identification of environmental barriers conjoined with a conspiracy theory regarding the interests of professionals engaged in rehabilitation. In line with many other activists in both Britain and the USA, Zola recognised the undermining power of the dominant ideology of disability which regarded 'it' - that is the thing from which the individual 'suffers' - as a personal tragedy. However, in contrast to much of the work in this field, Zola recognised that the oppression experienced by people with disabilities was a complex matter. Contrasting disability with race, for example, he argued that:

> '..the social invisibility of people with a disability develops more insidiously. Children spontaneously express an interest in wheelchairs and leg braces, but as they grow older they are taught that "...it's not nice to ask such things"....But why all this effort? Why this distancing of the chronically ill and handicapped? Why are we so threatening that we must be made socially invisible?' (Zola, 1982, p. 200).

The threat to be removed, Zola suggests, lies not just in society's failure but in the inevitability of one's own:

> 'When the "able-bodied" confront the "disabled", they often think with a shudder, "I'm glad it's not me"... The threat to be dispelled is the inevitability of one's own failure. The discomfort that many feel in the presence of the aged, the suffering, and the dying is the reality that it could just as well be them' (Zola, 1982, p. 202).

In some of his later work, in particular, he discussed the enormous implications of ageing societies peppered with chronic illnesses for the development of the disability movement (Zola, 1988b), pointing out that the processes of ageing were something that linked the interests of 'the able-bodied' to those of 'the disabled'. However imperative it may be politically to define people with disabilities as a minority group, it is a curious minority which will include us all if not today, then tomorrow, or the day after, and that:

> '....only when we acknowledge the near universality of disability and that all its dimensions (including the biomedical) are part of the social process by which the meanings of disability are negotiated, will it be possible fully to appreciate how general public policy can affect this issue' (Zola, 1989, p. 420).

It was Zola's '...conviction that it is impossible to create a society without disease and disability' (Zola, 1988b, p. 380). There is no all-encompassing master-slave narrative, there is no simple schema - Marxist, Freudian, or Foucauldian - which will illuminate the matrix of power and knowledge within which disability exists, and there will be no simple revolutionary change in medicine or in politics which will deliver liberation. The oppression is not easy to see or articulate, and people speak in different voices:

> 'If one has been oppressed for thousands of years, one does not gain a voice overnight. One of the features of oppression is the loss not only of voice but of the tools to find it...It will take us time to speak out, to learn what we have lost, to articulate what we need. But as I have tried to state here and elsewhere, the numbers trying to speak out are ever growing and the chorus of voices is increasingly diverse' (Zola, 1994, p. 65).

In place of the monochrome languages of the 'medical model' on the one hand and the 'social model' on the other, we find in Zola a willingness to examine disability from many points of view, and a desire to understand the contribution the different voices have to make to our discussions about disability. In the context of an occasionally intolerant debate over the correct language to use in talking about disability, Zola's work was a bold attempt to hold firm to the politics of disability while remaining free to explore its darker phenomenological waters. He wanted to place at the forefront of any discussion of disability the bleak realities of economic deprivation, disenfranchisement, and marginalisation, while insisting on the continuing need to find a place for research in clinical rehabilitation and an interpretative social psychology of the personal worlds of people with disability and chronic illness. Zola believed, in short, that you could not deal politically with disability without confronting it personally. He was committed to a civil rights perspective on disability, but he recognised that an understanding of disability also required an anthropology of the body and the emotions.

What marked Zola out was his willingness to be pluralistic without losing sight of the need for taking a position on issues of moral and political importance. He recognised that neither the life of a disabled individual nor the history of disabled people could be understood without understanding both. Neither medical sociology nor disability theory were of any use unless they made connections with the world of policy and politics on the one hand and the realm of personal experiences and narratives on the other. The 'voice' which was so important to Zola within the disability movement, was the voice which told a story that connected with other peoples stories, providing the foundation for a collective identity, a common agenda, and a shared strategy for social change.

CONCLUSION

In this paper I have described some of the complex issues to be addressed in writing about or representing disability as a social phenomenon. Like other areas of social and political analysis, there is a tendency to veer towards either an 'undersocialised' or an 'oversocialised' conception of human life. Moreover, these conceptualisations are not neutral. They reflect fundamental interests, and one cannot pretend that these interests do not have implications for the way in which people are likely to be treated on the basis of them. It seems to me that the medical model is reductive. It is rooted in biology and it serves the interests of the medical profession and those professions and other economic and political groups allied to it. It is an intellectually and politically limited model for responding to the problems covered by the term 'disability' in the modern world.

It is limited for two reasons. First, it neglects the subjective experience of illness and impairment and reduces it to a set of discrete problems requiring technical interventions. In this sense the clinical approach to rehabilitation is dehumanising. Secondly, it deflects attention from many of the material and social bases of the difficulties people experience. In these terms it depoliticises disability. For this reason, the critiques of both medical sociologists and disability theorists are important. However, they too have their pitfalls. I have shown that the work of many sociologists starts off by viewing the experience of chronic illness and disablement in its context of social and economic circumstances, but gets side-tracked into increasingly solipsistic explorations of identity and self. With regard to disability theory, many of those writing from the perspective of the 'social model' seem so concerned to retain a tough political line on social oppression, that they are unable to accommodate the subtleties of social experiences of chronic illness.

In the struggle for equality in an unequal world simple positions need to be taken. However, we should not allow the strategic imperatives of disability politics to deflect our attention from the many needs experienced by people with chronic illnesses and the multiple perspectives they bring to bear on their situations. These perspectives reflect differences in bodies, interpretations and the degree of social exclusion and disadvantage people experience. In the harsh and uncertain welfare world of the late twentieth century we need to go beyond the fragmentation of post-modern political radicalism and forge new alliances across bodies, experiences and socio-economic structures.

REFERENCES

ANDERSON, R. and BURY, M. (1988) *Living with Chronic Illness: the Experience of Patients and their Families,* London: Unwin Hyman.

BARBELLION, W. N. P. (1984) *Journal of a Disappointed Man and a Last Diary,* London: The Hogarth Press.

BARNES, C. (1992) 'Institutional discrimination against disabled people and the campaign for anti-discrimination legislation', *Critical Social Policy*, 34, 20, 5-22.

BURY, M. (1982) 'Chronic illness as biographical disruption`, *Sociology of Health and Illness*, 4, 167-182

BURY, M. (1991) 'The sociology of chronic illness: a review of research and prospects', *Sociology of Health and Illness*, 13, 451-468.

CHARMAZ, K. (1991) *Good Days, Bad Days: the Self in Chronic Illness and Time*, Berkeley: University of California Press.

COLLEGE COMMITTEE ON DISABILITY (1986) 'Physical disability in 1986 and beyond: a report of the Royal College of Physicians', *Journal of the Royal College of Physicians*, 20, 160 194.

CORBIN, J. and STRAUSS, A. (1991) 'Comeback: the process of overcoming disability' in: G. Albrecht and J. Levy (eds.) *Advances in Medical Sociology (vol. 2)*, Connecticut: JAI Press.

FRANK, A. W. (1991) *At the Will of the Body: Reflections on Illness*, Boston: Houghton Mifflin.

FRANK, A. W. (1995) *The Wounded Storyteller: Body, Illness, and Ethics*, London: The University of Chicago Press.

GLOAG, D. (1985) 'Severe disability - tasks of rehabilitation', *British Medical Journal*, 290, 301-303.

GRANGER C.V., ALBRECHT G. L. and HAMILTON B. B. (1979) 'Outcome of comprehensive medical rehabilitation: measurement by PULSES profile and the Barthel Index', *Archives of Physical Medicine and Rehabilitation*, 60, 145-154.

LOCKER, D. (1983) *Disability and Disadvantage: the Consequences of Chronic Illness*, London: Tavistock.

MACINTYRE, A. (1981) *After Virtue: a Study in Moral Theory*, London: Duckworth.

MAIR, A. (1972) *Medical Rehabilitation: the Pattern for the Future. Report on the subcommittee of the standing medical advisory committee, Scottish Health Services Council on Rehabilitation*, Edinburgh: HMSO.

MATHIESON, C. M. and STAM, H. J. (1995) 'Renegotiating identity: cancer narratives', *Sociology of Health and Illness*, 17, 283-306.

MURPHY, R. F. (1987) *The Body Silent*, New York: Henry Holt.

OLIVER, M. (1990) *The Politics of Disablement*, London: Macmillan.

RADLEY, A. (1993) *Worlds of Illness: Biographical and Cultural Perspectives on Health and Disease*, London: Routledge.

RICOEUR, P. (1991) 'Life in quest of narrative' in: D. WOOD (ed.) *On Paul Ricoeur: Narrative and Interpretation*, London: Routledge.

SACKS, O. (1985) *The Man who Mistook his Wife for a Hat*, London: Duckworth.

SCAMBLER, G. (1989) *Epilepsy*, London: Routledge.

STRAUSS, A. and GLASER, B. (1984) *Chronic illness and the Quality of Life* (second edition), St. Louis: Mosby.

THOMPSON, D. and HARAN, D. (1983) 'Living with an amputation: the patient, International Rehabilitation Medicine', 5, 165-169.

TUNBRIDGE, R. (1972) *Rehabilitation. Report of a subcommittee of the standing medical advisory committee*, Department of Health and Social Security, London: HMSO.

WILLIAMS, G. (1983) 'The movement for independent living: an evaluation and critique', *Social Science and Medicine*, 17, 15, 1003-1010.

WILLIAMS, G. (1984) 'The genesis of chronic illness: narrative reconstruction', *Sociology of Health and Illness*, 6, 175-200.

WILLIAMS, G. (1987) 'Disablement and the social context of daily activity', *International Disability Studies*, 9, 97-102.

WILLIAMS, G. (1988) 'Independent living: rolling back the frontiers of the state?', *Disability Studies Quarterly*, 8, 50-54.

WILLIAMS, G. (1991) 'Disablement and the ideological crisis in health care', *Social Science and Medicine*, 32, 4, 517-24.

WILLIAMS, G. and WOOD, P. (1988) 'Coming to terms with chronic illness: the negotiation of autonomy in rheumatoid arthritis', *International Disability Studies*, 10, 128-132.

WORLD HEALTH ORGANISATION (1980) *International Classification of Impairments, Disabilities and Handicaps*, Geneva: WHO.

ZOLA, I. K. (1972) 'Medicine as an institution of social control', *Sociological Review*, 20, 487-504.

ZOLA, I. K. (1982) *Missing Pieces: a Chronicle of Living with a Disability*, Philadelphia: Temple University Press.

ZOLA, I. K. (1983) *Socio-medical Inquiries: Recollections, Reflections and Reconsiderations*, Philadelphia: Temple University Press.

ZOLA, I. K. (1988a) 'Whose voice is this anyway? A commentary on recent recollections about the experience of disability', *Medical Humanities Review*, 2, 6-15.

ZOLA, I. K. (1988b) 'Ageing and disability: toward a unifying agenda', *Educational Gerontology*, 14, 365-387.

ZOLA, I. K. (1989) 'Toward the necessary universalizing of disability policy', *The Milbank Memorial Fund Quarterly*, 67, Supplement 2, 401-428.

ZOLA, I. K. (1993) 'Self, identity and the naming question: reflections on the language of disability', *Social Science and Medicine*, 36, 167-173.

ZOLA, I. K. (1994) 'Towards inclusion: the role of people with disabilities in policy and research in the United States - a historical and political analysis, in: M. H. Rioux and M. Bach (eds.) *Disability is not Measles: New Research Paradigms in Disability*, Ontario, Canada: Roeher

INDEX